BEGINNING
WITH BRAILLE

Firsthand Experiences with a Balanced Approach to Literacy

ANNA M. SWENSON

AFB PRESS
American Foundation for the Blind

Printed in the United States of America.

Library of Congress Cataloging-in-Publication Data
Swenson, Anna M., 1952–
    Beginning with braille : Firsthand experiences with a balanced approach to literacy / Anna M. Swenson
            p.   cm.
    Includes bibliographical references (p.   ) and index.
    ISBN **978-0-89128-323-2**
    1. Braille—Study and teaching (Elementary)—United States. 2. Children, Blind—Education—United States. 3. Children, Blind—United States—Books and reading. I. Title.
    HV1672.S94   1999
    411—dc21   98-35342
                                                                                                          CIP

Credits

Excerpt from *Lions and Gorillas,* by JoAnne Nelson, © 1989 by Modern Curriculum Press, Simon & Schuster Education Group, New York. Used with permission.

"Jelly in the Bowl" reprinted from *Sally Go Round the Sun,* by Edith Fowke. © 1966, McClelland & Stewart, Inc., The Canadian Publishers, Toronto, Ontario, Canada. Used by permission.

Ice Cream, by Joy Cowley, © 1986 by The Wright Group, 9201 120th Avenue, NE, Bothell, WA 98011, (206) 486-8011. Used with permission.

Photographs: American Printing House for the Blind, 49; David Snider/InSight Photo/Video, 28, 29, 30, 33, 55, 62, 63, 67, 74, 75, 76, 78, 79, 94, 103, 107, 111, 112, 157; The Wright Group, 44.

Dedication

To Mrs. Gooch,
    who introduced me to braille at the age of 11,

and to Linda and Donna,
    who continue to guide and inspire me in my teaching.

Contents

Foreword

About ten years ago, I started hearing about a revolutionary approach to teaching literacy skills that was becoming popular in Australia and New Zealand. I was quickly intrigued by key elements of this new "whole language" approach, such as immersing children in written language and using naturally occurring literacy events and authentic literature for the purposes of instruction. As someone interested in high-quality literacy instruction for all students, I saw the immediate value of these and other elements of whole language instruction. I felt that the emphasis on meaning and authentic literacy events would be superior to the synthetic and "dry" approach that was all too characteristic of basal readers.

As a specialist in teaching students who were blind, I joined with many of my colleagues in wondering and even worrying about how the whole language approach could be used with students who were learning to read braille. As an illustration, if one were to uphold the principle of immersion in written language, then all of the print that was available in the environment should be made available in braille. Largely because of the challenges of matching the amount of print information with braille information, many educators of blind children were at first overwhelmed by the thought of using a whole language approach with their students or mainstreaming their students in whole language classrooms.

Many of the concerns of educators of students who were blind centered on how to capitalize on the meaningfulness of whole language instruction while still providing instruction in the unique skills needed to read efficiently in braille. Those concerns have never been fully addressed until now. With publication of *Beginning with Braille: Firsthand Experiences with a Balanced Approach to Literacy*, Anna Swenson shares with us her many years of experience in teaching students to read braille and, in particular, how she learned to strike a balance between meaning-centered and skills-centered approaches to literacy instruction. She shows us, in clear and understandable ways, how these approaches can be balanced—sometimes tilting more to one end of the continuum or the other—to address the individual needs of students.

Much of what has been written on braille literacy instruction leaves the reader wanting more of the "nitty gritty" details on teaching braille literacy skills. That will not be the case here. In each chapter, creative and practical strategies are provided for designing and delivering high-quality braille literacy instruction. Extensive teacher-friendly strategies are offered for areas such as reading aloud to young children, selecting and making early tactile books, teaching tactile and hand movement skills, designing worksheets to meet the needs of braille readers, introducing braille contractions, teaching use of the braillewriter, facilitating the writing process in braille, and using tactile editing marks in braille writing instruction. In addition to strategies for teaching beginning reading and writing skills in braille, chapters also address the literacy needs of students with additional disabilities and assessment of student progress in developing literacy skills.

Consistent with the overall theme of balance in this book, Ms. Swenson never strays from a consistent emphasis on fostering in students the meaningfulness and true understanding of written text that is fundamental high-quality literacy instruction. While those who read this book will be thrilled by the sheer number of practical teaching ideas that are presented, they also will gain a fuller appreciation for the importance of skillfully selecting, interweaving, and balancing approaches to teaching literacy skills. Her approach to achieving this balance is illustrated powerfully through the case studies presented in the book. One chapter is devoted to month-by-month anecdotal records on two students, culminating with her reflections on these students' literacy development. These comprehensive case studies, as well as the other "mini" case studies throughout the book, allow the reader to get into the mind of a highly skilled educator and learn how she addresses the real needs of her students. Rarely does a book provide such a valuable learning experience.

The publication of this book is a valuable and significant contribution to the literature on braille literacy instruction. It provides a comprehensive guide to the teaching of beginning braille reading and writing skills, joining the ranks of a select few publications. Furthermore, it was written by a practicing educator. Ms. Swenson is a highly experienced, creative, practical, and articulate educator who shares freely her successful teaching ideas and strategies. AFB Press is to be applauded for its highly visible role in promoting braille literacy and for making this book available as a resource to teachers around the world.

The book you have in your hands is a treasure. You will be personally enriched and professionally rewarded as you read Anna Swenson's ideas for achieving the highest quality of literacy instruction for children who are blind. Reading *Beginning with Braille* will feel as though you have a wise and trusted mentor by your side, helping you tackle the challenges of ensuring your students' growth in literacy skills. Your ultimate goal as an educator is to nurture a love of and excitement for literacy among children who read braille. Using the ideas and strategies in this book will help you realize that goal for each of your students.

Alan J. Koenig, Ed.D.
Professor
College of Education
Texas Tech University
Lubbock, Texas

Acknowledgments

The lengthy process of writing this book would have been impossible without guidance and support from many people along the way. It really began in the late 1980s, when a fellow Fairfax County teacher, Linda Bowlin, welcomed four successive braille readers from my resource room into her first-grade class. Her meaning-oriented, child-centered approach to literacy transformed my idea of teaching reading and writing. Linda has continued to keep me up to date on the latest developments in general education over the span of our 12-year friendship. Two other Pine Spring Elementary teachers, Martine Pistell and Sandy Hluboky, have also worked with many of my students in their kindergarten and first-grade classes, devoting extra time and effort to make mainstreaming a success for each child. Their willingness to collaborate has provided my students and me with learning opportunities we never could have experienced in a self-contained setting. Another longtime friend, Donna Pastore, has taken a special interest in each of my students and spent many hours sharing her expertise in braille with me; her common sense and natural teaching ability have been invaluable resources.

I am grateful to teachers from the Fairfax County Vision Program who took the time to encourage me in my writing and to review drafts of my book: Carol Norrish for collaborating with me in three workshops that led to the conception of the book; Anne Spitz for her suggestions from the perspective of a new teacher; and Cathie Krebs for her review from a "seasoned" teacher's viewpoint, as well as her suggestions for using the braille eraser and magnets. I would also like to extend my appreciation to other professionals who contributed their creative ideas: Adrienne Mosumade for her concept books and "finger wake-up" exercise; Denah Burnham for her "Songs for Beginning Braillists"; Martine Pistell for her braille writing worksheet; Janie Humphries for her bibliography of "Books Featuring Characters Who Are Blind or Visually Impaired"; and Catherine Hula and Emily Calvert for their "Braille Talk" suggestions. In addition, Alan Koenig of Texas Tech University provided me with continuous support, reviewing my initial outline, reading the first draft of the manuscript, and answering the numerous questions of a novice in the publishing world. From Alan, the manuscript made its way to AFB Press, where my editors, Natalie Hilzen and Ellen Bilofsky, spent countless hours guiding me through the steps of the writing process in much the same way that I attempt to assist my students with their writing. It was truly a learning experience to be on the receiving end of so much invaluable advice.

Like many teachers, I feel I have learned as much from my students and their families as they from me. I am particularly indebted to the children I have taught at Pine Spring Elementary in Falls Church, Virginia, and Centreville Elementary in Centreville, Virginia. I would also like to acknowledge the many general education staff members and administrators in the Fairfax County Public Schools who shared their expertise, recommended books, and invited me to workshops. Because of them I have always felt a part of the regular education mainstream, and my students have benefited from this foundation.

Finally, I would like to thank my husband, John, for his technical support, encouragement, and sense of humor throughout this project.

Prologue

About ten years ago I had a second-grade student named Trinh in my resource room. Trinh was totally blind and had come from Vietnam three years earlier speaking no English. She was a determined little girl who made remarkable progress. In fact, by second grade she was placed in a mainstream class for language arts. In October of Trinh's second-grade year, the classroom teacher told me that she would be piloting a recently developed "whole language" reading approach—which she explained as a child-centered philosophy of learning that emphasizes meaning over isolated skills—and she presented me with a print copy of the brand new textbook her class would start using the following week.

I was not happy. Up until that time my students had used Patterns: The Primary Braille Reading Program, *published by the American Printing House for the Blind, or a transcription of the regular education basal reader, both of which were readily available in braille. I had never heard of whole language. Changing books in midstream meant that I would need to braille hundreds of pages very quickly. As I looked at the book, I developed more reservations. It seemed to be a collection of children's stories by different authors. There was no semblance of a controlled vocabulary or sequence of difficulty. The workbook consisted of open-ended questions and creative-thinking activities that demanded a great deal of writing from the students. There were no drills, no fill-in-the-blank exercises, and only a few token pages devoted to phonics.*

I expressed my concerns to the classroom teacher. Both the English language and the braille code were relatively new to Trinh, and I felt that she needed the structure of a traditional basal reader. However, in the end, I had no choice if Trinh was to remain in her mainstream class for language arts.

I brailled—and Trinh read . . . and read . . . and read. It was not long before she wanted to take the stories home so that she could read them again and again. I had never had a student ask to take the basal reader home. As I reviewed the stories with Trinh and watched how writing assignments were integrated with the reading, I began to share her enthusiasm. The stories were not only enjoyable for Trinh to read, they were exciting for me to teach. Each story presented a myriad of creative possibilities for instruction.

At the end of the year the students in Trinh's class took a standardized reading test as part of the pilot study. Trinh scored above grade level in reading.

Furthermore, she was more excited about reading and writing than any other student I had taught.

When I began teaching braille reading to young children 20 years ago, it was accepted practice to use transcriptions of the basal readers and workbooks found in most regular classrooms. All students moved through the same sequence of stories, each of which was written to teach particular skills or sight vocabulary. The *Patterns* series continued in the tradition of the basal readers, with a highly controlled vocabulary and numerous ready-made worksheets designed to reinforce reading skills. Although my early students learned to read well enough to pass the end-of-level tests, my own enthusiasm for basal readers waned as I taught the same stories over and over again, year after year.

Trinh's whole language reading experience marked the beginning of my conversion to a meaning-oriented philosophy of teaching language arts. Over the next few years I discovered that children who were strongly motivated to read often acquired tracking, decoding, and comprehension skills by reading extensively and writing about their reading; they didn't need the stacks of worksheets I had used in the past. With few regrets, I abandoned basal readers and began using children's literature as the basis for reading instruction, borrowing and adapting many ideas from general education classes. I continued to reinforce the skills that all beginning braille readers need, such as phonics and the rules of the braille code; however, I constantly searched for ways to teach them in context, rather than as isolated drills. I also encountered students with additional disabilities who required a great deal of structure, repetition, and vocabulary control to learn to read braille. Keeping their learning meaningful became a major challenge for me.

Looking back on the students I have taught, I find that those who have participated in the meaning-oriented instruction characteristic of whole language are without a doubt the most motivated readers and writers. They are interested in a wide variety of fiction and nonfiction; they enjoy writing, while appreciating the time and effort involved in the writing process; and they feel empowered by the opportunity to make many of their own choices in reading and writing tasks. Watching the enthusiasm and confidence of these learners, I feel they have the best chance of becoming the lifelong readers and writers that we teachers strive to create.

This is not to say that learning to read braille is easy, whatever the approach. Beginning braille readers face many challenges as a result of such factors as limited experiential background and lack of incidental learning, as well as the intricacies of the braille code itself. They undoubtedly require more structure and individual guidance in general than many of their sighted classmates. The scarcity of braille materials also places increased demands on teachers who elect to use children's literature for some or all of their reading program.

This book is intended to provide teachers of young braille readers with a variety of practical guidelines and activities for promoting literacy at the beginning stages of braille instruction. Although oriented toward a whole language philosophy, it includes a balance of traditional teaching techniques that have worked well for generations of students. The activities and observations throughout the book are drawn from my own teaching experiences in both itinerant and resource settings. Since this book largely reflects a personal perspective, it does not attempt to address all aspects of teaching braille, nor does it provide a comprehensive overview of teaching reading. Whenever possible, I have tried to refer the reader to other sources that may be helpful in learning more about specific topics. Teachers reading this book will undoubtedly take a "smorgasbord" approach, picking and choosing those ideas that may be effective with a particular student. Over the years I have found that no single method or set of activities meets the needs of all children who are learning braille. Each new student presents unique challenges, and each makes different demands on our expertise and creativity.

As teachers of students with visual impairments, we serve a diverse population of young braille readers, many of whom have additional learning problems. Sharing teaching philosophies, strategies, and materials among ourselves can only benefit our students and give each of us more time to tackle new issues. My purpose in writing this book is not to present the "right way" to teach braille. Rather, I hope my ideas will increase options for instruction and spark others' imaginations as we all work toward the common goal of expanding braille literacy.

CHAPTER 1 Balancing Literacy Instruction

Approaches to teaching reading and writing vary widely from one district to another throughout the United States and are constantly changing. Even schools within a district or classes within a school may rely on different techniques and materials for language arts instruction. For many years the pendulum has swung between traditional "skill-oriented" instruction characteristic of basal reading programs and "meaning-oriented" approaches to instruction such as whole language. (For definitions of terms used in this discussion that have special meaning in writing on literacy, see "The Language of Reading.")

Itinerant or resource teachers of blind and visually impaired students working in mainstream settings often adapt the general education curriculum as they teach braille reading so that their students can benefit from group learning with sighted peers. However, if their students have additional learning problems or if the mainstream curriculum does not appear to meet all their needs, teachers may choose to supplement or replace portions of the regular instructional program with more appropriate activities (see Chapter 4). Teachers of self-contained or residential school classes have the opportunity to design their own programs. An understanding of the major characteristics of skill-oriented and meaning-oriented instruction can help teachers select, adapt, and create techniques and materials to meet the needs of individual students.

CHARACTERISTICS OF SKILL-ORIENTED AND MEANING-ORIENTED INSTRUCTION

Skill-oriented (traditional) language arts instruction is characterized by a focus on discrete skills that may not have immediate meaning or use for students; for example, completing exercises in a phonics workbook or learning to track lines of braille before applying the skills within the context of a story. It may include some or all of the following:

- basal readers
- teacher-directed instruction
- controlled vocabulary in reading materials
- a "part-to-whole" approach, in which the focus is first on sounds, letters, words, and rules rather than their meaning in context.
- worksheets, workbooks, spelling books, and grammar books
- fixed reading groups
- limited individual student choice of reading materials or writing topics
- little relationship between writing and reading activities

Among the materials available to teach braille to beginning readers, *Patterns: The Primary Braille Reading Program* (Caton, Pester, & Bradley, 1982c) and the *Mangold Developmental Program of Tactile Perception and Braille Letter Recognition* (S. Mangold, 1977) represent traditional methods of reading instruction. *Patterns* is a typical basal reader with a controlled vocabulary and extensive worksheet drills. The Mangold program teaches tracking (the use of the hands to follow a line of braille) and letter recognition in isolation; other instructional materials must be used to allow students to apply these skills to meaningful reading contexts.

Meaning-oriented instruction, such as whole language, focuses first on the meaning of a text for the child rather than its component parts. It may include any of the following components:

- the use of children's literature as the major source of instructional material
- participation of students in decision making (for example, choosing reading materials and writing topics, conducting self-evaluations)
- meaningful vocabulary rather than controlled vocabulary
- a "whole-to-part" approach in which students comprehend a meaningful whole, such as a story, before breaking it down into phonetic and grammatical parts
- focus lessons using literature and the children's own writing to teach specific strategies and concepts
- fluid instructional groups, which change according to students' needs or interests
- daily opportunities for the children to write
- a close relationship between reading and writing activities
- integration of language arts with all areas of the curriculum

TRADITIONAL OR WHOLE LANGUAGE INSTRUCTION?

Although the debate between traditional and whole language reading methods continues in the news media, many educators are recognizing that a flexible, balanced

Teachers of visually impaired children teach much more than the braille code: They provide instruction in the fundamental skills of reading and writing as well. Understanding some of the theory behind literacy instruction helps teachers match techniques and materials to the needs of their students. The following key vocabulary occurs frequently in professional literature related to the teaching of reading and writing.

- **Basal reader** A teacher-directed reading series composed of textbooks, workbooks and/or worksheets, and a teacher's manual. In the traditional basal system, students progressed sequentially through all the stories at each level and completed extensive skill-oriented exercises to practice what they had learned. Many more modern basal readers make increased use of children's literature and include a better balance of meaning-based and skill-based activities.

- **Controlled vocabulary** A carefully planned sequence of new words, such as that used in a traditional basal reading series. Each story introduces a set of new words and reinforces previously learned vocabulary.

- **Cueing system** A way of obtaining information needed to identify an unfamiliar word. Good readers rely on phonics, meaning (semantics), and language structure (syntactic) clues interdependently.

- **Decoding** The process of sounding out words using sound-symbol relationships.

- **Fixed reading groups** Traditional reading groups, usually organized by ability, whose membership does not change during the school year.

- **Focus lesson** A short lesson designed to teach a specific reading or writing strategy. It often involves modeling by the teacher, with follow-up reinforcement using children's literature or samples of students' writing.

- **Meaningful vocabulary** Uncontrolled vocabulary found in stories of high interest to children. These words should be in the children's listening and speaking vocabulary. Students use pictures, phonics, meaning, and language structure clues to identify unfamiliar words.

- **Phonemic awareness** The ability to recognize and manipulate the sounds in words. Phonemic awareness includes skills such as identifying rhyming words, isolating the sound at the beginning of a word, segmenting words into syllables and sounds, and blending sounds and syllables to make words.

- **Phonics** The association of a letter or group of letters with a corresponding sound.

- **Skill** (In whole language and related literacy theory) An isolated unit of knowledge, such as knowing that the letter *b* makes the sound /b/.

- **Strategy** (In whole language and related literacy theory) A skill applied in practice, such as using one's knowledge of the sound made by the letter *b* to decode the word *ball* in a sentence.

- **Whole language** A child-centered philosophy of learning that emphasizes meaning rather than isolated skills and espouses instructional activities that are relevant to the individual learner's experiences, needs, and developmental level. It advocates integration of listening, speaking, reading, and writing into the entire curriculum and views teachers and students as a community of learners. Whole language encompasses a greater range of instructional possibilities than other meaning-oriented methods such as literature-based instruction or the language experience approach.

approach best meets the needs of the wide variety of students in both general and special education (Sanchez, 1998). Whole language philosophy has opened up a vast repertoire of new teaching materials and strategies that are extremely motivating to children. At the same time, traditional methods, including direct, skill-oriented instruction, are particularly effective for certain students. What is primary is that learning remains functional and meaningful.

Language arts teaching can be viewed as a continuum (see Figure 1.1). Meeting an individual student's needs for braille instruction requires the teacher to move back and forth along the continuum, selecting a balance of skill-oriented and meaning-oriented activities appropriate for that particular child at that time. Some students may benefit from the structure, repetition, and controlled vocabulary found in traditional methods of instruction. However, the teacher can enrich this type of literacy program with bookmaking and other activities from the meaning-oriented end of the continuum. Students who are learning braille in a whole language program using children's literature rather than a traditional basal program like *Patterns* may still need to practice certain skills in isolation, such as tracking or recognition of contractions. The key is to integrate these skills into an authentic reading or writing activity as soon as possible. Even when using traditional methods, a meaningful context enhances learning for all students. Chapter 4 provides a more detailed discussion of the choices to be made in implementing different approaches to braille literacy.

Figure 1.1   THE CONTINUUM OF APPROACHES TO LANGUAGE ARTS TEACHING

Skill-Oriented Instruction
(traditional basal reader approach)

Meaning-Oriented Instruction
(whole language)

SUMMARY

Students with visual impairments vary widely in their learning styles, abilities, and interests. A balanced approach to literacy instruction offers a broad continuum of possibilities for meeting individual needs. Many students learn best when the instructional balance is tipped toward the meaning end of the continuum; others may require a heavier emphasis on skills within a meaningful context. The balance between skill-oriented and meaning-oriented instruction may also change for individual learners as they become more proficient in braille. The next chapter discusses general and practical guidelines for teaching young braille readers, regardless of the type of reading program they are using. Options for selecting or designing a language arts program are presented in greater detail in Chapter 4.

CHAPTER 2

Guidelines and Strategies for Teaching Beginning Braille

Learning to read braille is a time-consuming and complex process that requires daily instruction by a teacher of visually impaired students. This frequent, intensive level of intervention is necessary to provide young students with consistent access to adapted classroom materials and to give them sufficient practice to master the braille code and correct reading techniques. A number of general guidelines, practical teaching strategies, and essential supplies can facilitate a student's braille literacy learning during both individual and group instruction. In a mainstream setting, close collaboration with the general education teacher (and paraprofessional, if available) ensures that appropriate reading strategies are taught and that the student has many opportunities to share literacy activities with sighted classmates. The involvement of parents also enhances students' opportunities for success. Parents who take the time to learn braille, supervise homework, and become involved in the school program communicate the importance of braille literacy to their child.

Many children who are learning braille spend all or part of their day in a general education classroom. Although mainstreaming may be defined differently by educators in different parts of the country, for the purposes of this book it refers to the time a child spends in the regular classroom participating in the general education program—including both academic and nonacademic activities—with appropriate accommodations. The itinerant or resource teacher may be present to assist, or the child may function independently within the peer group.

In the example that follows, Eva, a first grader, is mainstreamed for a majority of the school day, with support during the language arts instruction period, or block. However, her itinerant teacher also provides her with specialized instruction in braille and spelling during a daily "pullout" session. Eva's story illustrates a typical lesson for a mainstreamed student and introduces many of the ideas and concepts that will be presented throughout this book. In particular, it demonstrates the collaboration between the classroom teacher and the itinerant teacher, how the itinerant teacher adapts the class's approach to reading and writing for a student who is learning braille, and how braille instruction is integrated with classroom work. Moreover, the balanced approach to language arts instruction that is followed in Eva's classroom is demonstrated by meaningful reading and writing activities that provide the context for instruction in specific skills and strategies.

A TEACHER'S DIARY
A MORNING IN THE MAINSTREAM

Eva is a totally blind 6-year-old with abundant energy and a mischievous streak. She has just completed her first semester in Ms. Schroeder's first-grade classroom and is functioning in the middle of the group of 22 students. Ms. Schroeder follows a balanced language arts program, which includes children's literature as the major source of reading material, daily opportunities for students to write, and an emphasis on phonemic awareness and phonics. As an itinerant teacher, I usually spend 1½ to 2 hours daily with Eva during the language arts block before dashing off to my next four schools.

It is Wednesday morning. Ms. Schroeder and I meet briefly before school for an update on scheduling and materials. I've already brailled the packet of materials for the week that Ms. Schroeder gave me on Monday, but there is an additional activity related to today's lesson on compound words that needs adapting. Ms. Schroeder also tells me that she would like to do a short reading evaluation with Eva today as part of her ongoing assessment program. I look over the schedule of activities for Readers' and Writers' Workshops to decide when to give Eva her daily block of individual braille instruction. Readers' Workshop generally includes a read-aloud story time and a variety of reading activities, which may involve the whole group, small groups, or independent reading. During Writers' Workshop, children write on topics that they select themselves, following a specific sequence for revising, editing, and publishing their work. Sometimes Ms. Schroeder begins this workshop by modeling a writing skill or strategy that the children need to work on. At the end of the writing time, students may share their pieces with the whole group and receive feedback.

It's always a juggling act to keep Eva up with the mainstream activities and still provide her with the individual attention she needs to master the special skills related to braille. Today, since I have to leave early to take another student to a low vision exam, I decide to work with Eva at the very beginning of the morning when the teacher is reading to the class. Tomorrow I will try to pull her out later on, perhaps during part of Writers' Workshop, so that Eva won't miss story time two days in a row.

Eva bounces into the room at 9:00 a.m., puts her homework folder on her desk, and hangs up her coat and backpack. She stays for opening exercises, then brings her homework with her to the adjoining room where she and I have our lessons. We begin by reviewing Eva's individualized spelling list, which includes words from her own writing and words I've chosen to teach contractions and rules of the braille code. This week Eva is learning words with the *o-n-e* contraction from her writing piece about a trip to Discovery Zone, the children's indoor play center. Eva also has *McDonald's* on her spelling list—her choice!

The main focus of today's individual lesson is editing Eva's Discovery Zone writing. Eva proofreads her draft for errors in spelling, capitalization, and punctuation, and I help her correct them with tactile editing marks (described in detail in Chapter 7). Then Eva reads her edited piece over again to me so she will be ready to copy it independently during Writers' Workshop later in the morning. Before returning to the classroom I listen to Eva read part of the book *Rosie's Walk* (Hutchins, 1968), which she had chosen for last night's reading homework. She reads fluently, with expression and obvious enjoyment. Eva chooses a new braille book to read tonight, and takes *Rosie's Walk* to her reading basket in her classroom.

Back in the classroom, the students are reading to their "reading buddies" in pairs while Ms. Schroeder assesses individual children. She picks a short unfamiliar braille book for Eva to read to her and records her miscues (reading errors) on a running record sheet while I listen and make my own notes. When she is finished, we share our observations with Eva before she joins a friend for buddy reading. We comment on how well Eva is moving her hands using a new two-handed tracking pattern. I point out that Eva's confusion with *his* and *have* relates to the positions of each character in the braille cell and tell Eva we will review this tomorrow.

During the next part of Readers' Workshop, Ms. Schroeder calls her students together for a group lesson on compound words. The students contribute examples from their reading for Ms. Schroeder to write on a large piece of chart paper. I braille the words for Eva as we sit on the rug with the class, then turn the brailler over to her when I have to leave for my next student's low vision exam. Ms. Schroeder continues to spell each word so that Eva can write it correctly. When the list is complete, each child chooses a compound word to write and

illustrate on a strip of specially folded paper. Eva completes her activity using paper fasteners and three pre-punched index cards, one for the first part of the word, one for the second, and one for the entire compound word. A friend shows her how to attach the cards using the paper fasteners so that the parts of the word separate and come together.

During Writers' Workshop, Ms. Schroeder confers individually with students while the rest of the class works on their current writing pieces. Everyone is at a different stage in the writing process (discussed later in this chapter and in Chapter 7). Eva takes her edited draft out of the work folder taped to the side of her desk and writes her final copy, remembering to work slowly and carefully so that there are no mistakes. When she finishes, she reads it over to herself and then shares it with the rest of the class just before lunch.

Not every language arts block goes as smoothly as this one, even when I'm able to be at the school for the entire time. Some days I have to spend most of my individual lesson previewing math skills; or the brailler may "eat" a piece of paper when I'm not there and be out of commission until I return; or I may have to develop a behavior plan for a student who has difficulty attending to group instruction or working independently. All of this, however, is the mainstreaming trade-off. Not everything in the general education classroom is perfectly designed for a child who reads braille, but for many students the benefits outweigh the disadvantages. Participating in the mainstream, *as long as there is adequate support from a teacher of visually impaired students,* teaches children about flexibility, problem solving, and working with others. And, keeping up with the general education curriculum, while stressful at times, compels the itinerant or resource teacher to expect the very best performance from his or her student.

GENERAL GUIDELINES FOR INSTRUCTION

Regardless of the approach to language arts adopted by their school system, teachers can strengthen children's acquisition of braille literacy using techniques from the meaning-oriented end of the language arts continuum. The result is a child-centered mode of instruction that provides students with choices and gives them a measure of control over their own learning. Listed here are some general guidelines for providing a meaning-oriented introduction to literacy for beginning braille students. They will help to promote effective instruction for both mainstreamed students and students with multiple disabilities.

Immersing Students in Braille

Just as very young children learn to talk by hearing and practicing spoken language constantly, so many school-aged children learn to read and write by being immersed in print (Butler & Turbill, 1987). Sighted children acquire numerous literacy concepts from their print-filled school and home environments. Because of the scarcity of braille materials, children who are blind or have very low vision (that is, whose visual impairment is severe enough to interfere with their daily functioning) do not automatically participate in this type of literacy learning. Instead, their "braille immersion" must be deliberately orchestrated by teachers and parents.

Young braille readers benefit from opportunities to use braille across the curriculum throughout the day. Children can read class schedules, daily messages, cassette tape labels, recipes, menus, notes from teachers, transcriptions of classmates' writing, and a wide variety of children's books transcribed into braille. They can write thank-you letters; telephone numbers; labels for lunch boxes, chairs, and coat hooks; shopping lists for mobility lessons; holiday cards; reading logs; journal entries; and certificates of appreciation for classmates who have served as sighted guides. It is also critical that children spend 20 to 30 minutes each night at home reading a braille book to someone or reading independently, if they are ready. These varied opportunities to practice literacy skills develop the concept that braille is an enjoyable and important means of communication.

Integrating Listening, Speaking, Reading, and Writing

Beginning reading activities are often most effective when they develop children's abilities in two or more areas simultaneously. Young students can listen to, read, and discuss high-quality children's literature daily and then imitate the rhythm and pattern of language they hear and read. These imitations, or retellings (see Chapter 7), may be oral or written. For example, after learning to read the rhyme, "One, Two, Buckle My Shoe," children can write their own version: "One, Two, We Went to the Zoo." In this way, reading and writing instruction occur together, reflecting the belief that each reinforces the other (Rex, Koenig, Wormsley, & Baker, 1994).

Focusing on Meaning

Providing children with meaningful contexts to develop literacy skills often increases motivation. In meaning-oriented programs, students read children's literature rather than the controlled-vocabulary stories found in traditional basal readers and practice writing by composing stories, journal entries, and personal letters, rather than completing exercises in grammar or spelling books. Children often learn reading skills such as phonics in context instead of using worksheets and may use their own writing to practice the mechanical skills of capitalization, punctuation, and spelling.

One way that beginning writers can be helped to focus on meaning is by encouraging them to use their own approximations of conventional spelling, often called invented or temporary spelling. Invented spelling is a logical system of sounding out words that can be read back by the writer and others. Since learning to spell is a developmental process, children's invented spelling moves through defined stages until nearly all words are spelled correctly (Bolton & Snowball, 1993a). In the following sentence, written about the book *The Snowy Day*, by Ezra Jack Keats (1976), a kindergartner uses invented spelling to represent the sounds that she hears:

Per   pt   the   so   b   in   the   pk

⠠⠏⠻   ⠏⠞   ⠮   ⠎⠕   ⠃   ⠔⠝   ⠮   ⠏⠅

(Peter put the snowball in the pocket.)

Invented spelling enables young children to write independently about any topic and focus first on the message, rather than on mechanics. However, mastering conventional spelling should be an important part of any language arts program. Some schools require that students master an increasing number of high-frequency words by the end of each grade level from first grade on. Spelling approximations are accepted at beginning levels, but correct spelling of most common words should be expected by the middle grades. Specific ideas for teaching spelling are discussed in Chapter 7.

Modeling Literacy Behaviors

Having the teacher model behaviors intrinsic to literacy is important for all learners, but particularly for the child who is blind or severely visually impaired and whose incidental literacy learning is limited. Teachers can model such behaviors and strategies as efficient tracking skills, invented spelling, and writing a friendly letter. Modeling helps students view the teacher as a fellow reader and writer, one who uses a variety of strategies to decode text and compose clear, meaningful written messages.

Emphasizing Process as Well as Product

Giving a correct answer, reading a book, or completing a piece of writing is only part of the overall learning objective. Students also must become aware of the *process* they have used in achieving a desired end. While reading, students can be asked to describe how they were able to decode a difficult word or figure out the main idea of a passage, so that they can apply the same strategy next time.

Beginning in first or second grade, many students learn the multistep approach to writing known as the "writing process" (Fowler & McCallum, 1995b). The steps may include prewriting or planning, drafting, conferring, revising, editing, and publishing the piece for others to read. (Adapting the writing process for students who read braille is discussed in detail in Chapter 7.) Work on a selected piece often culminates in publishing it as a student-authored book, a valuable learning experience involving the integration of reading and writing. Even very beginning readers de-

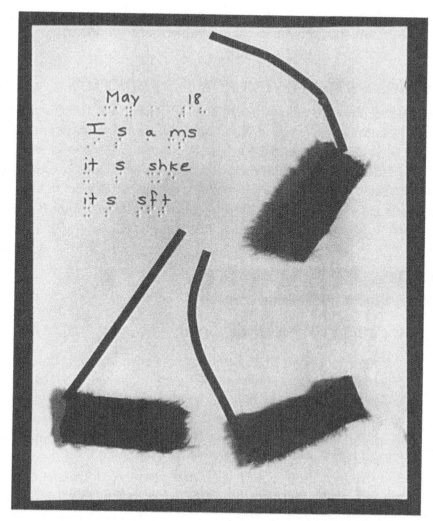

A 5-year-old student uses invented spelling to write a journal entry about visiting some mice in another classroom: "I saw a mouse. It was shaky. It was soft." Pieces of fur and graphic art tape were used to create simple pictures that were meaningful to the student.

velop positive images of themselves as readers and writers when they participate in the process of creating a simple book with braille text and tactile pictures.

Encouraging Students' Participation in Decision Making

In traditional classrooms, teachers (in conjunction with the basal reading program) often make all the major decisions about what children learn. The teacher's manual may even tell the teacher exactly what to say during each lesson. Teachers in meaning-oriented classrooms, however, view themselves more as facilitators, rather than the sole directors of learning. They observe children carefully to discover what motivates them and integrate individual interests into reading and writing activities. Teachers also encourage students to select some of their own reading materials and writing topics. As a result of their involvement in decision making, children develop a vested interest in the reading and writing that they do.

PRACTICAL STRATEGIES FOR INSTRUCTION

Maximizing students' achievement involves more than the creation of a classroom climate conducive to learning. Figuring out the nitty-gritty details of how to present braille to young readers, make accommodations for classroom activities, and adapt or create materials can consume much of a teacher's time. No set of practical teaching strategies will be appropriate for all learners or classroom situations. However, the ideas listed here are intended to provide a starting point for teachers who are beginning braille instruction with a young student.

■ SUGGESTIONS FOR TEACHERS

INTRODUCING THE BRAILLE CODE

- Decide whether to begin with grade 1 (uncontracted) braille or grade 2 (contracted) braille. Traditionally, young children learn grade 2 braille contractions from the beginning. In this author's experience, most students master these contractions with ease when given frequent opportunities to read and write; they also find the contractions for common letter combinations helpful in decoding new words. (See Chapter 4 for a sequence of steps to introduce grade 2 braille.) Some teachers do report success in teaching grade 1 braille first (Burton, Ormerod, & Kelzenberg, 1997; Troughton, 1992). It should be noted, however, that the transition from grade 1 to grade 2 braille involves a significant amount of relearning, which must be carefully sequenced by the teacher. Also, since most braille books are published only in grade 2 braille, the use of grade 1 braille may limit children's reading options in a literature-based program unless books are custom made using only the contractions the child knows. Research is needed to compare the effect of teaching grade 1 or grade 2 braille on children's reading speed, comprehension, and spelling abilities. The possibility that grade 1 braille may be more effective for children with reading disabilities also needs to be studied.

- Consider using a slightly modified version of the grade 2 braille code in teacher-made materials for very young readers so that they clearly see the correlation between each spoken word and the corresponding braille word. Avoid using the contractions for *to, by,* and *into* (which are attached to the next word), and leave a space between *and, for, of, the, with,* and *a* (which are attached to each other without a space if they appear together in braille) until the student has established a one-to-one voice-to-braille match. In these early materials, each word will be clearly defined by having a space before and after it. When the student is able to read simple sentences with fingers on the correct words (not just from memory), standard contracted forms can be introduced. Very often children are ready for fully contracted braille by mid- to late kindergarten, or when they begin using commercial materials such as transcriptions of simple emergent reader books discussed in Chapter 4.

- Use a minimum of punctuation in very early reading materials, since punctuation marks are easily confused with letters. Always precede names and the word *I* with a capital sign.

- Double or triple space between lines for beginning readers and those with additional learning problems. Double space between words if necessary.

- Braille on plastic, self-adhesive sheets, such as Braillabels or ClearLabels (see the Resources section at the back of the book for availability of products) to enhance legibility and increase the longevity of frequently used materials such as flash cards.

- Attach materials, such as sorting trays, braille paper, flash cards, puzzles, and worksheets, firmly to the work surface with masking tape or Velcro; or place them on a nonslip material such as Dycem (see Resources)—a rubber sheet with a sticky texture—or commercially available Rubbermaid shelf liner.

ADAPTING VISUAL MATERIALS

- Before adapting, ask yourself if this material serves a meaningful instructional purpose for your student. Remember that it is not possible or necessary to adapt everything. For example, common primary-level activities such as dot-to-dot worksheets and word searches may not be worth the time it takes to create them in tactile form. Substitute a different activity to provide a better learning experience for the student.

- Try to adapt materials so the student can complete the assignments independently.

- Use self-adhesive file folder labels or round stickers as the blank spaces on worksheets, rather than a braille line, to make it easier for the student to position the insert. The student locates the sticker, positions the embossing head of the brailler over it, and writes the answer on the sticker. If an answer requires a whole sentence, a small sticker is often helpful to show where to start writing, although the sentence will extend beyond the sticker. In the following example the student is asked to write a one-word answer on the file folder label:

Directions: Fill in the blank with your own idea.

I   like   ice   cream   in   the   _____

- Substitute a three-dimensional object and verbal explanation for a diagram, if this would be more meaningful to the student. For example, bring in a real tulip to show the parts of a flower, rather than creating a tactile diagram.

- Redesign webs (diagrams) and charts that organize information in graphic format so they are in linear form, leaving space for the child to write answers (see Figure 2.1).

- Keep tactile diagrams and pictures as simple as possible. Leave out unnecessary details.

- In general, don't spend more time adapting the material than the child will spend using it, unless you plan to save the material for future students.

WORKING ONE-ON-ONE

- Establish a daily routine to practice certain literacy skills. This might include, for example, reviewing a schedule of activities, marking the date on a calendar, and reading a message.

- Vary work positions to provide young children with opportunities to move throughout the instructional period, if appropriate. Students can stand at a counter for short writing activities, sit on the floor to read with a lapboard or snack tray, or stand to match and sequence cards on a vertical pegboard (see Chapter 5 for a description of this activity).

- Include daily independent literacy activities in each student's program, even when working one-on-one, and even for the youngest students. Move away from the work area, refrain from talking, and see if the student can complete the assigned activity on his or her own. The ability to work independently demonstrates true mastery of a targeted skill and should transfer to a larger classroom setting with sufficient practice.

WORKING IN A CHILD'S MAINSTREAM CLASSROOM

- Provide your student with two desks, side by side, so that the brailler can be moved to the empty desk when not in use and still be conveniently close at hand. Be sure, however, that the student is seated next to other children on the side without the empty desk.

- Check the child's posture when seated. Feet should be flat on the floor or on a footstool.

- Braille all the print vocabulary found on the walls and bulletin boards in the room and put the pages in a binder. Very often children are expected to use the "wall words" as a spelling reference during writing activities. Group the braille words on separate pages, with a different page for each category (for example, months, number words, classmates' names, and so forth), to make it easier for the student to locate them quickly.

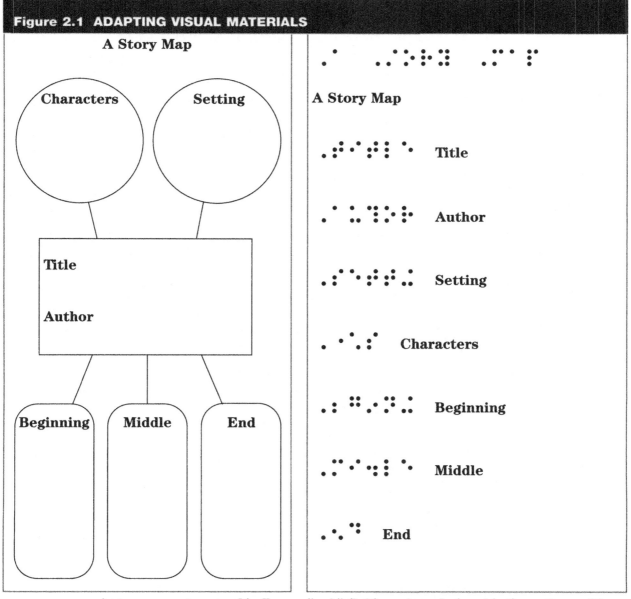

A story map set up graphically as a "web" (left) can be redesigned in linear form, with space left to complete the answers in braille (right).

- Interline (write in print) exactly what the student writes in braille, including mistakes, before giving the work to the classroom teacher. Indicate errors that are common in braille but not in print and that the teacher may not understand. (For example, "have" and "his" have the same dot configuration but are made in different parts of the braille cell and are easily confused.)

- Listen to your student read orally with the classroom teacher to check tracking techniques and, again, to explain braille errors. A child who confuses upper and lower signs (such as "have" and "his") or does not self-correct for confusing letters that are reversals of each other will need extra individual reading sessions with you.

■ Provide your student with braille copies of all "big books" and other print materials used in the mainstream classroom. A "big book" is an extra large copy of a book with enlarged print text and pictures that the teacher displays to the class during group instruction. Sighted children follow along as the teacher reads or read the text aloud themselves while the teacher points to each word. Children who read braille require their own individual braille copies of the big book during this type of instruction so that they can participate in the lesson. However, very beginning braille readers may have difficulty following when the teacher or other students read aloud. Children who race across the lines with their fingers in a frantic effort to keep up very often do not feel the individual words and may not be able to give their full attention to the meaning of the text. Previewing a braille book individually with a student is always desirable. Even when a child has heard the book before, however, it is sometimes more advantageous for beginning braille readers simply to *listen* to the book or story being shared in a large mainstream group for the first time. In this way they absorb the rhythm and pattern of the language, which are so important for future reading and writing success. The itinerant or resource teacher can read the braille copy of the book individually with the child before and/or afterward, taking time to focus on decoding skills (see Chapter 4) and specific aspects of the braille code. As the child's braille skills improve, keeping up during shared reading will become easier.

■ When the mainstream teacher is writing a message on the board or information on a wall chart, copy the words on the brailler as they are written. At the end of the activity, be sure to have the student read the braille back to you.

■ In most primary classrooms, reading and writing occur throughout the day during both planned and spontaneous activities. Good communication with the classroom teacher can ensure that most worksheets, books, and overhead sheets are brailled in advance. However, the itinerant or resource teacher is not always present to transcribe spontaneous written language instantly for a student, and many school systems do not provide paraprofessionals or on-site braille transcribers. Some classrooms may be equipped with technology that permits general education teachers to input text on a regular computer that is attached to a refreshable braille display (Koenig & Farrenkopf, 1994). In many cases, however, less high-tech solutions must be found. If the classroom teacher spells orally while writing a list of related words on chart paper or on the board, the mainstreamed student can often keep up on the brailler (although the result may not be perfect grade 2 braille). The list can be rebrailled before it becomes a part of the student's "wall words" binder. When the teacher writes more extensively—for example, taking notes while the class brainstorms about a topic—the teacher may need to save the writing in print to be brailled later and reviewed individually with the child when the itinerant or resource teacher returns.

■ Maintain frequent communication with the members of the student's Individualized Education Program (IEP) team—including the mainstream teacher, paraprofessional (if one is assigned to assist the student), other educational and service professionals, and parents. This group plans the students' long- and short-range educational goals, specifies necessary accommodations, and determines the frequency of special services. Each member of the IEP team has important insights to contribute, and each benefits from understanding the others' concerns and priorities (see "Guidelines for Collaboration").

■ GUIDELINES FOR COLLABORATION

Itinerant and resource teachers of mainstreamed students need to work with a number of other people besides the individual child—most notably the classroom teacher, possibly a paraprofessional who may be assisting the child, and, of course, the parents. The more cooperative these relationships, the better the results for the child. Keeping the following basic guidelines in mind will facilitate collaboration with school personnel and parents. The book *Classroom Collaboration* (Hudson, 1997) provides more detailed suggestions for promoting cooperation and understanding among the members of a child's educational team.

With Classroom Teachers

■ Review each week's objectives and activities with the mainstream teacher in advance to allow time to preview specific content and skills with the student. Some general education teachers agree to meet once a week for this purpose; others prefer to photocopy their lesson plans and provide a packet of work to be brailled.

■ Negotiate a reasonable turn-around time for preparing materials in braille and providing other adapted learning materials.

■ Communicate daily with the mainstream teacher about last minute-needs, schedule changes, and brief observations related to the student's progress. Be sensitive to the multitude of demands made on the regular classroom teacher, however, and make these contacts as efficiently as possible.

■ Schedule longer staffing conferences as needed that include all teachers and therapists working with the student. These meetings can be used to share observations concerning the student's progress in academic, social, self-help, and motor skills and to plan strategies that everyone can use with the student.

■ Solicit input from the classroom teacher when writing the student's Individualized Education Program (IEP) and be sure that the teacher is a part of the IEP team.

■ Be aware that occasional impromptu activities are an unavoidable part of mainstreaming. Flexibility is the key for both you and your student.

■ Evaluate the student's work with the mainstream teacher, taking into account the progress of the sighted children and the specific learning characteristics of a child who reads braille.

(continued on next page)

GUIDELINES FOR COLLABORATION (*continued*)

With Paraprofessionals

■ Be flexible in your expectations of the paraprofessional, and capitalize on his or her strengths. Some paraprofessionals are expert braillists or have a flair for adapting materials; others work extremely well with students in their mainstream classrooms.

■ Since independent functioning is a goal for your student, encourage the paraprofessional to sit next to the mainstreamed child only when really necessary (for example, to braille information that the classroom teacher is writing on a chart or to assist with an assignment that the child cannot complete independently). Gradually decrease the student's dependence on the assistant in as many areas as possible. Be sure the student understands how important it is to work independently.

■ Plan activities in which the paraprofessional can work with a small group of children that includes the mainstreamed student. The classroom teacher will appreciate the additional attention the general education students receive, and the mainstreamed student benefits socially and academically from actively participating in a group learning situation with peers.

■ Include paraprofessionals in staff conferences and other meetings regarding the students, as appropriate. Often they can provide valuable insights into a child's work habits, social skills, and level of independence.

■ Provide the paraprofessional with such appropriate resources as *A Paraprofessional's Handbook for Working with Students Who Are Visually Impaired* (Miller & Levack, 1997).

With Parents

■ Encourage parents to participate fully in the IEP process. Discuss goals and objectives over the telephone and send home a draft of the written IEP before the IEP meeting.

■ Provide a braillewriter for the child's home, beginning when the child is in preschool. Encourage the parents to use it themselves and to allow their child to "scribble" on it long before formal homework is assigned.

■ Inkprint all homework assignments or send home a print copy so that parents can work with their child even if they do not know braille.

■ Give parents a print copy of each textbook to refer to at home.

■ Refer parents to sources of print-braille books (see "Sources of Braille Books for Children" in the Resources section).

■ Provide parents with resources to learn braille such as *Just Enough to Know Better* (Curran, 1988).

■ Provide parents with resources that will help them help their children. For example, *The Bridge to Braille: Reading and School Success for the Young Blind Child* (Castellano & Kosman, 1997), gives parents an excellent overview of what to expect for their child in school. (See the Resources section at the end of this book for a list of suggested resources for parents.)

ESSENTIAL SUPPLIES

A variety of supplies and materials facilitate both teaching and learning. Many of the office supply and craft items listed in "Essential Supplies for Teaching Beginning Braille" will help teachers streamline the process of adapting or creating learning materials. Others, such as the clipboard, snack tray, and three-ring binder, will enable students to work more efficiently in class. The Resources section at the end of the book lists sources for specialty materials that are not widely available commercially.

■ ESSENTIAL SUPPLIES FOR TEACHING BEGINNING BRAILLE

The following list of materials comprises an essential part of every braille teacher's toolkit:

- graphic art tape or graphic charting tape, such as Form-A-Line or Letraline Flex-a-Tape, for making instant raised lines. These are available in a variety of widths from large office and art supply stores. (Tape with a textured "crepe" finish rather than a smooth "matte" finish is recommended because it can be used to form curves and is easier to discriminate tactilely.)

- self-adhesive plastic sheets, such as Braillabels or ClearLabels, which can be inserted in the brailler and used like regular pieces of paper. When the sheet is removed from the brailler and the back is peeled off, the sheet will stick to any surface.

- double-sided tape, a great substitute for glue

- restickable adhesive glue sticks for making movable word and number cards

- Wikki Stix (also known as Stikki Wikkis)—stiff, waxed cord that sticks to paper—for creating quick tactile pictures or for marking answers

- puff paint for making raised lines and dots

- box of miscellaneous materials for making tactile pictures, such as felt with self-adhesive backing; spongy packing sheets; textured paper; buttons; fabric scraps, including fur and lace; bubble wrap; sandpaper; ribbon; shiny "noisy" paper; and popsicle sticks

- sandpaper for making quick raised-line drawings by placing a sheet of regular copy paper over the sandpaper and drawing with a crayon

- different sizes of braille paper, including whole and half sheets and long, skinny "list sheets," for worksheets and writing activities

- self-adhesive file folder labels, round dots, and stars to use as blanks on worksheets and as tactile editing marks on student-brailled drafts (see Chapter 6)

- small bulletin board (17" x 11") and pushpins for marking braille worksheets (see Chapter 5) and graphs

- index cards for making flash cards

- poster board for book covers and more durable flash cards

(continued on next page)

ESSENTIAL SUPPLIES FOR TEACHING BEGINNING BRAILLE (*continued*)

- small containers or baskets for sorting flash cards

- masking tape, self-adhesive Velcro strips, Dycem, or other nonslip materials such as Rubbermaid shelf liner for securing materials to the work surface

- large cookie sheet or magnetic board and self-adhesive magnetic strips for sequencing and matching activities

- flat-sided crayons (such as Crayola Anti-Roll Crayons) that can be labeled with the braille color names

- glitter crayons, available in toy stores or art supply stores, which make a good tactile mark

- clipboard, snack tray, or lapboard for reading while seated on the floor

- separate three-ring notebooks for journals, reading response logs (written reflections on material read), and other collections of writing

SUMMARY

Teaching braille to a young student requires time, flexibility, and teamwork. It is essential that a braille reader receive daily intervention from a qualified teacher to build the literary foundation needed to compete with sighted peers. Even with a large block of instructional time each day, it is still a challenge to be sure the mainstreamed child masters all necessary braille competencies without missing parts of the general education curriculum. Close collaboration among the members of the IEP team can maximize the use of available time and provide the child with ongoing opportunities to use braille throughout the day.

CHAPTER 3
Promoting Early Literacy: First Experiences with Reading and Writing Braille

Before beginning readers can benefit from formal instruction in braille, they require a foundation of literacy skills that must be taught individually by teachers and parents at the preschool level, or possibly later for students with additional learning problems. These skills relate to tracking, tactile discrimination, basic positional concepts, and, most important, a familiarity with the processes of reading and writing in braille.

Children who are blind or visually impaired need to learn that spoken words can be written down in braille and read back. They acquire this essential concept by observing adults' modeling of literacy behaviors and by having frequent opportunities to imitate them. As children observe others and participate in reading and writing experiences themselves, they begin to connect oral language to writing and writing to reading. Providing a literate environment equivalent to that experienced by sighted children requires significant time and effort on the part of teachers and parents. Although a few high-quality braille books are available at the preschool level, such as the *On the Way to Literacy* series from the American Printing House for the Blind (see the Resources section), teacher-made materials based on a young child's own immediate experiences are often the most effective teaching tools. Young children's early attempts at reading and writing braille may include running their fingers across a word or sentence and "reading" it from memory, turning the pages of a book and retelling a story using the tactile pictures, or "scribbling" random dots on the braillewriter. Teachers and parents need to applaud these approximations of literacy, knowing that they represent the first stage in the development of competent readers and writers (Miller, 1985).

This chapter offers suggestions for promoting early literacy, with a special emphasis on bookmaking. As children participate in the process of creating books with tactile pictures and simple braille text, they practice oral language skills, strengthen literacy concepts, and develop a strong interest in books. By connecting writing and reading in a meaningful context, bookmaking establishes a solid foundation for future literary pursuits in the primary grades.

PROMOTING EARLY LITERACY

The activities suggested here help to create an atmosphere that promotes literacy, teaching specific skills such as tracking and tactile discrimination as well as important concepts related to reading and writing. They involve a relaxed, informal interchange between the adult and the child using simple, motivating materials.

SUGGESTIONS FOR TEACHERS

ACTIVITIES TO PROMOTE EARLY LITERACY

- Read aloud to young children (as well as to children of all ages) as often as possible. There is no better way to develop vocabulary, thinking skills, and a feel for the rhythm and pattern of language. Preschoolers who are blind or severely visually impaired may require explanations of words and concepts that sighted children grasp easily from pictures, so a one-on-one or very small group story-time setting is desirable. For example, they may not understand specific vocabulary like *porridge, bat* (the animal), or *flour;* they may need models or verbal descriptions of unfamiliar animals or unusual characters, like those found in books by Dr. Seuss; they may require a verbal explanation of events that are illustrated but not described in the text (one character giving another a hug); or they may benefit from an explanation of concepts such as a groundhog seeing its shadow or a hen laying an egg.

- Assemble separate "book bags" that each contain objects featured in a particular story to add interest to storytelling and convey important concepts (Miller, 1985). Pull each object out of the bag at the appropriate moment in the story. A child's understanding of a book like *If You Give a Mouse a Cookie* (Numeroff, 1985) is enhanced when real objects, such as a glass, a straw, a napkin, a mirror, and a small broom, are used to illustrate the text.

- Adapt favorite print books at the early reading level by sticking a key braille word related to the story on each print page along with a very simple tactile picture—for example, a round felt circle to represent a cat. Be sure the child has experienced the real object so that the picture will be meaningful. You can put the same word and picture on each page or vary them. As you read the book aloud, have the child search each page to find the picture and the braille word.

- Model braille reading with the child's hands on yours, even if you are not a tactile braille reader. Use print-braille and Twin-Vision books (books in which text is written in both print and braille; these are available from a variety of sources; see Resources) or braille familiar nursery rhymes and read them aloud to the child as you track the lines.

- Model writing on the braillewriter frequently and for a variety of different purposes. Make a shopping list, label cassette tapes, write a short story, or jot down someone's telephone number. Speak words and sounds aloud as you write, and read your message back after the child helps you take the paper out of the braillewriter. Encourage the child to "scribble" on the braillewriter by pressing random keys and "reading" the writing back to you.

■ Help the child label belongings and important landmarks—such as a storage cubby or a coat hook—in braille. Pair the braille name with a tactile marker, such as a square of corrugated cardboard or stick-on felt, if the child needs a larger tactile clue to find the object independently.

■ As a child develops the skills to discriminate braille words and letters, introduce meaningful written language: the child's own name; the names of family members and friends; letters found at the beginning of favorite words (for example, *l* for *lunch*). (Specific beginning reading activities are presented in Chapter 5.)

■ Talk about letter sounds at every opportunity to develop phonemic awareness and phonics skills. Make them a part of your conversation as you walk to the bus, fix a snack, or introduce your student to a new friend. Emphasize the initial consonant sound of each word you talk about, and name the letter that makes that sound. Play rhyming word games.

■ Play simple tracking games to help children begin to master the hand movements of braille reading.

   • Use strips of ribbon, sandpaper, corrugated cardboard, and full braille cells stapled to sheets of braille paper or cardboard. Children enjoy snipping these "roads" to various lengths with scissors and stapling them to the backing with help. Insert a paper fastener at the left as a starting point and place the sheet on a bulletin board or a piece of nonslip material such as Dycem so it won't slide. Encourage left-to-right movement and keeping all reading fingers "on the road."

   • To add interest to tracking activities for very beginning readers, stop the raised line partway across the page and insert a small textured shape, the child's name in braille, or a scratch-and-sniff sticker (see Figure 3.1). The child tracks from left to right looking for the "surprise" hiding in the line. Be sure the child continues to the end of the line after finding the shape or word.

■ A variety of meaningful tracking activities can be designed using braille characters to represent people, places, animals, and other objects of interest to the child (Lamb, 1996) (see Figure 3.2).

BOOKMAKING WITH YOUNG CHILDREN

Bookmaking is one of the most satisfying literacy experiences an adult can share with a child. The process of creating a book promotes oral language skills and develops many important literary concepts:

Figure 3.1 TRACKING PRACTICE

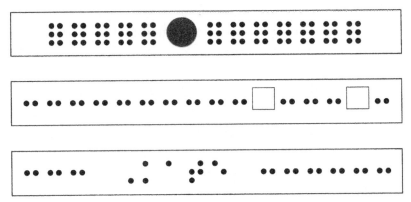

Inserting a surprise to look for in the line of braille, such as a sticker, a small textured shape, or the child's name in braille (here, "Kate"), adds interest to tracking practice.

Figure 3.2 MAKING TRACKING PRACTICE MEANINGFUL

Directions: The bus is going to school. Follow the road with your fingers and see how many children [full cells] it is picking up.

As the bus [represented by the braille for bus] gets nearer to school, it meets up with more and more buses. Can you find all the buses on the roads? Don't get the buses mixed up with the cars! [represented by the braille letter c]

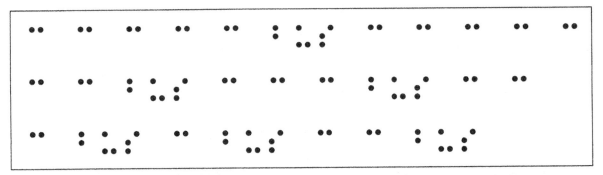

Routine tracking practice can be more meaningful to a young child when the braille characters are made the "actors" in a little story.

- Books come in different sizes and shapes.
- Books have parts: a front cover, a back cover, a title page, and other pages.
- Pages are turned one at a time from the front of the book to the back.
- Pages are numbered in order.
- Books contain meaningful pictures and writing.
- Braille words are read by tracking from left to right and top to bottom.
- Books are written by a person (the author) who has a message to share.

The key to successful bookmaking is having the child participate fully in the process of creating the book. Even very young children can select materials for tactile pictures; help staple or glue the pictures to the pages; suggest a word or sentence to tell about each picture; assist the teacher in sounding out each word as it is written; number the pages; and bind the parts of the book in order using rings, paper fasteners, or plastic binders. This process usually takes place over a period of several days, so that the child gains an appreciation for the time necessary to produce a book. Once a book is made, the teacher and the children read it over and over again together, reinforcing the concepts of front and back, turning pages one at a time, and examining each page to find the picture and the braille writing.

SUGGESTIONS FOR TEACHERS

CREATING A BOOK WITH A CHILD

- Spend time talking about the subject before writing.
- Compose words and sentences together with the child. Repetitive sentence patterns make the book easier for the student to read independently (see Chapter 5 for some examples).
- Verbalize sounds and words as you write on the braillewriter.
- Let the child write a "word" or "sentence" below yours by pressing random keys on the brailler.
- Extend the process of making the book to maximize learning. Complete only one or two pages each day, reviewing previous pages at the beginning of each lesson.

There are many of types of simple books that a teacher and a preschool student can make together. The examples listed here focus on basic concepts and familiar experiences; they help to build a foundation for the comprehension skills children will need during listening and reading activities later on.

Texture Book. Prepare a front and back cover in the shape of a large hand, and cut five to ten pages from braille paper to fit inside the covers. (See Appendix A for a hand pattern and page sizes). Assemble a collection of small pieces of textured material: felt, sandpaper, ribbon, corrugated cardboard, braille, spongy foam, cotton balls, rubber bands, a flat piece of wood, and so forth. Ask the child to choose a texture for the first page and think of a word to tell about it. Put the page in the braillewriter and model sounding out the word as you write it. Help the child glue or staple the texture to the page and read the word. Continue to make several pages a day, until you both agree that there are enough pages for a book. Compose a title for the book together (for example, *My Touching Book* or *My Finger Book*), stick the title and the author's name on the cover, organize the pages, and bind the book. You may also wish to include a title page, page numbers, and a sentence about the author.

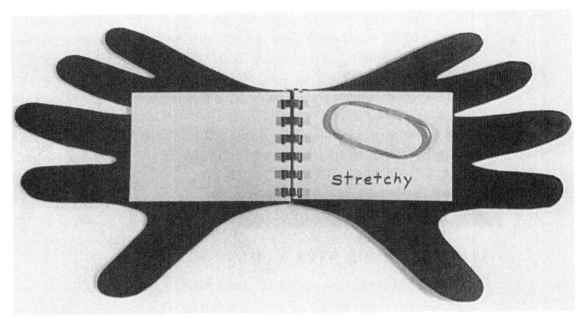

My Finger Book: **Making and reading this simple texture book teaches a child many important literacy concepts.**

Counting Book. Prepare five to ten rectangular poster-board pages, a front cover, and a back cover. Assemble objects that can be counted: shapes cut from sticky-backed felt and other textured materials, paper fasteners, large paper clips, toothpicks, and the like. You will also need a hole punch and a stapler. Have the child select and count objects for each page, increasing the number by 1 for each, for example: 1 fuzzy circle, 2 holes, 3 large paper clips, 4 staples, 5 paper fasteners, and so on. Attach the corresponding braille number below each set of objects.

Experience Books. An experience book may focus on a daily activity such as lunch time or a special event such as a field trip. Brainstorm possible book topics together and let the child make the final decision. Keep the following points in mind when creating the pictures for the book:

• Use real objects for pictures whenever possible; for example, a spoon, piece of milk carton, straw, and napkin for a lunch book.

- Keep other pictures very simple—for example, a long, narrow strip of smooth plastic placed diagonally on the page to represent a playground slide. Be sure the child has had extensive experience with the real objects that are being represented so that the pictures are meaningful.
- If the book's content includes people (the child, family members, classmates), a simple human figure made from poster board can be stapled to the page to represent each person. The child may wish to add clothes or facial features, but complex details are not usually necessary. Often a single characteristic, such as a strip of textured cloth for a belt or several pieces of yarn for long hair, is sufficient to identify the picture. (A pattern for a human figure is included in Appendix A.)

Concept Books. Encourage children to note similarities in environmental objects by focusing on particular attributes, such as points, curves, or textures. Or, target positional concepts by using a motivating tool such as a stapler to make horizontal, vertical, and diagonal tactile lines. Have the child participate in creating each page. Then write a braille word or sentence to describe the picture. Suggested books include the following:

- *Point Book.* Include a fork, toothpick, pushpin, triangle, paper fastener, unfolded paper clip, and so forth.

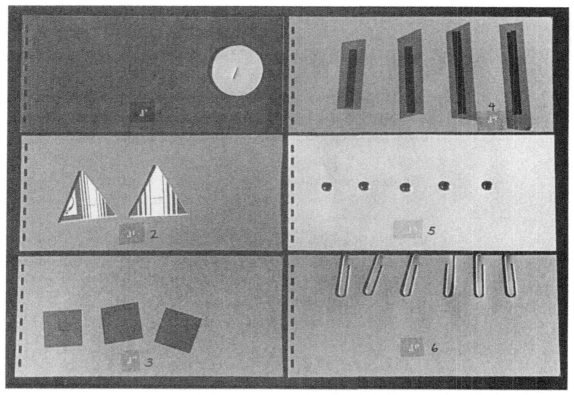

Children practice counting, number recognition, and fine motor skills as they assemble the pages for a counting book.

Experience books, based on real activities, are particularly motivating to young authors. Objects on the covers, such as a lunch tray and a strip of film representing a playground slide, make these books easy to recognize.

- *Book of Curves.* Include a plastic lid, bottle top, toy wheel, textured circle, and penny.

- *Gooey Book.* Attach zipper-type plastic bags containing such sticky substances as clay, cooked spaghetti, chewed gum, cookie dough, toothpaste, and hand lotion to each page. (This is a real *process* book, but not guaranteed to last!)

- *Staple Book.* Make lines of staples going across the page, down the page, diagonally from one corner of the page to the other, and in a circle. Vary the length of the lines to reinforce the concepts of long and short. Use a long arm stapler for larger pages. (Similar books can also be made using graphic art tape or a hole puncher.)

- *Fastener Book.* Fasten a textured shape to each page in a different way: staple, glue, paper fastener, metal ring, paper clip, tape, twist tie, and so on. Write the name of each type of fastener in braille.

- *Pipe Cleaner Book.* Attach a different shape of pipe cleaner to each page: straight, bent, twisted, circular, and so forth.

- *Cutting Book.* Have the child independently cut a different textured material for each page. Write a word or sentence to describe what the cut shape looks like.

SUMMARY

Parents and teachers can promote braille literacy in young children by integrating braille into everyday experiences as often as possible. At this level, modeling of reading and writing behaviors in a relaxed, informal setting provides the best motivation for children to experiment with braille.

The process of bookmaking in particular introduces young children to important aspects of literacy. They begin to make the connection between oral and written language, developing the basic understanding that anything they say can be written in braille. Creating books provides opportunities for young braille readers to master the book-handling skills that sighted children acquire so easily through observation. As they compose, assemble, and read their own books, children also gain firsthand knowledge of what it means to be an author. This experience can be an empowering one for them, promoting creativity, a feeling of competence, and enhanced skills. In time, it will also help children develop an interest in the authors of the trade books they read and contribute to their understanding of an author's composition, style, and message. This, in turn, will continue to foster the development of literacy at more advanced levels throughout their schooling.

CHAPTER 4
Teaching the Beginning Reader

Implementing a formal braille reading program with a young student involves many decisions and extensive planning. Teachers need to choose a reading approach or become familiar with the one used in the mainstream classroom. They must decide how and when to introduce braille letters, words, and contractions and plan activities to reinforce the student's learning. If a child who is severely visually impaired or has low vision is learning both print and braille, sufficient practice must be provided in each medium to develop reading proficiency. In the remaining time, there is a never-ending list of instructional materials to be created, adapted, or transcribed into braille.

This chapter describes a three-step approach to teaching braille reading that has been used successfully with mainstreamed students and with children who have additional disabilities. It includes suggestions for teaching skills within a meaningful context, as well as for using materials from the meaning-oriented end of the language arts continuum. Special considerations related to mastering the braille code and reading mechanics are discussed in the second half of the chapter.

THE READING-WRITING CONNECTION

Although this chapter focuses on reading braille and the following chapter on writing, these two components of literacy are not separate "subjects" taught in isolation. Rather, in a well-designed language arts program, reading and writing reinforce each other (Anderson, Hiebert, Scott, & Wilkinson, 1984). When young students begin to write they become more aware of sound-symbol relationships and develop the concept that written text must make sense. Over time children can apply the insights they gain as writers to better understand the structure and message of what they read. In short, through writing, "they learn how reading is put together . . . they learn the essence of print" (Hansen, 1987, p. 179)—or braille.

Children who are learning braille can discover a great deal about reading when provided with daily opportunities to write. Some children initially find writing on the

Reading and writing reinforce each other. A young author reads his book—shaped like a shoe—about a walk to the playground. The student's story is a retelling of *Rosie's Walk*, by Pat Hutchins, which he had read earlier.

braillewriter easier than making the fine discriminations necessary in reading braille characters; as a result, their writing skills may actually surpass their reading skills for a time. Insisting that children always read back their writing, first to themselves and then to a peer or adult, provides them with the opportunity to apply reading strategies to the text that is most familiar to them: their own writing. Teachers can enhance the impact of their instruction by helping students make frequent reading-writing connections in literacy activities. These can be as simple as writing a shopping list for a mobility lesson or as complex as publishing a student-authored book.

CHOICES FOR IMPLEMENTING A LANGUAGE ARTS APPROACH

Whether a young braille reader is enrolled in a self-contained, resource, or mainstream class, there are several important programming decisions to be made when implementing the language arts curriculum:

- Will the child use instructional materials created exclusively for students who are learning braille, or will materials and methods be adapted from the general education curriculum?

- Will the child's instruction be primarily one-on-one, or will it include group learning with sighted peers? Or, in a self-contained or resource setting, will there be group learning with peers who are also visually impaired?

- If the child is fully mainstreamed, how should the teacher balance the demands of the general education curriculum with the need for specialized instruction related to braille?

- If a student has low vision and is learning to read in both print and braille simultaneously, what portions of the curriculum will be presented in each medium?

The answers to these questions will depend on many factors, including an individual child's abilities, academic level, behavior, placement, and classmates. Whether or not they are working in a mainstream setting, teachers of young braille readers can benefit from learning more about recent developments in the teaching of literacy skills to young sighted children. (See, for example, Bolton & Snowball, 1993a, 1993b; Graves, 1983; Routman, 1988, 1991; and many other books published by Heinemann Press [see Resources]. Many school systems also produce their own resources, such as language arts curriculum guides with goals, benchmarks, and recommended activities for each grade.) Teaching braille to young children involves far more than the signs and symbols of the braille code; it encompasses the much larger task of teaching reading and writing, and students learning braille deserve the same up-to-date techniques that their sighted peers receive.

Using Materials Created for Teaching Braille

Several programs exist that are designed specifically for students who are learning braille. The two most widely used are *Patterns: The Primary Braille Reading Program* (Caton, Pester, & Bradley, 1982c) and *The Mangold Developmental Program of Tactile Perception and Braille Letter Recognition* (S. Mangold, 1977).

The *Patterns* program, published by the American Printing House for the Blind, is a traditional basal series with a controlled vocabulary, isolated skill practice, and little choice of reading material for students. At the readiness level, it consists of two small student books, a teacher's manual, review worksheets, and assessment materials. In the first student book, *Go and Do*, children learn to read common one-cell whole-word contractions (such as *go, like,* and *and*) and a few other simple words (for example, *we, get,* and *ride*). This enables them to read meaningful material immediately, an important step for those who may not fully comprehend the reading process. In the second book, *Letters and You,* children learn the letters of the alphabet. Subsequent books take students through the preprimer (grades 1–2), primer (grades 1–2), first-reader (grades 1–2), second-reader (grades 2–3), and third-reader (grades 3–4) levels. Skills and concepts are reinforced by having students complete numerous worksheets.

The traditional skill-oriented focus of *Patterns* makes it very different from the literature-based reading programs many sighted children are experiencing today.

Portions of *Patterns* may be useful in teaching specific skills related to the braille code, or for working with students who have additional disabilities (Erin & Koenig, 1997). However, students whose entire language arts curriculum is focused on this program miss out on the opportunity to read high-quality children's literature, integrate reading and writing, and share literacy experiences with peers.

The Mangold Developmental Program of Tactile Perception and Braille Letter Recognition (S. Mangold, 1977) is a traditional program that teaches efficient tracking skills and recognition of the letters of the alphabet in isolation. Students complete daily drills and games, keeping a tactile record of their progress. The Mangold program can be used in conjunction with other less traditional materials, such as a literature-based reading program, to provide daily practice in skills unique to reading braille.

Working with the Mainstream Curriculum

Teachers who work with mainstreamed children typically find that many of the materials, activities, and teaching strategies used in general education classrooms are appropriate for children who read braille, regardless of the approach taken to teaching reading. Special considerations for integrating a braille reader into different mainstream reading approaches and for using transliterated materials are discussed in *Instructional Strategies for Braille Literacy* (Wormsley & D'Andrea, 1997) and *Foundations of Braille Literacy* (Rex, Koenig, Wormsley, & Baker, 1994). Participating in group learning, whether in the mainstream or in a self-contained class, allows children who are learning braille to interact with other students during literacy activities. They are motivated to read books they hear their classmates enjoying and develop a sense of audience (whom they are writing for) very early in their writing careers as they share their writing pieces with others. With daily support from a teacher of visually impaired students, many young braille readers can participate in nearly all aspects of the regular language arts program, from group brainstorming to shared reading to publishing their own written work.

Balancing the Mainstream Curriculum and Special Needs

Children who learn to read braille in a mainstream class or in a self-contained special education class with sighted peers require supplemental individual instruction from their itinerant or resource teacher. Skills such as tracking efficiently, writing correctly on the braillewriter, and mastering the braille code demand extra time and attention from a specialist on a daily basis (see the section on "Special Considerations for Teaching Braille Reading" later in this chapter).

If a child is receiving language arts instruction in a self-contained or one-on-one setting, the teacher has the flexibility to choose strategies, activities, and materials that best match the child's learning style and needs (see "Choosing an Approach to Reading Instruction"). Frequently, however, students are mainstreamed into regular classrooms with a predetermined curriculum and expected outcomes. In such instances, the itinerant teacher must carefully balance the general education pro-

■ CHOOSING AN APPROACH TO READING INSTRUCTION

Choosing or adapting a reading approach for a student learning braille involves a number of considerations, including the student's learning style and needs, the classrooms teacher's approach if the child is mainstreamed, and maintaining a balance between the general education curriculum and specialized instruction in braille skills. Certain suggestions will be helpful in determining the reading approach to use with students in any setting:

■ Obtain a copy of the objectives and performance expectations for sighted students who are working on the same level as your students.

■ Examine work samples from regular education students to gain perspective on the level at which your students might be expected to perform.

■ Consult references such as *Instructional Strategies for Braille Literacy* (Wormsley & D'Andrea, 1997) and *Foundations of Braille Literacy* (Rex, Koenig, Wormsley, & Baker, 1994) to review the implications of using different reading approaches with students who are learning braille.

■ Refer to the *Assessment of Braille Literacy Skills* (ABLS) (Koenig & Farrenkopf, 1994–95), a comprehensive checklist of braille reading and writing skills, to be sure that the student is mastering all necessary braille-related skills. (See Chapter 10 for more details about assessment and the ABLS.)

The following additional suggestions will be particularly useful when selecting a reading approach for a student who is learning braille in a self-contained or one-on-one setting:

■ Expand your choice of instructional materials beyond those written exclusively for students who are learning braille. Ask general education teachers to share some of their materials with you, and adapt them for your students, if appropriate.

■ Observe a regular kindergarten or first-grade class to learn more about up-to-date approaches to teaching language arts.

■ Consult with the reading teacher or a teacher of children with learning disabilities if your students appear to have additional learning problems.

■ Find ways for your students to share literacy experiences with peers, even if it is only once or twice a week. For example, they can participate in story time in a general education class, join group discussions about literature, or read their writing to sighted classmates.

gram with specialized instruction in braille skills, and integrate the two whenever possible. Sometimes this feels like doing two jobs in the time allotted for only one! The amount of "pullout" time for individual instruction away from mainstream learning will depend on the student's performance level, the appropriateness of the general education activities to the student's needs, and the itinerant teacher's philosophy about working in a mainstream setting. Some teachers are most comfortable adapting nearly every activity and rarely removing the student from the room for specialized instruction; others prefer to allot a certain amount of individual instructional time each day to specific braille-related tasks that reinforce, supplement, or enrich the regular curriculum. (The case study of Sharon in Chapter 9 illustrates the latter approach.)

Mainstreaming at the Kindergarten Level

Under ideal circumstances, children who have begun to learn braille in preschool using a sequential approach such as the one described later in this chapter enter kindergarten with the same emergent literacy skills as their sighted peers. These may include reading and writing at least some letters of the alphabet; recognizing common sound-symbol relationships (the letter s makes the sound /s/); reading simple sentences using one-cell whole-word contractions (for example, "Mommy can go."); and writing their names. Children who begin kindergarten with these skills can continue their literacy learning using mainstream materials, such as braille transcriptions of stories and poems. They also have the advantage of being able to write simple journal entries and responses to questions independently when the sighted children may be drawing pictures for the same activities. Itinerant teachers will still need to spend individual time with their students, however, to teach and reinforce skills specific to braille, such as recognizing contractions, writing on the brailler, and tracking.

For a variety of reasons, many young children who are candidates for braille instruction do not start kindergarten with the same emergent literacy skills as their sighted peers. They may have additional disabilities, speak English as a second language, lack appropriate preschool experiences, or be immature. These children will have a difficult time following along on braille copies of kindergarten reading materials and, in most cases, will not "pick up" braille by mere exposure. Direct teaching is necessary to help them catch up and join their sighted peers in group learning experiences. In this situation, the itinerant teacher may decide to replace some of the general education curriculum with an individualized approach to teaching

■ BRAILLE LITERACY SKILLS FOR KINDERGARTNERS

By the end of kindergarten, students who are working on grade level in braille may demonstrate most or all of these skills:

- reading and writing the letters of the alphabet (some reversals may still occur)
- reading and writing a core of tactile sight words in grade 2 braille, such as names of family members and friends; common one-cell whole-word contractions such as *can* and *go;* and color and number words
- reading and writing some common part-word contractions in grade 2 braille
- matching voice to braille words with one-to-one correspondence
- beginning to use phonics, meaning (context), and structure (grammar) cues for word recognition
- tracking braille text from left to right and from top to bottom with an efficient return sweep from line to line
- using sound-symbol relationships (mainly consonants) to write words and sentences in invented spelling
- using some spacing between words when writing

braille, such as the one described later in this chapter. By the end of kindergarten, students should be expected to demonstrate the same competencies required of their sighted classmates (see "Braille Literacy Skills for Kindergartners") if they are to succeed in first grade.

Mainstreaming in the Primary Grades

Most sighted children "take off" with reading and writing once they enter first grade. Expectations for the quality and quantity of independent work increase significantly compared with kindergarten. Children who read braille *can* keep up with the mainstream pace if they have a strong foundation of literacy skills, access to all instructional materials in braille, and daily support from an itinerant or resource teacher. Parental assistance with homework (especially reading) also contributes greatly to a child's learning. As in kindergarten, the itinerant or resource teacher will have to balance the demands of the general education curriculum with the need for specialized instruction (see "Balancing the Mainstream Curriculum with Specialized Instruction"). Often it is helpful to preview the day's work with the child during an individual session at the beginning of the day. Those children who are not performing on grade level will continue to need longer pullout sessions and teacher-designed activities appropriate for them.

Teaching Braille and Print Reading Simultaneously

The decision to teach braille as a primary or secondary reading medium to a child with low vision is made by the educational team after a careful analysis of the child's current and future educational needs (Wormsley & D'Andrea, 1997). Several excellent commercially available materials can assist teachers and parents in making this decision. These include *Learning Media Assessment of Students with Visual Impairments* (Koenig & Holbrook, 1995), *Print and Braille Literacy: Selecting Appropriate Learning Media* (Caton, 1991), *TOOLS for Selecting Appropriate Learning Media* (Caton, 1994), and the *Braille Assessment Inventory* (Sharpe, McNear, & McGrew, 1996).

The balance between print and braille instruction is highly dependent on the individual child and requires frequent reassessment. In this author's experience, some children with low vision begin instruction with less proficient tactile skills than those who have been blind since birth. Teachers working with students who are learning both print and braille need to be sure that children have sufficient practice in tactile discrimination to become fluent readers. Over time, students may develop a preference for completing certain types of tasks in one medium or the other.

A THREE-STEP APPROACH TO BEGINNING BRAILLE INSTRUCTION

Students who acquire a foundation of literary understanding during their preschool years are ready for more formal braille instruction by late preschool or early kinder-

■ BALANCING THE MAINSTREAM CURRICULUM WITH SPECIALIZED INSTRUCTION

Itinerant or resource teachers of mainstreamed students in the primary grades must carefully balance their instructional focus between the demands of the general education curriculum and the child's need for specialized skills (primarily braille) to access this curriculum. The following suggestions will help teachers work as efficiently as possible during language arts instruction.

■ If the student is working on grade level, focus on teaching skills unique to braille. Whenever possible, integrate instruction in specific braille skills with regular classroom activities and materials. Use braille transcriptions of books and poems that the other children are reading to reinforce tracking, tactile discrimination, and recognition of letters or contractions.

■ Children who are on grade level may still benefit from specialized instruction in certain subject areas. For example, mainstream spelling programs often require students to learn words that are unrelated to their writing needs. Replacing this approach with an individualized spelling program designed by the itinerant or resource teacher can be an effective way to teach contractions and help students learn to spell words they really use in their writing. (Individualized spelling strategies are described in more detail in Chapter 7.)

■ Use pullout time to preview stories and activities that the mainstream teacher has planned for the day. Young students will understand story content better if they have the opportunity to learn new braille contractions, discuss concepts, and examine tactile models ahead of time. Also, previewing written assignments and practicing the first question or two may enable the student to complete the work independently when it is assigned later.

■ Consider substituting braille-related activities such as bookmaking or tactile discrimination exercises for highly visual assignments involving cutting, pasting, and coloring. Remember that not every mainstream activity needs to be adapted (see the section on "Adapting Visual Materials" in Chapter 2).

■ If a student is working significantly below grade-level expectations, increase the amount of time devoted to individual instruction. It may be necessary to replace some of the general education curriculum with an individualized approach to teaching braille, such as the one described in this chapter. Keeping students in the mainstream full time for self-esteem purposes when they are unable to benefit academically will lead to major learning deficits and less mainstreaming later on.

■ In general, pullout sessions should not replace the entire language arts curriculum. Children whose braille skills are very delayed can still benefit from learning involving listening and speaking with the whole group.

■ Remember that a pullout lesson does not have to be lengthy, nor does it have to take place in a separate room. Sometimes a 5- or 10-minute meeting with a child in a corner of the regular classroom to review skills or preview material is all that is needed.

■ Build as much flexibility into your schedule as possible. Being at school for the entire language arts instruction period enables you to work individually with a student for short or long periods and individually or in the large group, depending on the day's activities.

■ Keep in mind that the purpose of specialized individual instruction is to provide children with the skills that they need to participate as fully as possible in the general education curriculum. They will be expected to pass the same competency tests and meet the same objectives as their sighted peers as they move through school. The ultimate goal of individualized instruction is entry into the educational mainstream.

garten. In the three-step approach described here, children read and write common tactile "sight words" in grade 2 braille *before* they learn the letters of the braille alphabet. The purpose of this sequence is to give students hands-on experience with real reading from the very beginning. As they read simple sentences about themselves and people they know in step 1, children learn to match one spoken word to each braille word; they refine their tactile discrimination skills; and, most important, they realize that braille text has meaning for them. Once children internalize these basic reading behaviors, they can turn their attention to learning to recognize and write the letters of the braille alphabet and numbers in step 2. Sometimes learning this information can be a lengthy process, and students need to use their expanding knowledge of letters and sounds to continue reading high-interest materials at this stage. When students have mastered a core of basic tactile sight words and the letters of the alphabet, they are ready to read commercially available emergent reader books in step 3.

When they are working on the readiness level of *Patterns* (Caton, Pester, & Bradley, 1982c), children also read words in grade 2 braille before learning alphabet letters and numbers. However, the approach described here differs from the *Patterns* method in that the teacher selects vocabulary words and teaching strategies that capitalize on a particular child's interests, abilities, and experiences. For example, instead of reading about the fictional characters Tim and Pam in the *Patterns* readiness book, the child reads teacher-made sentences and stories that tell about his or her own family members and friends. (Examples of teacher-made stories are included in Chapter 5.) Children are encouraged to participate in choosing words and letters to learn next. The teacher uses materials and activities from both ends of the language arts continuum to teach words, letters, and numbers in a variety of ways. Chapter 5 describes specific beginning braille reading activities that can be used with this approach.

The three-step sequence described in this chapter teaches braille reading skills within a meaning-oriented framework. Children with unimpaired cognitive ability and strong early literacy skills are typically ready to begin steps 1 and 2 in their last year of preschool (see, for example, the case study of Sharon in Chapter 9). Students whose development is delayed may not be ready to begin the sequence until kindergarten or the primary grades (see the case study of Eddie in Chapter 9). If children are participating in the mainstream language arts program at the kindergarten or first-grade level, the itinerant or resource teacher may choose to supplement portions of the general education curriculum with some of the strategies and activities from this three-step sequence. Note that steps 1 and 2 may overlap for some students who learn words and letters simultaneously. Adapted approaches for teaching braille reading and writing to students with multiple disabilities are discussed in Chapter 8.

To summarize, in the three-step sequence of beginning braille reading instruction, the child learns to:

1. read and write a core vocabulary of tactile sight words and familiar names;

2. read and write the letters of the alphabet and the numbers 0–10; and

3. read commercially available emergent reader books.

The following sections describe these steps in more detail.

Step 1: Selecting Beginning Tactile Sight Words

In step 1, students learn a core of common tactile sight words and practice reading and writing them in meaningful contexts. Like a print sight word, a tactile sight word is one that a student recognizes instantly, without having to apply decoding strategies. The vocabulary list from the *Patterns* readiness book *Go and Do* (Caton, Pester, & Bradley, 1982a), consisting of common one-cell whole-word contractions and a few other simple words, includes most of the following core vocabulary words:

go	you	can
I	we	like
have	the	a
do	but	just
that	people	not
me	to (uncontracted)	and
with	get	will
for	it	in

A checklist for recording a student's progress in learning these beginning tactile sight words appears in Chapter 10 and Appendix B.

Make sure that each new word is mastered before introducing another. Depending on individual needs, you may choose to vary the sequence of this list, omit certain words, or teach other words that are meaningful to a particular student (for example, "lunch," which appears everyday on a brailled schedule). Have the student practice reading and writing these words daily using a variety of activities such as the ones described in Chapter 5.

It is important that the first words taught differ significantly in tactile configuration. Also, reversed or confusing pairs of contracted letters or words (such as the contractions for *and* and *you*) should not be introduced until the first member of the pair is well learned (see the section on "Special Considerations" later in this chapter). Words such as *go, like, I, you,* and *can* are easy for students to discriminate and can be used to create a variety of sentences and stories. Sample teacher-made stories composed of such core vocabulary words are found in Chapter 5.

The use of familiar names makes simple braille sentences meaningful to individual students. Teach the names of family members and classmates at the same time as basic tactile sight words. Discriminating one longer name from another is difficult for some beginning readers. See if these children can discriminate their own names from a group of five unspaced full cells, which you can call "Mr. (or Mrs.) Nobody":

Mr. Nobody

Once children are able to recognize their own names and Mr. Nobody, they enjoy helping to choose the names of family members and friends to learn. This is a good time to begin pointing out individual letters that give a word its special shape. The word *Joshua*, for example, has the letter *a* at the end, which is easy to find. Like sighted children, visually impaired students who are beginning braille readers first learn to recognize names by keying into one or two significant letters; they do not have to be able to identify all the letters and contractions in a word in order to read it. Distinctive letters (such as *y, l, g,* or *c*) at the beginning or end of words are easiest to spot, but sometimes a word also has a clue in the middle such as the double *m* in *Mommy* or the *a* in *Dad.* As children increase their repertoire of names and other words, they are obligated to make finer and finer distinctions to distinguish one word from another. No longer is the key letter *L* sufficient to read both *Laura* and *Larry*; the entire word needs to be examined. In this way children learn to recognize many letters and contractions using words that are meaningful to them. Thus, a sample sequence of words taught to a beginning reader might include the following:

> *Eddie, a, go, like, Mr. Nobody, I, you, can, get, lunch, work, Dad,* and *do.*

Step 2: Teaching Letters and Numbers

Begin to talk about braille letters in context as you help children examine easy-to-find letters in names, schedule and calendar words, classroom labels, and simple daily messages (see Chapter 5). Students may notice that certain letters and numbers have the same shape as the one-cell whole-word contractions they are learning; for example, the letter *l* and the word *like*; the number *7* and the word *go*. Introduce letters of the alphabet and numbers more formally when children are able to read and write some—but not necessarily all—of the tactile sight words listed in Step 1 and read them in teacher-made sentences and stories.

Different children will require different amounts of structure when learning letters and numbers. Many will need one or more daily activities from the skills-oriented end of the language arts continuum, such as short worksheets and flash cards, to provide sufficient practice in discrimination. Have the children learn to write each new letter or number as it is introduced. Reading back their writing will provide additional reinforcement of the shape of each new character.

It is important to continue meaningful reading activities when the instructional focus shifts to individual letters and numbers. Use the new letters to write more words, sentences, and stories of high interest to students and emphasize the relationships between the sounds and symbols to develop beginning phonetic decoding skills. Recognizing a braille letter or contraction in isolation on a flash card is much easier than discriminating it in the middle of a longer word. Ask students to spell written words from their reading to be sure that they are able to recognize letters and contractions in close proximity.

Step 3. Introducing Emergent Reader Books

During the initial phase of braille instruction, children read meaningful sentences and stories composed by the teacher or written jointly with the teacher. These materials reinforce specific sight words and letters that they are learning. Once students have mastered a basic set of tactile sight words and the letters of the alphabet, they can begin using commercial materials such as the emergent reader books available from a number of publishers. These generally come in sets of small books sequenced by reading level, such as the Storybox and Sunshine collections from the Wright Group and the Literacy 2000 Series from Rigby (see the Resources section).

At the very beginning levels, these books have one word or sentence on a page and often use patterned language or rhymes to assist the beginning reader. For example, the entire text of the book *Ice Cream* (Cowley, 1986) is as follows:

> We like ice cream in the car.
> We like ice cream in the plane.
> We like ice cream in the snow.
> We like ice cream in the rain.
> We like ice cream in the tree.
> We like ice cream on the hill.
> No more ice cream!
> We feel ill.

Many of these stories are meaningful to children who are blind or visually impaired, even without picture clues. Brailling the text on a self-adhesive plastic strip and placing it above or below the printed words enables parents and mainstream teachers to read with the child.

Techniques to Use with Emergent Reader Books

In primary classrooms with meaning-oriented reading instruction, children learn to use three cueing or information systems interdependently to identify unfamiliar words: the graphophonic, meaning (semantics), and language structure (syntax) systems (Routman, 1988). For example, in the following sentence a child needs to identify the word "growls":

> My dog *growls* when he is mad.

The reader simultaneously checks phonetic cues (the letter sounds for *bites* would not fit), the meaning of the sentence (*grows* would not make sense), and the language structure (a verb is needed, so an adjective like *grouchy* would not sound right) to narrow the range of possibilities and arrive at the correct word. Beginning

Emergent reader books can be enjoyed by beginning braille readers. Clear labels containing the braille text are affixed to the pages so that both braille and print can be read. These books are from the Sunshine collection published by The Wright Group.

print readers also make extensive use of picture clues to help in the identification process.

Children are encouraged to develop such reading strategies and to become independent readers by participating in activities derived from the whole language approach such as shared, assisted, and guided reading (Fowler, Jackson, & McCallum, 1995). During shared reading instruction, the students (usually the whole class) and the teacher share the reading of enlarged text in a big book or on a handwritten chart. The teacher points to each word as it is read so that the children develop a voice-to-print match. This activity also provides an opportunity for the teacher to demonstrate one or more reading strategies that will help children decode and comprehend the text. For example, the teacher may model how to figure out an unknown word by thinking about what word makes sense and begins with the right letter. Individual braille copies of books must be available for these lessons, and it is helpful for the itinerant teacher to preview the book with a student before the whole group lesson.

Teachers of students with visual impairments may use assisted reading when working one-on-one with a young student. The teacher begins by reading the entire story to the child and describing the pictures as the child follows along with the braille text. During subsequent readings, the teacher points out such features of the braille code as new contractions and unfamiliar punctuation marks. Other clues, such as beginning sounds or rhyming words, also help in the decoding process. The student repeats the words read by the teacher, imitates the decoding strategies, and gradually learns to read the story independently.

As children gain reading competence, guided reading instruction encourages them to become more independent readers. Using this technique, the teacher provides a small group of students with a carefully planned introduction to a book before asking them to read it independently. The introduction will include the reason the book was chosen for the lesson and may link background information with the students' own experiences, offer a description of the pictures, or focus on specific words or contractions that are unfamiliar to the students. As students read orally or silently to themselves at their own rate, the teacher listens to each one in the group for a few minutes and notes areas of strength and weakness in decoding and comprehension. At the end of the lesson, the group comes together again to discuss what they have read and to share successful reading strategies.

Routman's whole language classic, *Invitations: Changing as Teachers and Learners K–12* (1991), is highly recommended for teachers who wish to explore these whole language teaching techniques in greater depth. Adaptations for students who are learning braille are discussed in *Providing Quality Instruction in Braille Literacy Skills: Companion Guide to "Invitations: Changing as Teachers and Learners K–12"* (Koenig & Farrenkopf, 1994).

Teaching Braille Contractions with Emergent Reader Books

During the first two steps of braille instruction, when children are learning basic tactile sight words and letters, the teacher controls the vocabulary that learners encounter in teacher-made stories, on worksheets, and in other beginning reading activities. This controlled vocabulary gives children an opportunity to match spoken words to familiar braille words and to begin to grasp the reading process. However, once students start to read commercially produced emergent readers in Step 3, there is no more vocabulary control. Any book may contain a variety of new short-form words, single-cell contractions, and more difficult two-cell contractions. Although this may initially seem confusing, most young readers navigate the array of new contractions successfully with appropriate daily guidance. Teachers can use a variety of strategies with emergent reader books to help children learn contractions, develop decoding skills, and read with fluency and confidence.

◼ SUGGESTIONS FOR TEACHERS

TEACHING READING WITH EMERGENT READER BOOKS

◼ Insist that children keep their fingers on each word that they are reading, just as young sighted children point to words as they read. Emergent reader books are often easy to memorize because of their patterned language and rhymes, and children may be tempted to recite the words from memory. However, they need to "see" the written words over and over again by matching each one to a spoken word until they can recognize them automatically.

■ After children have read a book several times, ask them to turn to pages at random and read them. They will need to use reading strategies rather than their memory to make sense of the text.

■ Always spell contractions using letter names, such as the *i-n-g* contraction. Do not simply say the sound the contraction makes. This will help children learn conventional spelling and eliminate confusion when a contraction makes more than one sound (for example, the *o-n-e* contraction sounds different in *done* and *bone*).

■ For each emergent reader book, pick several common contractions as a focus for instruction. It is not necessary for a child to recognize every contraction in order to read a book fluently. For example, in the book *Ice Cream*, quoted earlier, the teacher might choose to introduce the *a-r, i-n,* and *t-h-e* contractions. The *e-a* contraction in "cream" is more difficult because of its position in the braille cell, so this contraction might be saved for later; however, *cream* is still easy to decode using the beginning *cr* blend and the ending consonant *m*.

■ Keep a running list of contractions that have been introduced and make note of the ones that students are recognizing independently in their reading and using correctly in their writing. The *Assessment of Braille Literacy Skills* (Koenig & Farrenkopf, 1994–95) includes a handy form for recording the contractions that students have learned (see Chapter 10; a copy of this form is also included in Appendix B).

■ Plan follow-up activities to reinforce the new contractions that students are learning. Whenever possible, connect students' reading to writing. Together with the student, write a list of words containing a particular contraction, and keep it for future reference and additions (see description of the *Words, Words, Words!* book in Chapter 5). For example, when focusing on the *a-r* contraction, list words like *star, car, far,* and *market*.

■ Have children practice writing the new contractions by using a sentence from the book to generate a "rewrite" or "retelling," in which they repeat the pattern of the sentence, but substitute new ideas. For example:

> *Where else do we like ice cream?*
> We like ice cream on a star.
> We like ice cream in a swimming pool.
>
> *What else do we like to eat?*
> We like pizza in a tent.
> We like pizza in the tree.

■ Be sure students write the target contractions correctly (*a-r, i-n,* and *t-h-e* in this example), but accept invented spelling for their own ideas (such as "swimming pool"). Having students read back what they have written reinforces the reading-writing connection. (See Chapter 7 for more detailed examples of rewrites or retellings.)

■ Include words containing new contractions in an individualized spelling list, especially if these are contractions that the students need for words they use in their daily writing (see the section on spelling in Chapter 7).

■ Keep a basket of books the students can read in the classroom, and encourage them to reread the books frequently. They will enjoy taping their reading when it is fluent.

■ Teach color and number words to introduce common part-word contractions. Give children a set of flat-sided crayons with braille labels (see Chapter 5 and the Resources section). Use braille transcriptions of children's literature such as *Brown Bear, Brown Bear, What Do You See?* (Martin, 1983) and the rhyme "Five Little Monkeys Jumping on the Bed" to reinforce color and number words.

Learning to read braille using children's literature is a highly motivating experience for many students. They enjoy the wide range of reading materials and derive satisfaction from reading individual books independently. In most cases, the uncontrolled vocabulary and grade 2 braille contractions do not hinder children's progress in reading, as long as they read extensively and integrate their writing with their reading.

SPECIAL CONSIDERATIONS FOR TEACHING BRAILLE READING

Regardless of the reading approach or instructional setting, learning to read braille entails special attention to certain details of the reading process. These include mechanics (the movement of the reader's hands), an understanding of the dot positions in the braille cell, and varied strategies to facilitate word identification.

Promoting Efficient Tracking Skills

An emphasis on efficient tracking (hand movements) at the beginning of braille instruction contributes greatly to the reader's long-term fluency and speed. Some teachers choose a formal program, such as the *Mangold Developmental Program of Tactile Perception and Braille Letter Recognition* (S. Mangold, 1977), to teach tracking skills in isolation. Others prefer to use a combination of teacher-made tracking sheets (featuring different textures, lengths, and widths of raised lines, as discussed in Chapter 3) and meaningful braille materials (for example, stories on the child's reading level), integrating tracking practice with the reading of familiar text. Whichever approach you choose, provide extensive modeling of tracking movements by having students place their hands on yours. If you are not a tactile reader yourself, also invite an older child or adult who knows braille to read to your students. It is not necessary for children to have perfect tracking skills before they begin to read teacher-made stories or commercial books. Tracking skills develop over time, and reading motivating materials is one of the more effective ways to practice them.

There is no single correct instructional sequence to develop tracking skills. In general, efficient braille readers use most of their fingers (except their thumbs) to read and move their hands independently to increase tracking speed. This outline presents a common sequence for developing tracking skills:

1. The student tracks across a single raised line, texture, or sequence of braille characters, two hands moving together (pointer fingers touching), four fingers of each hand on the line.
2. The student tracks across the top line, retraces the line, and drops vertically down to the beginning of the second line, two hands moving together.
3. The student tracks across the top line and drops diagonally down to the beginning of the second line, two hands moving together.
4. The student tracks halfway across the top line with the two hands moving together, separates hands, and continues to the end of the line with the right hand while the left hand drops diagonally to the beginning of the second line. The left hand starts reading as the right hand is lifted from the page and meets the left hand. This is known as two-handed independent tracking.

Students may progress through all of these tracking stages, or they may be ready to use two hands independently from the beginning. Always encourage children to keep as many fingers as possible on the raised practice line or line of braille text. Even with consistent prompting, however, not all children will read with six or eight fingers. In fact, some extremely competent adult braille readers use primarily their two index fingers for reading.

Some students with additional disabilities may track most accurately using their two hands together, retracing the line they have read, and dropping vertically to the beginning of the next line, as described in stage 2 of the tracking sequence. They may benefit from widely spaced lines and rote verbal cues such as "across, back, down to the next line."

Backtracking and Scrubbing

During backtracking, the reader returns to previously read characters or words if the text being read does not make sense. Many print readers, including adults, use this strategy to be sure they are comprehending the material they are reading. As long as backtracking does not occur so frequently that reading becomes inefficient, it can be regarded as a positive sign that a young reader is really focusing on the message of the text. However, frequent backtracking may indicate that the reading material is too difficult for the student (Wormsley & D'Andrea, 1997).

Scrubbing, or rubbing the fingers up and down or back and forth to aid in recognizing a braille character, may develop into a bad habit that hampers efficient braille reading. It may indicate that the child requires more practice in recognizing certain characters or contractions (Wormsley & D'Andrea, 1997). However, beginning readers, whether they read braille or print, need time to stop and examine unfamiliar words as they apply word-identification strategies. It is not uncommon to see young readers move their fingers over an unfamiliar word; return to the beginning of the word to spell it; suddenly recognize a new letter or contraction in the middle of the word; and finally apply phonetic, contextual, and syntactic clues to identify it. Although this may look like a combination of backtracking and scrubbing, it is often a necessary step in beginning reading. If children are given plenty of opportunities to develop their character-recognition skills and to reread familiar materials until they are fluent, word identification becomes automatic, just as it does for print readers.

Teaching the Dot Positions in the Braille Cell

Learning the positions of dots in the braille cell helps children discriminate letters and contractions when reading and copy them during writing activities. The Swing Cell, a simple six-hole pegboard available from the American Printing House for the

When closed, the Swing Cell, available from the American Printing House for the Blind, is a large-scale model of a braille cell. The halves swing open to represent the keys of a braillewriter.

Blind (see Resources section), provides an excellent model of the braille cell that children can use to make large-scale letters and contractions. The two vertical halves of the cell swing upward into horizontal positions to represent the keys of a braillewriter. Children are able to see the relationship between the keys on the braillewriter and the positions of the dots they write. Tack-Tiles (braille blocks that are interchangeable with standard Lego-type blocks), also make it easy for children to see the dot positions for each letter or contraction. Each Tack-Tile block has a jumbo-sized braille letter or contraction on it. Because the dots are large and easy to discriminate, children can clearly distinguish which dots of the braille cell are used to make a specific braille character.

Some teachers label the dots by number: dots 1, 2, and 3 on the left and dots 4, 5, and 6 on the right. Others recommend referring to the top, middle, and bottom dots in the first and second columns to facilitate learning to write with a slate and stylus later on (P. Mangold, 1993).

Not all children will be able to relate the peg configurations on the Swing Cell or the jumbo dots on the Tack-Tiles to the braille characters beneath their fingertips. Very young children or those with cognitive disabilities may be confused by the concept of dot numbers or positions. It is not necessary to be able to describe the positions of the dots in the braille cell in order to read braille, however. Children who have a grasp of basic positional concepts may find it easier to remember the spatial characteristics of braille letters and contractions. The following descriptions work well with many children, for example:

> *y* has a big hole on the left.
> *j* has a little hole at the top left.
> *r* has three dots on the left and one on the right.
> *e* slides down to the right.

Dot positions and spatial clues are most helpful when new braille characters are introduced or when two or more are confused. Frequent exposure to braille enables children to internalize the shape representing a particular letter or contraction so that thinking about numbered positions is no longer necessary.

Distinguishing Reversals or "Confusers"

Certain pairs of braille characters have the potential to cause discrimination problems for young readers. Some, like *b* and *c* or *p* and *f,* are very similar in configuration. Others, like *e* and *i* or *y* and the *a-n-d* contraction, are reversals, or mirror images of one another. Each member of these confusing pairs should be introduced at different times and practiced separately. Once students can consistently recognize each confuser without the other one present, they are ready to discriminate one from the other in exercises like the following:

Directions: Find one *i* in every row.

```
i

e        e        i        e

e        i        e        e

i        e        e        e
```

Even when care is taken to introduce the second member of a confusing pair only after the first is well-learned, some children do experience problems with reversals; in fact, this is normal for many 5- and 6-year-olds. It is helpful to determine whether children are unable to discriminate tactilely between two confusing shapes, or whether they simply are having trouble remembering which name to apply to which shape. Beginning readers often have particular problems with *e* and *i, m* and *sh,* and *k, st,* and *ch.* The letters *e* and *i* are especially critical because they are the same shapes as the Nemeth numbers 5 and 9, which appear without number signs in vertically oriented addition and subtraction problems. Use a simple worksheet such as the one just presented with the target letter at the top to determine whether the problem relates to tactile discrimination or memory.

If a child is unable to find the different letter in each row, it may be helpful to focus directly on the orientation of the two shapes. Use the Swing Cell or Tack-Tiles to show differences in dot positions and describe the characters' spatial orientations. Reading these characters in the context of a sentence or story will also help. If, after drill and practice, a child is still not able to discriminate the difference between two confusers like *i* and *e,* set this goal aside for a while and return to it in a month or so. Sometimes a little maturity is a big help in character recognition, especially when spatial orientation is involved.

Children who are able to tell which character is different in exercises, but who still mix up the names of reversed characters, may benefit from a braille alphabet strip stuck to the edge of their desks to check the orientation of the letters they are reading or writing. Knowledge of sounds and spelling patterns also helps when decoding words containing one or more confusing characters. For example, when confronted with the unknown word *five,* a child who confuses *e* and *i* might identify the last letter by knowing that a silent *e* is often found at the end of a word; the second letter has to be an *i* because only a long *i* sound (not a long *e* sound) makes a real word. (Additional strategies for dealing with reversal problems may be found in *Communication Skills for Visually Impaired Learners* [Harley, Truan, & Sanford, 1997], *Guidelines and Games for Teaching Efficient Braille Reading* [Olson, 1981], and *Instructional Strategies for Braille Literacy* [Wormsley & D'Andrea, 1997].)

Introducing Punctuation Marks

Punctuation marks may be confusing to beginning braille readers because they are the same size and configuration as letters and contractions. When preparing early reading materials using tactile sight words and familiar names, teachers can omit punctuation marks altogether. Periods may be introduced in emergent reader books, with other punctuation presented as a child is ready. First graders who are learning Nemeth Code for mathematics often find it easy to remember punctuation marks by relating them to Nemeth numbers: a question mark looks like a Nemeth 8; an exclamation point looks like a Nemeth 6.

Developing a Voice-to-Braille Match

During preschool literacy activities, children are encouraged to imitate the tactile reading behavior modeled for them. They move their hands quickly over a line of braille, often repeating the text from memory, but not discriminating individual words, letters, or contractions. Sighted preschoolers display a similar behavior when they use pictures and their memory to "read" a familiar book to an adult.

As children begin to read their names and a few single-letter contractions in sentences and stories, they need to slow down and match each braille word to a spoken word. This process can be tedious for a child with strong auditory memory skills who memorizes a simple story after hearing it once, but it is an important step toward independent reading. Only by focusing on individual words can readers develop accurate word-recognition skills that will transfer to unfamiliar materials. Regular education teachers help sighted children develop a voice-to-print match by asking them to point to each word as they read. When teaching braille you can encourage a voice-to-braille match by carefully monitoring oral reading to be sure the student's fingers are on the right word and by having the student reread the sentence if more practice is needed. You may also wish to leave a space between the words *and, for, of, the, with,* and *a* and avoid using the contractions for *to, by,* and *into* until the student has mastered the matching skill.

Teachers may discover that it is unrealistic for young braille readers in kindergarten or first grade to follow along on a braille copy while a mainstream teacher is reading a big book to the class during shared reading and really "see" each braille word; the pace is just too fast. Providing one-on-one assisted reading of classroom materials in braille gives the student the opportunity to examine individual words, learn new contractions, practice decoding strategies, and develop fluency.

Distinguishing Among Letters, Contractions, Words, and Sentences

Young children often do not understand the difference between a letter and a contraction or a word and a sentence. Ask students to show you a letter, contraction, word, and sentence during their reading to be sure that they understand the concepts. Have them count the letters in a word or the words in a sentence. You may wish to explain contractions as a short way of writing words or parts of words; some contractions have familiar shapes (such as *g* for the word *go*) and some have a special shape all their own (*s-h* and *o-u*). Point out that when writing on the computer we spell words the "long way" as in print, but when writing in braille we should use contractions to save space.

Tack-Tiles can be used to illustrate contractions. Spell a familiar word that contains a contraction, perhaps the child's name, in both contracted and uncontracted form using the tiles. Compare the length of both words. You can also have the child remove the individual letter tiles that make up a specific contraction in a word and replace them with a single tile showing that contraction.

Phonics and Phonemic Awareness

As noted earlier, good readers use three cueing or information systems interdependently to aid them in recognizing written language; they are semantic, syntactic, and graphophonic (Routman, 1988). The graphophonic system, or phonics, refers to the association of a letter or group of letters with a corresponding sound. Phonemic awareness, the ability to break words apart into syllables or sounds and blend these parts together again, is also critical to reading success. Despite general agreement that young readers need phonological instruction, there is often a wide discrepancy in the type and amount they receive from one regular education class to the next.

Although children who read braille should be expected to use all three information systems as they read, an emphasis on phonics and phonemic awareness remains critical for many beginning braille readers because of their inability to use picture clues. The braille code lends itself naturally to phonics instruction because it has special signs for digraphs (two consonants that represent one sound, such as *th* and *sh*) and common spelling patterns (frequently occurring sequences of letters that make a distinctive sound, such as *ound* and *ong*). In meaning-oriented programs, phonics skills are frequently taught in context, rather than as isolated drills. For example, vocabulary from *The Three Billy Goats Gruff* can serve as the basis for several focus lessons such as these:

- Discuss the "long e" sound made by the *y* at the end of *Billy* and relate it to familiar words such as *mommy, funny,* and *daddy.*
- Provide practice reading consonant blends such as *gr* in *Gruff, tr* in *troll,* and *br* in *bridge.*
- Discuss the sound made by *th* in *three;* have the student begin a list of words containing the *th* digraph.

All children, whether visually impaired or sighted, benefit from instruction in spelling patterns and sounds within the context of their reading. Some of them internalize sound-symbol relationships naturally and use them easily in conjunction with meaning and structural clues. Others require more extensive work in skills related to phonics and phonemic awareness, particularly if they have a reading disability in addition to their visual impairment. These students may struggle during the decoding process and lose the meaning of the text; or they may rely too much on context clues and become adept "guessers," rather than paying attention to sound-symbol relationships. The reading teacher is often a valuable resource in situations such as these, suggesting materials and teaching techniques that can be adapted for braille readers. If students are using a traditional workbook or isolated skill drills for phonics instruction, the teacher should be sure that they are applying phonics skills in meaningful contexts—that is, in their reading and writing. Teachers will also need to adapt the picture-oriented format of most phonics workbooks by presenting the exercises orally or on tape.

Using Tactile Picture Clues

Beginning braille readers use simple tactile pictures in the same way that sighted children use pictures. When reading a page with a tactile picture, children often examine the picture first, then read the braille text. Tactile pictures may be symbolic, rather than looking exactly like the object or action they represent; however, a real-life concept must precede the use of tactile representations. For example, dots of puff paint can represent rain, even though they bear little resemblance to drops of water falling from the sky. As long as children are familiar with the concept of rain, they quickly learn the meaning of the symbolic dots and use this picture clue when reading. The picture is not teaching the concept; the child should already have this. Rather, the picture provides an additional clue to enable a young child to read simple text.

Children enjoy making tactile pictures using a variety of textured materials and small objects. Choosing materials provides them with an opportunity for oral language development and an outlet for creativity. Activities such as cutting, taping, gluing, or stapling the pieces of a picture develop fine motor skills. In general, the simpler the picture, the easier it will be for the child to create, remember, and use in decoding text. A diagonal strip of old film serves as a slide, or a piece of fur as an animal; complicated, time-consuming details are not necessary.

Choice of Reading Materials

Books for sighted children differ in size, shape, texture of cover and paper, and type of illustrations. Young children often choose books based on these characteristics as much as on subject matter. Children who read braille are equally fascinated by variety in the books they read and learn to recognize favorites by the way they feel or from a special tactile picture on the cover.

A simple cardboard shape illustrates the spiral slide in the playground.

Provide children with a choice of braille books to read, books that differ both in subject matter and in tactile characteristics such as binding, shape, and size. Include commercially made books from the American Printing House for the Blind, Seedlings, and other sources (see the Resources section), in addition to books you braille and bind yourself. When making a braille copy of a print book for a child, cut the cover in an unusual shape or attach a tactile picture to the front to make the book easier to find quickly. Adapt regular children's books and emergent readers by sticking the braille text directly on the pages (see "Print Books with Tactile Features"). When presenting a choice of two or three books to a child, provide a short synopsis of each book while the child holds and examines it.

Permitting children to choose some of what they read provides them with control over their own learning. Children begin to evaluate their choices and develop preferences for certain authors and types of books. Braille readers are often highly

■ PRINT BOOKS WITH TACTILE FEATURES

Many print books for young readers have tactile features that make them attractive to braille readers. The following are just a few such examples. (See the list of Children's Books cited at the end of this book for the full references.)

- *The Very Hungry Caterpillar,* by Eric Carle (1969), has interesting page shapes and holes in the pictures where the caterpillar has eaten through different foods.
- *The Very Busy Spider,* by Eric Carle (1984), contains tactile pictures of the spider and its web.
- *The Secret Birthday Message,* by Eric Carle (1972), has interesting page shapes.
- *Dear Zoo*, by Rod Campbell (1984), is a lift-the-flap book with pictures of animals hiding under the flaps. The animals' names can be brailled and placed under the flaps for children to find.
- *Go Away, Big Green Monster!* by Ed Emberley (1992), has holes of different shapes illustrating the monster's facial features.

motivated to read books they hear their classmates or teacher reading. Whenever possible, follow the child's lead in choice of books and provide a braille copy. The goal is not to master a prescribed list of stories or books, but rather to instill habits characteristic of life-long readers. Choosing one's own reading material is one of these habits.

SUMMARY

The beginning stages of braille reading require a balance between skill-oriented and meaning-oriented activities and, in general education settings, between mainstream and individual instruction. Many skills related to tactile discrimination, mechanics, and word recognition can be taught in context using simple, high-interest materials created especially for a particular student. In the author's experience, however, most children also need some direct work on skills, such as worksheets and sorting tasks, to become proficient braille readers. Chapter 5 describes a variety of beginning reading activities from both halves of the language arts continuum that will help students learn words, letters, and numbers.

5 Beginning Reading Activities

The language arts continuum offers a broad spectrum of teaching strategies and materials, ranging from traditional to whole language. Most beginning braille readers benefit from a balance of meaning-oriented and skill-oriented activities as they master a core vocabulary of tactile sight words, the letters of the alphabet, and numbers.

This chapter begins with a description of six types of materials that teachers can use on a daily basis as part of the instructional routine. Controlled-vocabulary stories, calendars, schedules, and messages teach reading in context, while worksheets and flash cards tend to focus more on isolated skill development. The remaining activities and materials presented in this chapter reinforce children's learning in a variety of ways.

DAILY ACTIVITIES

Teacher-Made Controlled-Vocabulary Stories

Beginning braille readers benefit from the opportunity to read meaningful sentences and stories composed by the teacher as soon as they can recognize their own names and a few tactile sight words. As noted in Chapter 4, these words can come from the *Patterns* readiness book *Go and Do* (Caton, Pester, & Bradley, 1982a) or they may be words of particular interest to a child, such as *lunch*. Words that are not a part of a child's core reading vocabulary may be included to add interest to sentences and stories, along with tactile pictures or objects.

The amount of control the teacher needs to exert over the vocabulary in the reading material depends on the child's ability to read independently. Some students will require extensive drill and repetition of core vocabulary words in highly controlled materials characteristic of traditional instruction. Other students who are making good progress recognizing common words in a variety of sentences are

■ GUIDELINES FOR WRITING CONTROLLED-VOCABULARY STORIES

- Give the story an oral title or theme of interest to the child. Precede reading with oral discussion related to the theme.
- Focus on tactile sight words and names the child is learning.
- Use repetitive sentence structure and predictable text.
- Omit punctuation if it is confusing to the child.
- Use non-controlled vocabulary to add interest to the story, if appropriate.
- Make sure that the student can read the story accurately with a perfect voice-to-braille match before introducing another controlled-vocabulary story. This may necessitate several days of practice.
- Review previous stories to develop fluency.

ready to use context (meaning), phonetic, structural (grammatic), and tactile picture clues to identify unfamiliar words.

Consider the accompanying "Guidelines for Writing Controlled-Vocabulary Stories" when creating sentences and stories for children to read in braille during the first two steps of the three-step approach to teaching braille reading described in Chapter 4—that is, when they are learning a core vocabulary of tactile sight words and learning letters and numbers. Following are some examples of controlled-vocabulary stories.

Example 1

Oral title: "The Race"
Words the child knows: *go, Kate, Molly, Edward* (family names)

go   Edward   go

go   go   Molly

go   Kate   go

go   go   go

At the end, the teacher asks, "Who won?" The child picks a flash card containing a name from a choice of three in the teacher's hand and reads the name.

Example 2

Oral title: "My New Scooter" (a story based on child's own experience)
Words the child knows: *I, can, ride, with, me, Jay* (brother's name)

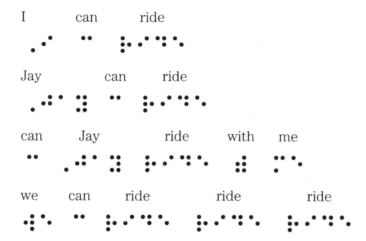

I	can	ride

Jay	can	ride

can	Jay	ride	with	me

we	can	ride	ride	ride

Example 3

Oral title: "Who Can Go to the Birthday Party?"
Words the child knows: *I, like, Albert, Daddy, do, not*
Uncontrolled vocabulary: *Lion* (prop: toy lion), *Rrrrrrrrr*

I	like	Albert

Albert	can	go

I	like	Daddy

Daddy	can	go

I	do	not	like	Lion

Lion	can	not	go

Rrrrrrrrr

Example 4

Oral title: "Things I Like"

Words the child knows: *I, like, work, lunch, you, do*

Example 5

Oral title: "Lunch"

Words the child knows: *I, can, get, a*

Uncontrolled vocabulary: *milk, straw, napkin, spoon, eat, mmmmmmmm*

Tactile pictures: milk carton, straw, napkin, spoon, mouth

Calendar Activities

Daily work with a calendar helps young students develop time and number concepts; spatial orientation to a page; left-to-right tracking skills; and letter, word, and number recognition in braille. A daily sequence of simple calendar activities might include the following:

- locating and spelling the name of the month
- tracking across the days of the week while reciting: *S* for "Sunday," *M* for "Monday," and so forth
- reading the numbers already on the calendar, using efficient tracking from line to line
- attaching the number for the date in the appropriate place
- reciting the entire date

The Individual Calendar Kit from the American Printing House for the Blind (APH) (see the Resources section) comes with many excellent suggestions for additional activities. Students stick the braille number for each day on their calendars using a glue stick, sticky tabs that are provided, or double-sided tape. They can also braille numbers directly onto the calendar. Carolyn's Enhanced Living Products also offers a Perpetual Calendar that consists of a raised grid and individual magnetic pieces with raised large-print and braille numbers. (However, the raised large-print numbers may be confusing to some students.)

Students who participate in opening exercises or morning circle time with their mainstream classes need an individual braille calendar to mark the date while their classmates are looking at the large classroom calendar. During this activity the children often sit on the floor in a large group, and it may be difficult for a student to attach a braille number to the calendar quickly and independently with tape or glue. This can be facilitated by separating the calendar numbers for one month from the APH calendar kit. Use a restickable glue stick to attach them in sequence to a plastic or wooden clipboard. (Be sure to allow the glue to dry for at least 30 seconds before sticking the numbers to the clipboard so that they can be removed and restuck.) Then clip the calendar to the board over the numbers. Each day the child can flip up the calendar, pull off the appropriate number, and stick it in the correct place on the calendar grid. Since restickable glue is not as adhesive as regular glue, the teacher may prefer to prepare the calendar ahead of time by placing sticky tabs or horizontal strips of double-sided tape on the empty squares to ensure that the numbers stay on the calendar all month. The child can still use this calendar independently by pulling each number off the clipboard and placing it on the correct space. If you are using the magnetic calendar, the magnetic number pieces can be placed in sequence on a separate magnetic board so that the student can easily locate the number needed for the day.

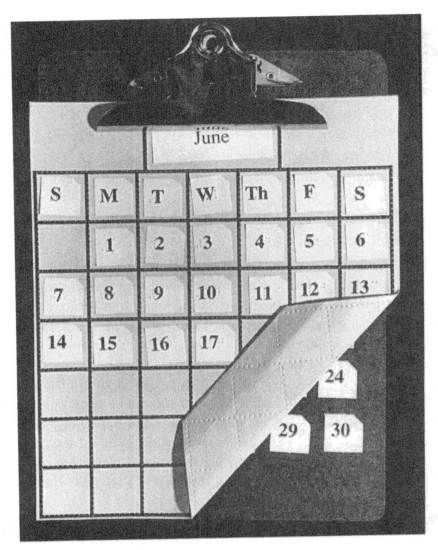

Attaching numbers to a clipboard with restickable glue allows a child to mark the date on a calendar quickly and independently.

Daily Schedule

Like the calendar, the schedule is an essential part of each child's daily lesson. Reading the schedule provides children with an opportunity to practice tracking, letter and word identification, and sequencing. They also enjoy finding out whether today will be a regular day or one with special events. Mainstream classroom teachers usually provide a daily schedule on the board, which can be brailled. However, students in preschool or special classes may need individual schedules designed for them. For these students, the first type of schedule described here uses objects paired with braille words. The second schedule is designed for a student who recognizes some braille letters and words.

For the very beginning reader or the student with multiple disabilities, use schedule cards with objects and braille words to represent daily activities. Hang the cards on a pegboard or stick them to a magnetic surface (such as a blackboard or the side of a tall filing cabinet) with adhesive magnetic strips. Attach simple objects from each activity that are meaningful to the child. One set of possibilities includes a bead (to designate occupational therapy), a toothbrush (daily living skills), a tactile circle representing a ball (gym class), small bells (music), a stick or twig (recess), a tactile picture of lips (speech), a plastic spoon (lunch), six textured braillewriter keys (braille lesson with the itinerant teacher), two long vertical rectangles representing legs (physical therapy), and a piece of corrugated cardboard that makes a bus sound when scratched with the fingernails ("go home").

As the child becomes more familiar with the concept of a schedule and develops beginning reading skills, fade out the tactile clues and use braille only. Gradually increase the amount of braille on the schedule throughout the year, moving from single words to phrases to complete sentences, as in the following progression:

Monday	Monday	Monday
circle	circle with Nina	I will have circle with Nina.
braille	braille with Carol	I will see Carol for braille.
snack	snack with friends	I will have snack with my friends.
play	play with friends	I will play with my friends.
go home	go home with Sam	I will go home on the bus with Sam.

For the more advanced reader, consider adding the times for each activity.

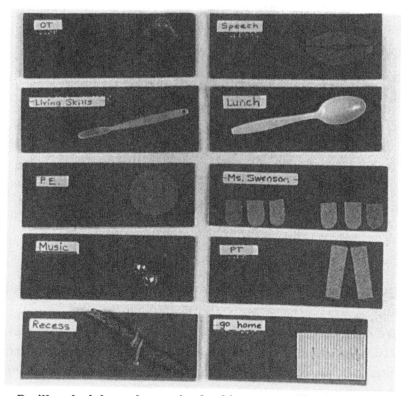

Braille schedule cards use simple objects or tactile pictures that are meaningful to the child to represent that day's activities.

Daily Message

Many teachers use a simple daily message to reinforce young children's awareness of the conventions of written language and to provide practice with a variety of writing and decoding skills. Sometimes the message is ready for the students to read as they walk in the door; at other times, the teacher writes the message with input from the students. The teacher often focuses the children's attention on a specific sound, type of word, punctuation mark, or reading strategy as the class reads the message together. The vocabulary is appropriate to the students' general reading level, but is not controlled for specific words.

Mainstreamed students usually read a braille copy of the daily message with their classmates, but may also require individual assisted reading with the itinerant or resource teacher to provide time to discuss specific aspects of the braille code. Students whose classwork does not include a daily message can benefit from one written especially for them in braille. Messages include a greater range of vocabulary than do controlled vocabulary stories, and they provide teachers with the opportunity to model many desirable braille reading and writing behaviors using high-interest material. Students may read the message through the first time with the teacher's assistance and the second time independently.

▬ SUGGESTIONS FOR TEACHERS

WRITING DAILY MESSAGES

▬ Choose a topic of interest to the child or one related to the daily schedule, for example:

> September 23
>
> Dear Eddie and Josh,
>
> It is a sunny day.
>
> We will play with balls in gym.
>
> We will read about a dog.
>
> It will be a great day!
>
> > Love,
> >
> > Ms. Norrish

▬ Vary your procedure: Sometimes write the message ahead of time, sometimes compose it with the child.

▬ Have a purpose for each message. Introduce or reinforce a particular spelling pattern, contraction, punctuation mark, or reading strategy using motivating content. In the following example, the *t-o* contraction is presented to a child in a message about her swimming lessons.

June 6

Ashley likes to go swimming.

She likes to jump and splash.

She likes to blow bubbles.

She likes to swim fast.

Ashley can go to the pool tomorrow.

- When writing together with the child, model writing behaviors (see Chapter 6) by sounding out words, choosing interesting words, deciding on punctuation marks, and occasionally making changes to your text. Vary the format— to include styles such as narratives, lists, letters, and poems.

- Use repetitive, predictable sentences, one sentence per line.

- Consider omitting some punctuation if it is confusing to the child.

- Make a line at the bottom of the message. Below it write five or six tactile sight words from the message that you want the child to be able to recognize in isolation, as in the following example:

September 23

I have 2 seeds.

I have a big seed.

I have a little seed.

We will put the big seed in the big pot.

We will put the little seed in the little pot.

_____

we I the in little have will

Unknown words can be reexamined in context by referring back to the message.

TEACHING WITH MESSAGES

- Read the message to the child. Model braille reading behavior by placing the child's hands on yours as you read.

- Have the child read the message; encourage the use of phonetic, contextual, and structural clues, but give help as needed so that the context of the message is not lost in the struggle for a word. Be sure the child's fingers are on the word being read.

- Have the child read the message again, this time more independently.

- Ask the child to read the tactile sight words at the bottom, referring to the text if he or she has difficulty.

- Talk about the number of letters in a word, the number of words in a sentence, the number of sentences in the message. Have the child find specific contractions or punctuation marks. In the previous example of the message about her swimming lesson, the teacher had Ashley mark each *t-o* contraction with a crayon.

■ Use the message as a springboard to a related writing activity. For example, after marking each contraction, Ashley wrote several more sentences with the contracted word *to*, using the pattern "I like to . . ."

Braille Worksheets

All beginning braille readers need a certain amount of drill and practice as they learn to discriminate letters, contractions, and words. Worksheets are a valid means of developing tactile discrimination skills, as long as the children's program also includes frequent opportunities for more meaningful literacy experiences, such as controlled-vocabulary stories, bookmaking, and journal writing. Most early worksheets contain lines of a few different braille letters or words. Students must distinguish a target word, letter, or contraction from the other "distractors" and mark it in some way—for example, with pins, crayons, or magnets. As they complete a worksheet, children learn to use efficient tracking patterns, manipulate the markers, and work independently. Children who use braille reading and writing frequently and for a variety of purposes may require fewer worksheets, since they learn many letters, contractions, and words in context. In the author's experience, those with additional learning problems may benefit from more extensive practice with worksheets, but, as noted, this can be paired with opportunities to use braille skills in meaningful contexts.

Children need to understand that marking the correct answer on a worksheet is not an end in itself, but a necessary foundation for the reading and writing that they want to do. Therefore, worksheets never make up a majority of the instructional time devoted to language arts; rather, they are short and focused on the target word or letter. Using the target word or words in conversation before beginning the worksheet is especially important for students with language deficits so that they make the connection between the written words and meaningful language. For example, if students are marking the word *go,* discuss places they like to go and people who might go with them. When discriminating among braille letters, ask students to relate the letters being learned to real words, or let them choose the next letter to be learned by associating it with the beginning sound of a familiar name or favorite word.

There are a number of ways to mark braille worksheets. If the worksheet is attached to a small desktop bulletin board, children can mark their answers with pushpins. It is easy for them to keep track of their place and to check their work when finished. Stick the pins along one side of the bulletin board so that the children can locate them easily with one hand while keeping their place with the other. As students improve their fine motor and page orientation skills, they can switch to marking answers with a crayon or pencil. Glitter crayons make marks that can be felt if firm pressure is used. Children can also indicate their answers using rolled-up pieces of masking tape, magnets on a magnetic board, or short pieces of Wikki Stix (Wormsley & D'Andrea, 1997).

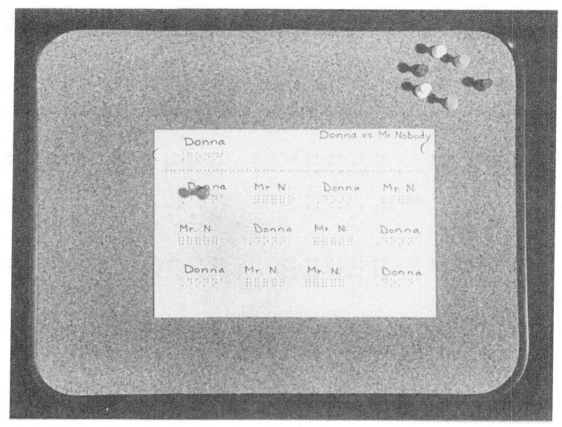

Pushpins and a small bulletin board enable students to mark answers independently on a braille worksheet.

However children complete their worksheets, it is important that they use both hands and continue tracking all the way to the end of the line after marking each answer. Children may develop the more efficient habit of reading with one hand and marking answers with the other, and there is a risk that the "marking hand" will not learn to read as well as the other hand. This uneven development is not usually a problem if children have plenty of two-handed reading practice with other types of materials. However, it is a good idea to assess the reading of the "marking hand" from time to time to be sure that both hands are reading equally well.

There are a number of different formats that can be used for worksheets. The target word or letter may appear at the top of the worksheet to use as a sample. Or, a different target can be supplied for each line. Following are some suggestions for different types of worksheets.

Name worksheet. Ask the child to pin his or her name. Intersperse the child's name with "Mr. Nobody"—a group of five unspaced full cells—as the distractor (see Figure 5.1). Note that the "checker" name at the top is not pinned so that the child can refer to it while working. A braille line (dots 2,5 across) can be used to separate the sample word from the rest of the worksheet.

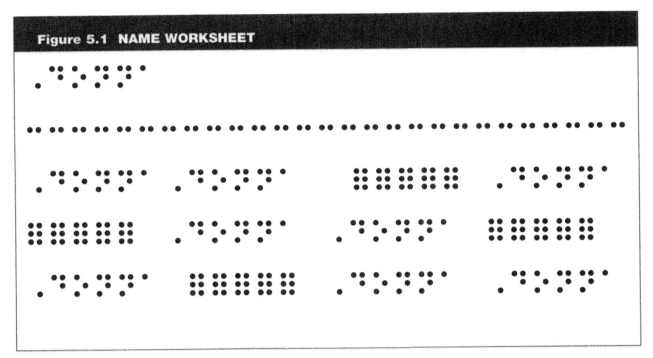

Figure 5.1 NAME WORKSHEET

Directions: Pin *Donna*, not *Mr. Nobody*.

New word or letter worksheet. Use the same format as for the name worksheet to practice the discrimination of new words or letters. Mix up the new target shape with previously learned characters and words (see Figure 5.2).

Letter- or word-matching worksheet. The format for letter or word matching demands greater skill from the student because the target letter or word changes

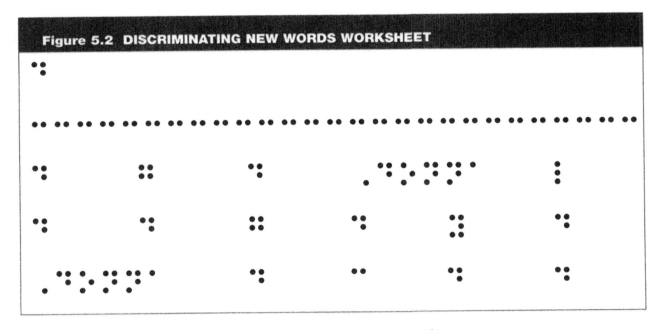

Figure 5.2 DISCRIMINATING NEW WORDS WORKSHEET

Directions: Pin the word *do*. Skip over any other words.

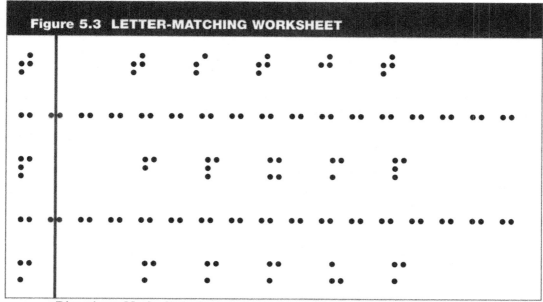

Figure 5.3 LETTER-MATCHING WORKSHEET

Directions: Mark all the letters in each row that are the same as the first one.

from line to line, and there may be more than one match in each line (see Figure 5.3). Include as many lines as the child can handle without skipping over any. Use graphic art tape for the vertical separation and a braille line for the horizontal separations.

Color-word identification worksheet. In this worksheet, the target is a number paired with a color. The child picks out the identified color from a set of flat-sided crayons with the braille color word written and marks the specified number of full cells (see Figure 5.4). To increase the difficulty, the numbers may be written as number words.

Focus worksheet. If a child is confusing two similar or reversed shapes, it sometimes helps to isolate them on a worksheet so that the differences are highlighted (see Figure 5.5).

Figure 5.4 COLOR-WORD IDENTIFICATION WORKSHEET

Directions: Mark the correct number of full cells with the right color of crayon.

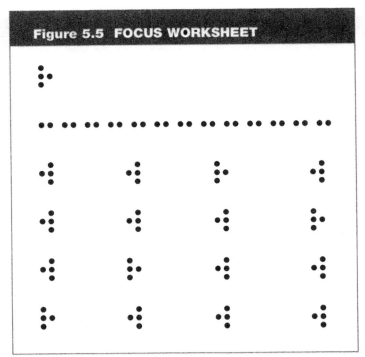

Figure 5.5 FOCUS WORKSHEET

Directions: This is a worksheet with lots of *w*'s. One *r* is hiding in each row. Can you find it?

Commercial worksheets. The *Patterns* readiness workbook *Letters and You* (Caton, Pester, & Bradley, 1982b) consists of letter identification worksheets. Children can complete these for additional practice if needed. The pages are easier to use if they are torn out of the book and completed one at a time. It may be necessary to rebraille some pages if the dots are squashed or faint.

SUGGESTIONS FOR TEACHERS

CREATING BRAILLE WORKSHEETS

- Keep worksheets short and focused on the target letter or word.
- Inkprint as much of each sheet as possible for the benefit of regular education classroom teachers and parents.
- Include a sample of the target letter or word at the top of the sheet or to the left of the row. Encourage the child to use this as a reference when completing the sheet. Having a "checker" promotes independence.
- Vary the size and shape of worksheets: use half sheets, long narrow sheets, or full sheets.
- Use only letters, contractions, or words the child has already had as distractors.
- Revise or repeat the activity the next day if the child cannot complete it independently.

TEACHING WITH WORKSHEETS

- Ask the child to read aloud the worksheet to you after the new letter or word has been introduced. Discuss any errors or uncertainties. Have the child reread the sheet, if necessary, until there are no oral errors.

- Have the child complete the worksheet independently using pushpins, a crayon, magnets, pieces of Wikki Stix, or rolls of masking tape to mark answers. The sample word or letter at the top or on the left of the row (the "checker") should not be marked so that the child can refer to it if necessary.

- Check the worksheet tactilely together with the child, locating each pin or other marker and reading the answer marked.

Flash Cards

Flash cards are a traditional means of drilling new letters and words in isolation. They serve as a useful transition to reading more meaningful material, such as controlled-vocabulary stories and daily messages. Students can use sorting tasks with flash cards—such as those listed in "Sample Flash Card Activities"—to develop independent work skills.

SUGGESTIONS FOR TEACHERS

MAKING AND USING FLASH CARDS

- Use index cards or braille paper cut to a similar size for flash cards.

- Cut off one corner of each flash card for orientation purposes, or use a hole puncher or stapler to make a tactile clue in that corner. (It can be any corner; just be consistent.)

- Braille one word, letter, or number on each card to practice recognition of tactile sight words and other braille characters in isolation, in one set of flash cards.

- To practice recognition of vocabulary in context, write a short sentence composed of familiar words on each card in a different set.

- If the cards will be needed for frequent practice, use adhesive braille labels for durability, rather than brailling directly on the card.

- Store flash cards in a "word box" that is accessible to the student.

- Tape sorting containers to a work tray or table surface, or use a nonslip material such as Dycem.

Additional strategies for creating and using flash cards can be found in *Instructional Strategies for Braille Literacy* (Wormsley, 1997).

Independent Sorting

Students can work independently with a set of flash cards. One activity is to distinguish two or more words, letters, or numbers from each other by placing each identical card in the same pile. For this activity, prepare approximately five identical braille flash cards of each word, letter, or number. If the student will be sorting by category (such as "girls' names" versus "boys' names"), prepare at least five different cards for each group. Mix up the cards and have the student sort them independently into two or more small trays or other containers. Categories for sorting might include the following:

Sorting into Groups of Identical Cards

- the student's name and full cells (Mr. Nobody)
- two or more different words (such as *and* and *the*) or letters (such as *q* and *t*)

Sorting by Category

- girls' names and boys' names
- the names of people at school and the names of people at home
- color words and number words
- words that are names and words that are not names
- letters and numbers
- words containing the letter *e* (such as *pet, set, fell,* and *peg*) and words containing the letter *i* (such as *pit, sit, fill,* and *pig*)
- two sets of rhyming words (such as words that rhyme with *get* and words that rhyme with *got*)

"Find It" Games

Give the student a set of 10 to 12 flash cards from the word box. These should be words that have already been introduced in reading and worksheet activities. Challenge the child to find the flash card with the word or words you describe. Award points for each correct word. You can try using a timer to encourage more fluent reading. Children may be asked to find words that

- describe a certain color (for example, "Find the word that tells the color of grass").
- contain a specific letter or contraction.
- rhyme with a given word.
- tell how many of something there are (for example, "Find the number word that tells how many people are in your family").
- mean the same as—or is the opposite of—a given word.
- name a boy (or a girl, or a pet).
- contain a certain number of syllables.

ADDITIONAL ACTIVITIES

The activities described in this section can be used to reinforce a variety of skills, such as recognition of letters, words, and numbers; matching and sequencing of words and numbers; and practice in reading, writing, and spelling. Most are multi-purpose, meaning that they can be used over and over again with different letters, words, sentences, or numbers. Most are also designed to be completed independently by the student once initial instruction has taken place.

Letter, Word, and Number Recognition Activities

Bingo

Many kindergarten and first-grade students play bingo games to reinforce simple language arts and math skills, such as letter and number recognition. Very often the braille characters can be written directly on top of the corresponding print symbols. If the bingo card will not fit in the brailler, clear self-adhesive braille labels can be attached over the print. The set of cards used by the caller can also be brailled so that the child who reads braille can take a turn calling out the numbers or letters to the class. Children using braille bingo cards need markers to cover the letters or numbers that are called that are easy to handle and that will stay in place. Magnets on a metal board, rolled-up pieces of masking tape, or small self-stick notes cut in half and lined up along the top edge of the card all work well for this type of game.

Coloring

Many children who read braille enjoy coloring just like their sighted classmates, even if they are totally blind. Drawing with crayons on paper placed over sandpaper creates a raised picture. Keep a piece of sandpaper and some regular copier paper in an accessible place in the classroom for impromptu scribbling. Flat-sided crayons can be labeled in braille with color words using self-adhesive braille labels, reinforcing recognition of color words. Crayons with different smells are also available commercially. Exceptional Teaching Aids sells a raised-line coloring book called *Touch and Color* (see the Resources section). Some teachers also make their own raised-line drawings for children to color using graphic art tape or glue.

Number Recognition: "Hats"

Young children, as well as older students with additional learning problems, may require extensive practice in recognizing braille numbers. A number-recognition block provides a fun twist to this practice. To make a number-recognition block, drill five holes, spaced about 2 inches apart, into a wooden block such as the ones found in kindergarten block centers. Glue pieces of thick wire (No. 12 stranded wire, available from the electrical department of hardware stores) into the holes, leaving about two inches sticking up out of the block. Sand the top of each wire until it is smooth. Cut a rectangle out of poster board with five holes to fit over the wires. Label each hole on this poster-board overlay with a braille number.

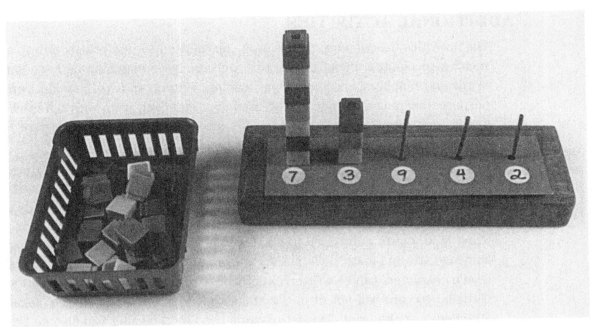

A number-recognition block helps children practice reading braille numbers.

Next to the number-recognition block, place a basket of objects with holes in them. The objects should be easy to manipulate and slide onto the wires; for example, beads, washers, or Unifix cubes (pictured; these are stacking blocks of different colors used to teach math concepts and are available from teachers' supply stores and catalogs). The student slips the correct number of objects over each wire, working from left to right. To add interest to the activity, have the child give each wire a name; the number associated with the wire tells how many "hats" that person would like to wear. Make new poster-board overlays with different groups of numbers as the student learns to recognize more numbers.

Students with additional disabilities may have difficulty working from left to right if the wires are too close together. When working with these students, bend down the second and fourth wires and secure them with strong tape so that there is more space between the three remaining wires. Make some overlays with only three holes to fit this variation on the number-recognition block.

Matching and Sequencing Activities

Matching-Board Activities: The Bus

The Bus is a simple word-matching activity that was originally designed to help students learn to read the names of family members and friends, but it can be used with any set of word or number cards. Its object is to place each "person"—represented by his or her name brailled on an index card or piece of poster board—in the correct place on the matching board, which is designated as the "bus."

To make the matching-board bus game, tape five or ten library card pockets to a piece of laminated poster board in one or two rows. These are the seats on the bus (or the airplane, train, or other conveyance). Prepare two identical sets of name

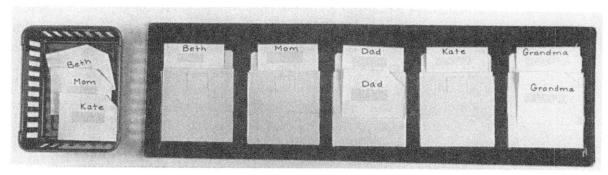

The names of family members are matched to their "seats" on the "bus" in this simple matching-board activity. Matching cards can be slid in the pocket or attached with Velcro, as shown here.

cards, with one of the words to be learned written in both print and braille at the top of each card. Using different colors of print writing for each set makes it easier for the teacher to sort them at the beginning of the activity. Place one card from the first set in each pocket to show where each person is to sit. Have the child read each name from the second set, and slide it into the correct "seat" pocket by matching the names.

Encourage systematic search patterns (left-to-right, top-to-bottom) as the child scans the board. If a child has difficulty sliding the matching cards in the pockets, attach Velcro to the front of the pockets and to the "people" cards so the child can stick cards onto the pockets. Mix up the cards in the pockets when repeating the activity.

Number Sequencing

Students who are learning to recognize the braille numbers 0 through 10 benefit from activities that allow them to arrange the numbers in sequence. Writing the braille numbers on small cards and using Velcro or self-adhesive magnetic strips to keep them in place lets students rearrange the cards without losing them. This technique works with letter or word cards as well.

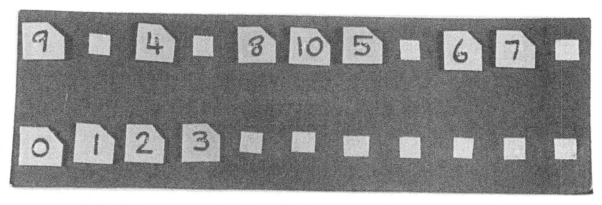

Using Velcro or magnetic strips makes it easy for the student to select numbers from the top row and place them in order on the bottom row.

The number cards can be made from 1-inch squares of laminated poster board or rubber foam (available in colored sheets from crafts stores). Write print and braille numbers from 0 to 10 on each, using markers and self-adhesive braille labels, and cut off the top right corners for orientation. Attach a piece of self-stick Velcro or a self-adhesive magnetic strip to the back of each square. If using Velcro, place 11 additional pieces of Velcro spaced out along both the top and the bottom of a laminated poster board to hold the number squares. If using magnetic strips, the squares can be arranged on a large cookie sheet.

For sequencing practice, mix up the numbers along the top edge of the poster board or cookie sheet. Then have the child put the numbers in order along the bottom edge, starting with 0 in the bottom left corner and continuing from left to right.

Scrambled Sentences

In this scrambled sentence activity, adapted from one designed for sighted students (Butler & Turbill, 1987, p. 68), children place words taken from a familiar braille sentence in the correct order. The steps to set up this activity are as follows:

1. Braille two copies of a sentence from the child's reading or writing on two strips of paper. Leave at least three spaces between each word in the second copy of the sentence.

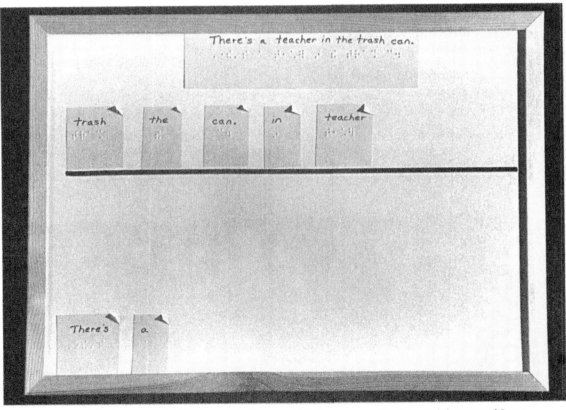

Reorganizing a scrambled sentence from a child's own reading or writing provides a meaningful matching activity.

2. Cut up the second sentence so that each word is on a separate piece of paper. Bend the top right corner of each piece for orientation and easy handling.

3. Use a restickable glue stick to attach the first sentence strip and the scrambled words to a dry erase board or other laminated surface. (Be sure to allow the glue to dry for at least 30 seconds before attaching the word cards so they can be removed and reattached.) The board should have a horizontal piece of graphic art tape or masking tape below the line of scrambled words to separate them from the child's work.

4. Have the child stick the scrambled words in the correct order along the bottom edge, using the sentence strip at the top as a reference, if necessary.

5. To repeat the activity using the same sentence, have the child stick the words to a blank strip of paper in the correct order. Staple the words to the paper so the student can take this strip home.

The task becomes more challenging when several of the words begin with the same letter.

Matching-and-Sorting Board Activities: "Hang It Up!"

A matching-and-sorting board lends itself to multipurpose activities that a child can complete independently while standing. A simple one can be made from a large pegboard approximately 3 feet by 5 feet; most hardware stores will cut one to measure. Prop the pegboard lengthwise on the tray of a chalkboard, and tape the top of the pegboard to the chalkboard to prevent it from falling over. Insert a row of 10 pegboard hooks, spaced three or four holes apart. The child hangs prepared index cards or small poster-board cards on the hooks to complete matching, sequencing, and sorting activities, such as the following:

- *Name matching.* Prepare two identical sets of braille name cards with a hole punched in the top of each card. Hang the cards from one set in random order on the hanging board. Mix up the second set and put them in a container on a nearby desk or table. The child picks up one card at a time, reads the cards already on the board from left to right, and hangs the matching card on the correct hook.

- *Rhyming word sort.* Prepare two or more sets of rhyming words (for example, *cat, hat, sat, mat, fat;* and *ride, hide, side, wide*). Hang one card from each set on the board. Mix up the remaining cards from both sets and put them in a container on a nearby desk. The child picks up one card at a time and hangs it on the hook with the word that rhymes with it. When the activity is completed, a full set of rhyming word cards will be hanging from each hook.

- *Number sequencing.* This activity can be done with numbers or with number words. Prepare one set of number cards or number word cards with a hole punched in the top of each card. Attach them in random order to a work surface using restickable glue, clothespins, or metal clips. The child scans the

A young student sequences the numbers 1 to 10 using a "Hang It Up!" board.

cards, looking for the number *1* or the word *one* and hangs it on the first peg-board hook. Then the child looks for the number *2* or the word *two* and hangs it on the second hook. The other numbers are hung in sequence. Children can also hang the numbers backwards; sequence by twos, fives, or tens; or hang sequences of higher numbers such as 11 through 20. Children who are not yet reading braille may be able to hang cards with different numbers of tactile shapes glued to them in numerical order, by first finding the card with one shape, then the one with two, and so on.

- *Alphabetical order.* Place a group of related words (such as children's names or animals) in random order on a nearby work surface. Have children hang them in alphabetical order.

- *Other sequencing activities.* Have children sequence the days of the week or the months of the year by hanging them in the correct order. Sentences or main events from a story may also be sequenced.

Writing and Spelling

Words, Words, Words! Book

Learning to recognize sound and spelling patterns in words helps children to decode unfamiliar words in their reading and to spell words correctly in their writing. In a

■ EXAMPLES OF WORD GROUPINGS

- rhyming words: *make, bake, cake, take, lake, rake, snake*
- *ea* with a long *e* sound: *eat, dream, peace, seat*
- *ea* with a short *e* sound: *ready, bread, heavy, head, healthy*
- *o-n-g* contraction: *wrong, long, song, dong*
- *e-v-e-r* contraction in compound words: *everyone, everything, everywhere*

Words, Words, Words! book, words that are related in some way are written together on one page. Rhyming words are easy to group because they end with the same sounds and often with the same letters. Other words belong together because they have the same sound for a particular spelling pattern. For example, words containing the letters *ea* with a long *e* sound might be written on one page and those with a short *e* sound on another (see "Examples of Word Groupings"). Word groups may also focus on specific contractions such as *o-n-g* or *e-v-e-r.*

Use the *Words, Words, Words!* book to plan lessons that target a specific spelling pattern related to a student's reading or writing. Encourage the child to add words to existing pages as they come across them during reading activities.

The pages of a *Words, Words, Words!* book, in which related words are grouped on each page, can be inserted into the brailler at any time to add new entries. Textured keys help some students maintain correct finger positions on the brailler.

To make a *Words, Words, Words!* book, bind 15 to 20 half sheets of braille paper at the top along the longer side. Include a front and back cover and a title page if desired. Individual pages of the bound book can be inserted into the braillewriter without removing the binding. One group of related words goes on each page, and more words can be added at any time.

Copying Lists

Copying short lists of interesting related words can be a valuable way for young children to learn to read and write new words and contractions. This activity should supplement, not replace, other types of written expression such as bookmaking and journal writing (see Chapters 3 and 6). It encourages young children to work independently and check their writing for accuracy.

Choose a category of words related to a current area of study, such as number words, color words, classmates' names, family names, or kinds of animals. Generate a list of five to ten words with the child; the child thinks of words to include, while the teacher does the writing using correct grade 2 braille. Number the words and place each word on a separate line. (The numbers help children keep their place, as well as acquainting them with standard list format.) Next, read through the list with the child, pointing out and practicing new contractions. Then tape the list to the desktop beside the braillewriter so that the child can refer to it.

Have the child copy the list, checking the "help sheet" as often as necessary. When the task is finished, the teacher and student check the list for accuracy by comparing it to the original. This activity can be repeated for several days with the same list of words until the child can complete it independently and accurately. Add each correctly copied list to a *Book of Lists* in a three-ring notebook.

As a variation of this activity, children who have learned to read and spell the color words on their flat-sided crayons can copy each color word directly from the crayon. Place the crayons in a container on the left of the brailler and an empty container on the right. To add interest, this can be the "swimming pool." The child picks up each crayon, spells the color word out loud, places it in the right-hand container, and writes the word. Each color word should start on a new line and be numbered. When all eight crayons are in the pool, the task is finished.

Mini-Worksheets

Children practice reading and writing a variety of simple words and numbers during this series of independent activities. It provides practice in manipulating the parts of the braillewriter and prepares them for the task of completing longer written worksheets later on.

Tape two small baskets or containers to a work surface, one on each side of a braillewriter. Several prepared index cards containing the activities are placed in the left-hand basket. The child picks up one card at a time, writes the requested information, and puts the finished card in the right-hand basket. The activities may be completed while sitting or standing.

This format lends itself to a variety of simple activities. For each of the following tasks, the teacher provides oral directions, demonstrates how to complete the first card, and assists the child as needed with the remaining cards. All the cards for a given activity focus on the same objective and require the same type of response.

- Braille from one to ten full cells, with spaces in between, on each card. Stick one file folder label below the row or rows of full cells to make a blank (see Figure 5.6). The child counts the full cells and writes the corresponding number or number word on the sticker.

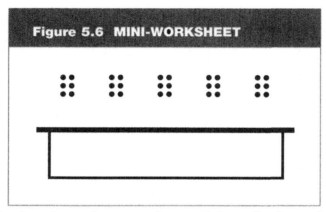

The child writes the number or number word that tells the number of full cells.

- Braille a number or number word on each card. The child brailles the corresponding number of full cells.

- Braille a number on each card, with a round sticker immediately following it (see Figure 5.7). The child reads the number and brailles the number that comes *next* on the sticker. Or, place the sticker to the left of the original number, and have the child braille the number that comes *before.*

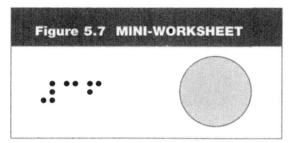

The child writes the number that comes next.

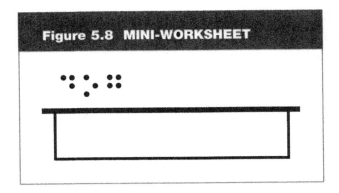

The child writes a word that rhymes.

- Braille a simple word on each card, followed by a file folder label (see Figure 5.8). The child writes a rhyming word on the sticker.
- Braille a color word, number word, or name on each card, followed by a file folder label. The child reads and copies the word.

SUMMARY

Learning the braille code adds another layer to the already complex process of learning to read. Unlike sighted children, beginning braille readers do not have unlimited opportunities to absorb words, letters, and numbers spontaneously from their environment. Many will require a certain amount of direct instruction with skill-oriented activities, controlled vocabulary, and repetition. Even in the beginning stages of literacy instruction, however, when children are learning a core braille vocabulary and the letters of the alphabet, the teacher can draw on the individual child's interests and experiences to create relevant and meaningful instructional activities.

As children gain proficiency in braille, much of their literacy learning can shift from a focus on skills to a focus on meaning. Composing journal entries, discussed in Chapter 6, provides an ideal way for young children to learn new vocabulary, contractions, sound-symbol relationships, and writing conventions within the meaningful context of their own writing.

CHAPTER 6 Teaching the Beginning Writer

Becoming a competent writer in braille requires much time and energy from the student, as well as continual modeling and feedback from the teacher. However, a daily focus on writing is time well spent. Young children who write frequently on topics of interest to them have the opportunity to reinforce their grasp of sound-symbol relationships, organize their thoughts so that they make sense to others, and practice their reading skills by reading back their own writing. As noted in Chapter 4, this reading-writing connection plays a critical role in the development of literacy in young children. Linking reading and writing strengthens skills in both areas and gives students a better understanding of how authors structure their writing to convey important ideas.

Oral language also plays a key role in children's success as writers. The opportunity to "feel it on the tongue first" (Graves, 1997) enables students to compose, revise, and experiment with their message orally before adding the mechanical components of writing. Young students who have a rich experiential background and strong oral language skills are well on their way to becoming successful writers.

This chapter discusses the prerequisite skills and concepts for braille writing as well as special considerations related to the mechanics of using the braillewriter. The second half of the chapter presents an instructional sequence for developing proficiency in writing through daily journal writing, a common activity in many primary classrooms.

PREREQUISITES FOR WRITING IN BRAILLE

Tools

Most young children receiving braille instruction learn to write first on the braillewriter. Pressing combinations of braillewriter keys is relatively easy to master and provides the instant feedback of what is written. However, children should also be exposed to other writing tools such as the slate and stylus, portable braille notetakers, computers with voice output, braille embossers, and standard printers. Familiarity with these tools helps students realize that writers have a variety of options for different tasks and that writing can be produced in print or braille, depending on the intended audience.

Skills and Concepts

A beginning writer requires a foundation of physical skills, hands-on experiences, and "braille awareness" in order to use the braillewriter to convey meaningful messages. (Detailed strategies for developing these prerequisite skills for writing in braille can be found in *Instructional Strategies for Braille Literacy* [Wormsley & D'Andrea, 1997]).

Developing physical strength and coordination. Many young children, especially those with low muscle tone, may benefit from specific adaptations and teaching strategies that help them master the mechanical aspects of braille writing. These are discussed in the section on "Special Considerations for Writing with a Brailler" that follows.

Developing experiential background and basic concepts. All writers, of any age, write best about what they know. Children who have had numerous "hands-on" experiences and the opportunity to talk about them can draw from a large repertoire of sensory images, vocabulary, and general knowledge when they write. Basic concepts develop through body movement and manipulation of materials, accompanied by verbal interchange.

Developing an awareness of why people write. Motivation plays a key role in the amount of time and effort children are willing to invest in writing. Preschoolers who have seen adults model braille writing frequently and who have had the opportunity to "scribble" on the braillewriter themselves will be more likely to persevere in writing tasks as kindergartners and first graders. They understand that people write for many different purposes, both functional (such as making shopping lists) and pleasurable (such as writing stories).

SPECIAL CONSIDERATIONS FOR WRITING WITH A BRAILLER

In some ways, children who write with a brailler have an easier task than their sighted classmates who must learn and practice many different stroke sequences to form lower- and uppercase letters. Once students have mastered a limited number of mechanical skills and can isolate their fingers to press the necessary combinations of keys, braille writing can be fast, efficient, and (for those who know braille!) easy to read. Nevertheless, learning to write in braille does require specialized instruction and monitoring to ensure that children develop good habits.

Inserting Paper into the Brailler

Inserting a piece of paper into a brailler is actually a more difficult skill for many children than writing letters and words. Some children are able to write successfully long before they can insert the paper independently. Mastering paper insertion is usually the result of daily hand-over-hand repetition. If a student is having particular difficulty inserting the paper, the following suggestions may be helpful:

- Teach the names of the braillewriter parts and verbalize the same sequence of steps each time you help the child insert the paper.

- Use only a half sheet of paper or a large index card.

- Remind the child to "lay the paper down" on the flat paper support bar at the back of the brailler; often children tend to hold the paper vertically rather than horizontally.

- Keep the embossing head centered so that the paper must slide horizontally under it. When the paper is in, the child can move the embossing head to the left before writing.

- Plan activities, such as those involving the mini-worksheets described in Chapter 5, that provide additional practice in manipulating the parts of the braillewriter.

Relating Dot Positions to the Braillewriter Keys

The Swing Cell (pictured in Chapter 4), available from the American Printing House for the Blind (see the Resources section), provides students with an excellent model showing the relationship between dot positions of the braille cell (in its closed position) and the braillewriter keys (when swung open). Younger children who may not be able to grasp this relationship can still learn the dot number associated with each finger and the corresponding key on the brailler. It is therefore important to refer to each finger by its dot number:

> left pointer—finger 1
> left middle—finger 2
> left ring—finger 3
> right pointer—finger 4
> right middle—finger 5
> right ring—finger 6

Knowing the number associated with each key and finger makes it easier to write combinations of keys for specific letters and contractions later on. The student who is told that the letter *t* is made with dots 2, 3, 4, and 5 can instantly write a *t* on the braillewriter using the correct fingers (see "Songs for Beginning Braillists"). With practice, finger positions become automatic, and students no longer need to think about key numbers.

Children who reverse or forget letters or contractions when writing can benefit from looking at the character they are trying to write. Attach a braille alphabet strip to the table edge in front of the braillewriter or stick problem letters or contractions on top of the braillewriter using self-adhesive braille labels. A quick check of the dots on the left and right sides of the cell is often the only clue a child needs to form the letter or contraction independently.

by Denah Burnham

These humorous songs are a creative way to motivate young children to use correct fingers when writing letters on the brailler. Students may enjoy making up more songs for other letters based on familiar tunes.

Letter *a*

(to the tune of *Yankee Doodle*)

On the brailler letter *a*
One finger does it all . . .
Left hand pointer on key one
To make the dot stand tall.

Letter *b*

(to the tune of *London Bridge*)

Letter *b* is easy to do.
Push one and two, just one and two.
Letter *b* is easy to do.
One and two.

Letter *c*

(to the tune of *Frère Jacques*)

Can you make it? Can you make it?
Letter *c*, letter *c*.
One and four together
Pointers do the work for
Letter *c*, letter *c*.

Letter *l*

(to the tune of *Camptown Races*)

Make that letter *l* with me
Doo-dah, Doo-dah
Left hand pushes one, two, three.
Oh, doo-dah day.
Now we're making *l*'s.
l's are one, two, three.
Work your left hand just this way.
Oh, doo-dah day.

Letter *g*

(to the tune of *Three Blind Mice*)

Letter *g*, Letter *g*
See how it's made; see how it's made.
It's one and two left, and four and five right.
You push them together with all your might.
So do it now and do it right.
It's letter *g*.

Full Cell

(to the tune of *Farmer in the Dell*)

It's easy can't you tell
To make the whole full cell.
Press ALL the keys if you please
And you will do it well.

Source: Reprinted with permission of Denah Burnham, Fairfax County Public Schools, Falls Church, VA.

Relating Dot Positions to Cells on the Slate

In his book *Teaching the Braille Slate and Stylus*, P. Mangold (1993) recommends referring to the two vertical rows of dot positions in the braille cell as "first side" (top, middle, bottom dots) and "second side" (top, middle, bottom dots). Teaching dot positions using these terms can make it easier to learn to write from right to left on the slate, since these terms are the same when used for both reading and writing.

Finger Positioning

It is extremely important that children use the correct finger on each key if they are to develop fast and efficient writing. Do not allow children to substitute a stronger finger for a weaker one. For example, discourage the urge to make the capital sign with any finger other than the right ring finger. If a child has difficulty keeping the correct fingers on the keys, stick material of a different texture—such as rough, smooth, and fuzzy—on each key to provide further tactile input. (Textured keys are pictured in the photograph of the *Words, Words, Words!* book in the brailler that appears in Chapter 5.)

Finger Isolation

The ability to move each finger in isolation is necessary to be able to press the different combinations of keys that make letters and contractions. Usually children are able to isolate the pointer and middle fingers before the weaker ring fingers. The following suggestions will help students develop this ability:

- A finger "wake up" exercise before writing helps develop the finger isolation necessary to press braillewriter keys one at a time. Have the child place both hands flat on the table, palms down and fingers slightly separated. Gently touch one finger at a time and ask the child to lift that finger.

- Letters and contractions with dots 1 and 3 (such as *y*) or 4 and 6 (for example, *e-d*) are especially difficult to write because the middle finger does not press a key. Try having the child put the middle finger "in the basement" below the middle key, rather than attempting to hold it up above the key.

- Some children bring the opposite hand over to help position the correct finger on a key, such as using the left hand to help the right ring finger locate key number 6 for the capital sign. Usually this is a preliminary step toward independent writing that disappears with practice. If it becomes an unnecessary habit, ask the student to feel your fingers as you write and point out how each finger does its own work without help from the others. Verbal or tactile reminders may be needed to encourage independent positioning of the fingers.

Developing Strength and Coordination

Young children may not have the physical strength to press the braillewriter keys without rocking their whole bodies back and forth. Provide back support and a footstool to facilitate good sitting posture if the child is unable to place both feet flat on the floor. Be sure that the brailler keys are positioned at or below elbow height. The child may also stand to write if more leverage is needed.

The mastery of mechanical skills is not an end in itself, but a necessary foundation for independent writing. Use short drills such as the following to increase strength and coordination, along with opportunities for more meaningful writing activities (see sections on "Talking Writing" and "Guided Writing" later in this chapter):

- Full cell drill 1: full cells across the page until the bell rings at the end of the line; "mix up" the child's fingers halfway across the line and see if the child can put them back on the correct keys and continue
- Full cell drill 2: full cell, space, full cell, space across the page
- Isolated finger practice in sequence: finger 1, 1, 1; finger 2, 2, 2; finger 3, 3, 3; and so on
- Isolated finger practice in random order as the teacher calls out the finger numbers: finger 4, finger 1, finger 6, and so on
- Systematic practice of the letters and contractions in the child's name, beginning with the capital sign

Spacing

Although an adult spaces with the thumb when using the braillewriter, this movement is very awkward for a young child, whose thumb is much shorter. Primary-aged children sometimes find it more comfortable to space with their right or left pointer finger. Later in elementary school they may switch to spacing with their thumb if they choose. (Note that on electronic braille notetakers, the space key is positioned lower than the other keys, which makes it much easier for a young child to space with the thumb.)

Like sighted children, students who write braille do not begin to space between words until they have had considerable experience writing unspaced strings of letters and words using invented spelling. This makes a child's independent braille writing difficult to read, because single-letter whole-word signs (such as *go*) and individual letters (such as *g*) look identical. When transcribing a child's work, ask the child to read it to you to be sure of the intended message. During guided writing sessions (discussed later in this chapter) when you are assisting the child with a writing activity, a slight touch on the child's hand can serve as a reminder to space.

Erasing

Children can erase their errors in two ways: by rubbing out the dots (with their fingernail or a braille eraser) or by brailling a series of full cells over the error. Generally it is easier for young children to read back their writing when they have used the full-cell approach. Rubbing out dots tends to leave some traces that may confuse the reader, especially if the correct characters are brailled over the erasures. When children are ready to learn to use a braille eraser, attach the eraser to the side of the brailler with a small square of Velcro so that it is easy to find.

Connecting Writing and Reading

Always ask children to read their writing after taking the paper out of the braillewriter, even if the "writing" is only a line of full cells. In addition to providing a review of what was written, this practice develops the concept that writing is intended to be read. As they read their own writing, students practice tracking, decoding, and proofreading skills. Children who are writing independently using invented spelling should be expected to read their work to themselves before reading to a teacher.

EARLY WRITING DEVELOPMENT

In many kindergarten and early primary classrooms, children write a daily or weekly journal on a topic of their choice. Sighted students often have a spiral bound notebook with lines for writing and blank pages for pictures; braille readers may use a three-ring notebook to hold their work. Journal writing allows children to write freely and to focus on their message; entries are not revised for content or edited for mechanical errors unless the writer decides to expand the piece for publication (see the description of the writing process in Chapter 7). Teachers may read and comment on the content of the entries, however, or make note of consistent errors that should be addressed in writing focus lessons.

Journal writing is an ideal activity for introducing young children to the process of writing and helping them to acquire written language skills in a meaningful context. In writing about what they know best—their own experiences—students develop early literacy skills related to oral language, reading, and writing.

In working with young braille students during journal writing activities, the author has identified three stages of development. As they pass through these stages, children benefit from different degrees of support from the teacher. Journal writing can be introduced when students are able to press random keys on the brailler and verbalize their message—the *talking-writing* stage. Gradually they move through the teacher-assisted stage of *guided writing* until they are able to do *independent writing* with only intermittent support from the teacher (see "Supporting Young Writers: Stages of Early Development").

■ SUPPORTING YOUNG WRITERS: STAGES OF EARLY WRITING DEVELOPMENT

Stage 1. Talking Writing: Teacher models writing; student imitates by "scribbling" on the braillewriter and speaking the message.

Stage 2. Guided Writing: Student does the writing; teacher assists verbally with spacing, sound-symbol relationships, and character formation.

Stage 3. Independent Writing: Student writes independently using a combination of conventional and invented spelling; teacher provides intermittent support and teaches focus lessons in areas of need.

Stage 1: Talking Writing

Very beginning writers develop an understanding of the writing process by observing others write and by having opportunities to make tactile marks on paper that have meaning for them. Because children do not read or write many real braille characters at this stage, if any, the focus is on the transfer of spoken language to tactile form. The writing lesson is in two parts: The teacher first writes a sentence dictated by the child, and then the child imitates the teacher's writing behavior. This level of support is most appropriate at the preschool level or early kindergarten level, although it may also be used with older children who have delays in fine motor or cognitive development.

Part 1: Modeling

In the first part of the talking-writing lesson, the teacher and student discuss an interesting topic to write about. The child dictates a sentence to the teacher, who writes the entry in braille. The student places his or her hands on the teacher's during the writing. The teacher uses conventional spelling and grade 2 braille, but models sound-symbol relationships by verbally accenting the dominant consonant sounds in words and stating the name of the letter or contraction written for each sound. Vowels are written but generally not mentioned at this stage. Gradually, the student learns to recognize the sounds made by different consonant letters and begins to help the teacher by orally supplying the beginning letter for many of the words. When the entry is complete, the student reads the sentence with assistance. The teacher points out easy-to-recognize consonant letters that help the child identify individual words.

For example, in the following talking-writing lesson, Alex, a 4-year-old preschooler, has just learned to button the large 1-inch buttons on a practice vest. This achievement becomes the topic for the day's writing lesson. During the first part of the lesson, the child dictates his sentence and the teacher writes, modeling sound-symbol relationships for beginning consonants. She encourages him to repeat both the sound and the name of the letter for each consonant to reinforce the connection.

Teacher: You're so proud that you can button the vest! What sentence shall we write today?

Alex (with some guidance): I can do big buttons.

Teacher (writing with student's hands on hers): Capital *I* (writes *I*) . . . "can" . . . /k/ . . . /k/ . . . That's the sound of the letter *c.* Can you make that sound?

Alex: /k/ . . . /k/.

Teacher: Yes, that's the sound of *c*! I'm going to write the letter *c* for *can* with fingers 1 and 4 . . . "I can **do** . . ." /d/ . . . /d/ . . . Can you help me with the letter for the sound /d/?

Alex: /d/ . . . /d/ . . . It's a *d!*

Teacher: Thank you! I'm going to write *d* for *do* with fingers 1, 4, and 5. Now, "I can do **big** . . ." /b/ . . . /b/ . . .

Alex: /b/ . . . /b/ . . . /b/ . . . It's a *b!*

Teacher: Right again! Here's a *b* for *big,* fingers 1 and 2 (writes whole word *big*). Next we have "buttons."

Alex: Buttons. /b/ . . . /b/ Another *b!*

Teacher: And here it is, *b* for *buttons* (writes whole word *buttons*). Now let's read our sentence.

Alex (reading sentence): "I can . . ."

Teacher: Here's the *c.*

Alex: ". . . do . . ."

Teacher: Here's the *d.*

Alex: ". . . big buttons."

Teacher: Can you find *b* for *big* and *b* for *buttons?*

Part 2: Imitation: Talking and Writing

In the second part of the lesson, the student writes freely on the braillewriter, usually about the same topic discussed earlier in the lesson. Very often the child will speak the message while writing (hence "talking writing"), imitating the behavior modeled by the teacher. The result may be lines of random dots that are equivalent to the scribbles and marks made by sighted children of the same age. The scribbles have meaning for the child, even though they cannot be read by anyone else.

During the second part of his lesson, Alex "scribbles" on the brailler while talking:

Teacher: Now it's your turn to write. (Helps child put paper back in brailler.) What would you like to say?

Alex: I can button my vest! (pressing random keys) "I . . . can . . . button . . ." /b/ . . . /b/ . . . How do you make a letter *b?*

Teacher: You know that /b/ is the sound of the letter *b!* Good for you! It's fingers 1 and 2, like this (demonstrates).

Alex: (continuing with random keys): ". . . my vest . . ."

Teacher: Now take your paper out and read your sentence back to me. Can you find the letter *b* that you wrote? (Student reads.) Let's glue a button to this page of your journal so you'll remember what we wrote about.

Together, Alex and the teacher produce the following sample of talking writing:

Teacher writes as student dictates:

| I | can | do | big | buttons. |

Student writes and verbalizes:

I can button my vest.

⠿ ⠿⠿⠿⠿⠿ ⠿ ⠿⠿⠿⠿⠿⠿⠿⠿ ⠿⠿⠿⠿⠿⠿⠿

It is important for teachers and parents to recognize that this tactile scribbling represents a valid literary behavior, just as sighted children's first efforts with crayons and paper are crucial steps in the development of literacy (Teale, 1985).

The talking-writing stage may last longer for students with delayed fine motor skills who have difficulty developing the finger isolation necessary to write correctly on the brailler. Many young children enjoy talking and scribbling on the brailler as a free-time activity.

Transition to Stage 2: Introducing "Book Writing"

The teacher's modeling during these early lessons helps children make the transition from tactile scribbling to an awareness of conventional writing, or "book writing." As children listen to strategies for sounding out words, feel their teacher's finger movements on the brailler, and begin to recognize a few braille letters, they are eager to write letters themselves. Students can learn to read and write many letters of the alphabet during the informal give and take of a daily writing lesson. The teacher conducts frequent assessments to determine how many letters the children are able to recognize and write (see Chapter 10). Students enjoy helping to choose the next letters to be learned, often by associating these letters with the beginning sounds of favorite words or names. As they move on to the guided-writing stage, children also learn to write their names.

Stage 2: Guided Writing

During guided journal writing, children do their own writing, but still benefit from the teacher's assistance with spacing, sound-symbol relationships, and the production of characters on the braillewriter. Like a talking-writing lesson, a guided-writing lesson begins with the teacher and child discussing possible journal topics and creating one or more oral sentences about the chosen subject. However, at this stage the child (not the teacher) does the writing, using invented spelling, while the teacher emphasizes new or difficult sounds and provides the finger numbers for unfamiliar braille characters.

Invented spelling (discussed in Chapter 2) is a logical system of sounding out words that can be read back by the writer and others. It is a temporary system, which gradually disappears as the child learns conventional spelling patterns. During guided writing the objective is not to write perfect grade 2 braille, but rather to create a message in invented spelling appropriate to the child's developmental level. When providing assistance during a guided-writing lesson, teachers may choose to focus on any of the following sounds:

- initial consonants only (including digraphs like *sh* and *th*)
- initial and final consonants
- initial, final, and middle consonants and named (long) vowels
- short vowels in consonant-vowel-consonant combinations

As children read and write more braille they become aware that special shapes called contractions may hide the letters they hear in words or have sounds of their own. For example, the letter *r* does not appear in the word *her* where the *e-r* contraction is used, and the contraction *s-h* makes a new sound altogether. As children encounter common contractions in their reading, they begin to use them naturally in their writing. New letters and contractions can be reinforced with a few warm-up writing exercises on a scrap piece of braille paper before the guided-writing lesson begins.

In the following example of a guided-writing lesson, a 5-year-old writes about flying a kite with her preschool class the day before. After discussion with the teacher, she decides to write the sentence, "I flew the kite." The teacher emphasizes initial, middle, and final consonant sounds and taps the child's hand lightly after each word to remind her to space.

Teacher: Do you remember how to write the word *I*? What does it always have in front of it?

Sharon: A capital sign. (Writes capital *I*.)

Teacher: Right! "I **flew**." . . . /f/ . . . /f/ . . . /f/ . . . What letter does *flew* start with?

Sharon: /f/ . . . /f/ . . . It starts with *f*. How do you make an *f*?

Teacher: That's a new letter for you. *F* is dots 1, 2, and 4. (Sharon writes *f*.) Do you hear any other sounds in the word *f-**l**-e-w?* (Stretches out word to emphasize *l*.)

Sharon: /l/ . . . /l/ . . . I hear an *l* and I know how to write it! (Writes *l*.)

Teacher: What word comes next?

Sharon: "I flew **the** . . ." How do you write *the?*

Teacher: We talked about this word yesterday. It's a braille contraction with a special shape. We use fingers 2, 3, 4, and 6. (Student writes *the*.)

Sharon: "I flew the **kite**." I can write the word *kite*! (Makes /k/ sound several times and writes *k*.)

Teacher: You're not quite finished! What do you hear at the end of "kite"?

Sharon: Kite. I hear /t/. (Writes *t*.)

Teacher: Let's read your sentence and make a picture.

Sharon (reading): "I flew the kite." (Cuts out a kite and attaches piece of yarn.)

The student's final journal entry in invented spelling read as follows:

    I   fl   the   kt

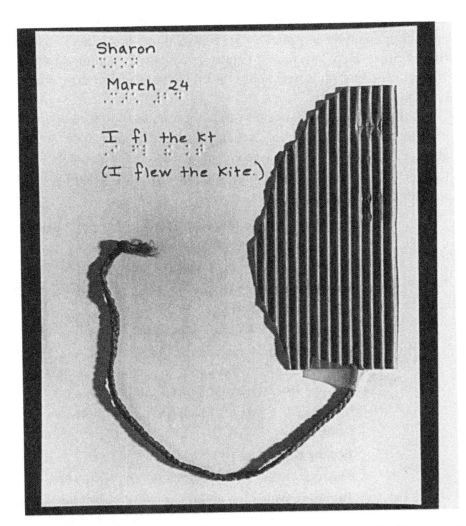

A preschool student wrote this journal entry in invented spelling during a guided-writing lesson.

The following longer sample of guided writing was written by a kindergarten student in the middle of the school year:

    I   like   fs   (I like flies.)

I   s   a   f   (I saw a fly.)

it   wsz   mn   the   wddow   (It was on the window.)

I   tch   the   fi   (I touched the fly.)

it   wsz   tiling   me   (It was tickling me.)

I   was   lafing   (I was laughing.)

The teacher provided guidance with

- spacing between words;
- hearing the *ch* sound and writing the contraction;
- hearing the short vowels in "tickling" and "laughing"; and
- writing the correct contraction for "was" in the last sentence.

Many children can learn to write most of the letters of the alphabet and common contractions within the context of daily journal writing, an activity from the whole language end of the language arts continuum. Students with additional learning problems may require more structured drill and practice with individual characters. However, they should also have the opportunity to use the letters and sounds they know during guided-writing activities (see Chapter 8).

Stage 3: Independent Writing

Sighted children can begin to compose independently when they know about six consonants (Graves, 1983). Children who are learning braille can achieve independence in writing on the braillewriter at the same time as their sighted peers. Beginning writers benefit from a balance of both guided- and independent writing activities. Guided-writing lessons provide students with opportunities for teacher-directed learning of specific writing skills, within a meaningful context. During guided writing, children are introduced to new sound-symbol relationships, new braille characters, and the conventions of writing (capitalization, punctuation, and spelling) as they write about topics of interest to them. Opportunities for independent writing reveal which of these elements a child has internalized. Teachers can use children's independent writing work to plan focus lessons that target specific areas of need in written language. (Focus lessons are discussed later in this chapter.)

This sample of independent writing, written by a kindergarten student at the end of the school year, reveals a great deal about what the child knows about writing:

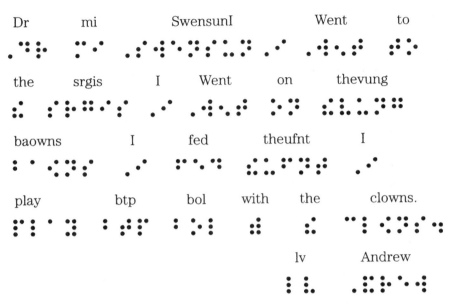

(Dear Ms. Swenson, I went to the circus. I went on the bungee bounce. I fed the elephant. I played beep ball with the clowns. Love, Andrew)

This sample shows that Andrew

- is beginning to use elements of the correct format for letter writing, such as starting with a greeting and moving his closing to the center of the line;
- knows the conventional spelling and/or grade 2 braille for such high-frequency words as *with, the, play,* and *went;*
- uses beginning, middle, and ending consonant sounds to write longer words (for example, *dr* for *dear; baowns* for *bounce*);
- uses some short vowel sounds in his invented spelling (e.g., *fed*);
- knows the *o-w* and *e-n* part-word braille contractions;
- usually spaces between words; and
- uses a period at the end of his message.

As young children move through the stages of writing development, from talking writing through guided writing to independent writing, they benefit from the teacher's constant modeling of conventional spelling, sentence structure, and the mechanics of writing. As children gain more proficiency, focus lessons, based on the student's individual needs as reflected in their writing, become increasingly valuable as an instructional strategy.

Conventional Spelling

In many early primary mainstream classrooms, teachers write the conventional spelling ("book spelling") lightly above each child's invented spelling. The itinerant or resource teacher can braille the correct grade 2 braille spelling at the bottom of the journal page and point out specific contractions, words, or punctuation marks to the child. However, young children should never get the message that their invented spelling is wrong. Rather, it is a developmental step toward the more mature writing they will do later.

Dialogue Journals

Another way to model correct spelling, punctuation, and sentence construction is to respond to the child's journal entry in writing with a question or a comment using some of the same words as in the original entry. The child reads what the teacher has written and writes back if a response is needed, as in the following example:

> Student's entry: I wgld mi tth (I wiggled my tooth.)
>
> Teacher's question: What happened to your wiggly tooth?
>
> Student's response: mi tooth fl out (My tooth fell out.)

The student spells tooth correctly after reading the teacher's sentence.

Focus Lessons

As children gain independence in writing, focus lessons, designed by the teacher based on the student's needs, replace guided-writing sessions. These lessons pinpoint a specific skill or aspect of writing. Examples of topics for focus lessons include the following:

- spacing between words
- differentiating between "question" and "telling" sentences
- varying the beginnings of sentences (avoiding "And then . . . and then . . . and then . . .")
- choosing interesting words
- including a beginning and an ending in a piece of writing
- providing more specific information about a subject
- using the contractions for the words *to, by,* and *into*
- learning when to use the uncontracted forms of whole-word lower signs such as *in, was,* and *his*
- using quotation marks in dialogue
- composing a main-idea sentence followed by supporting statements

During a focus lesson the teacher models the targeted skill or strategy and provides opportunities for students to practice it. Students then begin to apply what they have learned to their own writing.

SUMMARY

Children who are learning braille move through stages of writing development, just as their sighted peers do. Preschoolers scribble on the braillewriter, developing the concept that what they speak can be represented in tactile form. Kindergartners begin to make use of sound-symbol relationships—first consonants and then vowels—to write words and sentences in invented spelling that others can read. Over the next few years, students refine their written language skills by taking selected pieces of writing through the same multistep writing process that adults use. The next chapter will describe adaptations to the writing process for students who write in braille.

CHAPTER 7 The Developing Writer and the Writing Process

Both reading and writing in braille require daily support from a teacher of visually impaired students. However, once children begin reading braille transcriptions of commercial materials, they are able to complete many reading activities independently, as long as the teacher previews new contractions and braille code rules with them. Students in mainstream classes can join their classmates for shared and guided reading lessons (see Chapter 4) and participate actively in group discussions related to their reading. Writing instruction, however, continues to require intensive intervention throughout the primary grades from a teacher who knows braille. This is particularly true when writing is taught as a multistep process. This chapter presents a detailed look at the multistep approach to writing known as the writing process and ways that each step can be adapted for writers who use braille. It ends with suggestions for helping students learn to write grade 2 braille contractions and acquire conventional spelling skills.

Students with multiple disabilities can also benefit from participating in the writing process as well as other literacy activities described in previous chapters. Adjusting the balance between skill-oriented and meaning-oriented instruction for these students requires an understanding of their additional disabilities and their potential for using braille in educational and vocational settings. Chapter 8 suggests ways that teachers can help students who have additional learning problems, particularly those with cognitive disabilities, acquire braille literacy skills.

THE WRITING PROCESS

In meaning-oriented language arts programs, writing instruction is approached differently than it is in traditional programs. Students do not spend a majority of their writing time completing skill-development exercises from workbooks. Instead, they write daily on self-selected topics and learn grammar, handwriting, spelling, and other mechanical skills within the context of their own writing. This change reflects the belief that children learn to write only by actually writing, not by filling in blanks or copying exercises (Hansen, 1987).

As children develop independence in writing, they begin to look at some of their work more critically through the writing process familiar to most adult writers. The writing process includes six major steps (Fowler & McCallum, 1995b):

1. *Planning:* preparing for writing through activities such as oral discussion; reading; or constructing a list, web or diagram, or outline to follow during writing. Plans may change as the writer works on the piece.

2. *Drafting:* writing and refining the piece in successive trials (or drafts)

3. *Conferring:* talking with others, such as peers or teachers, about the content or mechanics of a piece and deciding whether or not to follow their suggestions for changing it

4. *Revising:* changing the content to make the message clearer to the reader

5. *Editing:* proofreading for errors in capitalization, punctuation, spelling, and grammar

6. *Publishing* (preparing for an audience): producing the work in its final form, such as a book or a tape

These steps do not apply to every piece a child writes, and some work, such as journal writing, is never revised, edited, or published. Often a child chooses the best of three or four drafts completed during Writers' Workshop, or writing time, to take through the writing process. The steps do not necessarily take place in fixed sequence. For example, a writer may revise a section before conferring with others, then revise it further and confer again. The writing process focuses first on the writer's message and how it is perceived by the reader. However, as part of the process, children are expected to edit their work for capitalization, spelling, and punctuation before it is published.

Advantages of the Writing Process

The writing process involves the integration of listening, speaking, reading, and writing. Students who hear, read, and discuss high-quality children's literature internalize vocabulary and writing styles that begin to appear in their own writing. Once they select a draft for publication, they have the opportunity to practice reading their own writing many times as they confer, revise, and edit. They learn to read new vocabulary, recognize writing conventions, and apply rules of the braille code that they will encounter in other reading and writing tasks.

The writing process promotes student-directed learning. Children make many of the decisions involved in writing instruction, such as which topics to write about, which drafts to take through the full writing process, what revisions to make, and how to publish their work. Students also develop independent work habits as they become familiar with the writing process.

Adapting the Stages of the Writing Process in Braille

Like sighted students, students who read braille benefit from guidance during each stage of the writing process, especially as they are becoming familiar with the procedures. In the case of the braille reader, however, much of this support must be given by a teacher who is familiar with the braille code; the classroom teacher can provide additional assistance orally during individual or small-group conferences. In a mainstream setting, the resource or itinerant teacher works closely with the regular education teacher, transcribing the child's work at each step along the way. One-on-one assistance is usually needed with manipulating braille text and creating tactile pictures during the revising, editing, and publishing stages. However, as students improve their writing skills, they can also work independently during much of the writing process. Techniques such as the use of invented spelling and tactile editing marks (described later in this chapter) enable children who are blind to work as efficiently as possible.

The following summary of the writing process provides suggestions that apply to any beginning writers as well as specific recommendations for adapting each stage for children who read and write in braille.

SUGGESTIONS FOR TEACHERS

ADAPTING THE WRITING PROCESS

Planning

- Remember that all writers write best about what they know well. Discuss possibilities for writing topics with your student and make a braille list. Encourage the student to write about an actual experience or a subject in which he or she is an "expert."

- If a topic is assigned (such as writing a fairy tale), be sure the student has had extensive experience with the particular genre or the type of information required for the piece. If the child doesn't have the necessary background, provide supplemental hands-on experiences or discuss the possibility of an alternate assignment with the student and the mainstream teacher. For example, if students are expected to describe the imaginary pictures they see in different cloud formations, it may be more appropriate for a student who is blind to listen to or read information about clouds and write a short nonfiction piece to summarize what she learned.

- Help the student plan for writing by discussing ideas and/or making a simple braille list or outline. Young students often benefit from rehearsing their sentences orally before they write them independently.

■ Work with the student to compile a short list of special or difficult words that may be needed for a particular piece of writing. Tape the braille list to the student's desk for easy reference. Include some or all of the words in an individualized weekly spelling list. (See the section on "Spelling" later in this chapter for more information.)

Drafting

■ Even very young students should be expected to write their first draft independently by sounding out words and using a mixture of invented and conventional spelling. This process builds sound-symbol relationships and independent work skills.

■ Remember that ideas take precedence over mechanics in the drafting phase. Certain spelling errors, erasures, crossed-out words, and false starts are acceptable, although carelessness is not. Depending on the student's level, a core of correctly spelled words should be expected (discussed in the section on spelling later in this chapter). The work must be legible enough so that the writer can read it back to others during the conferring stage.

■ Students should always double-space their work in braille to allow for revision and editing changes later on.

Conferring

■ The student may confer with the itinerant teacher, the mainstream teacher, or classmates in small groups or pairs, depending on classroom procedures.

■ During revision and editing conferences, the teacher may help the student make tactile changes directly on the draft, thus combining the stages of conferring and revising or editing.

■ Provide braille transcriptions of other children's work so that the braille reader can participate fully in peer conferences.

Revising

■ Revision may involve adding, deleting, or changing information to make the writer's message clearer to the reader.

■ Revision and editing may take place simultaneously when conferencing about short pieces with younger writers.

■ During a revision conference, focus on only a few stylistic points. Don't try to have the child change everything. The piece should sound like the student!

■ The revision step is generally not appropriate for kindergarten writers.

Revising with First-Grade Writers

■ Ask the child to read the draft aloud to you. Summarize your understanding of the writer's message and discuss the ideas orally.

■ Provide guidance in revising the content. At this stage, content revision often consists of deleting repetitive sentences and adding information, usually at the end of the piece. Help the child delete unwanted sentences by covering them with a piece of masking tape. Additional information can be written at the end of the piece or on a separate sheet if it is to be inserted into the text later.

Revising with More Advanced Primary-Grade Writers

- Have the student revise short pieces in one session with the teacher or peers. Longer pieces may need several revisions.

- As you focus on the clarity of the written message, first share your comprehension of the piece. Then question the student about parts you do not understand and discuss different ways of expressing the ideas.

- To change the sequence of ideas or to add new ones to the middle of a piece, cut the paper where changes are to be made and staple the pieces to a fresh sheet of paper with any new writing in the correct order.

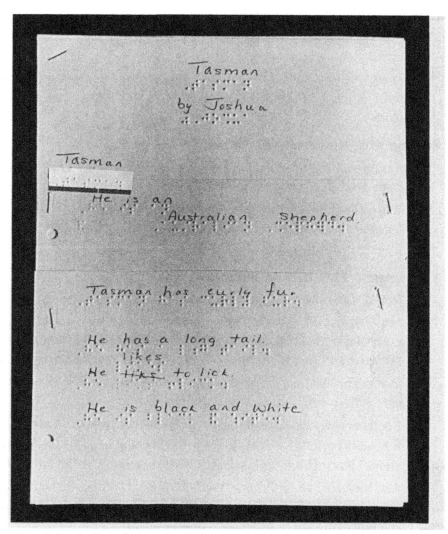

This first-grade author revised his story by moving the last sentence of his second draft to the beginning, so that his piece would start with a main idea. The itinerant teacher provided assistance with cutting and stapling.

- Use a thick vertical piece of graphic art tape to indicate that words have been inserted in the space above the original braille line.

- If two sentences say essentially the same thing, ask the student to choose the better sentence and to justify his or her choice.

- Use long pieces of masking tape to delete unwanted or repetitive ideas.

- If the piece is long and disorganized, try the following suggestions:
  - Help the student group similar ideas into sections orally or by cutting and stapling parts of the text.
  - List the main ideas of each section in a simple outline.
  - Then assign the student to work on only one section at a time.
  - Encourage the student to rehearse the revised text orally with you before writing it independently.

Editing

- Editing involves a careful search for errors in spelling, punctuation, capitalization, and grammar.

- Many writers, both children and adults, edit their work continuously as they write a piece. Others leave the editing step until final revisions have been made.

Editing with Kindergarten Writers

- In general, children at the kindergarten level should not be expected to edit their writing or to write perfect final copies.

- Write the child's words or sentences correctly in grade 2 braille beneath the invented spelling.

- Encourage children to read both their own writing and your "book spelling."

Editing with First-Grade Writers

- Revise and edit short pieces in one session, rather than in two separate steps.

- Have the child edit the piece independently for capital letters and ending punctuation before conferring with you. The child can either braille the capital signs and periods directly on the draft or mark errors with a crayon.

- Praise successful editing changes; some children like to count the number of errors they were able to find on their own.

- Focus on only one or two types of mechanical errors (for example, capital letters and periods), depending on the writing level of the child. First graders should learn the rule that after every period comes a capital letter.

- Ask the child to find three words that are spelled correctly and three that he or she would like to learn to spell. Discuss the correct spelling and help the student write them in grade 2 braille.

- Have the child revise and edit the draft orally by reading it aloud while you write a perfect braille copy. Do not avoid using contractions that the student has not yet seen; the best place to learn contractions is in the student's own writing.

- Ask the student to read your copy aloud, noting changes in spelling, capitalization, use of contractions, and punctuation. Practice brailling new contractions together on a piece of scrap paper.
- Have the student braille a final copy independently by carefully copying your corrected version.

Editing with More Advanced Primary-Grade Writers

- Have the student edit the piece independently before meeting with you. The student can braille changes (capitals, punctuation marks, and so forth) directly on the draft for future reference or mark errors with a crayon.
- Work together to edit remaining errors using simple tactile editing marks, such as those shown in Figure 7.1 (see "Suggestions for Using Tactile Editing Marks").
- Have the student copy from the edited draft independently, making a correction each time a tactile editing mark is encountered. The student may choose to use a portable braille notetaker, such as Braille 'n Speak or Braille Lite made by Blazie Engineering (see Resources), so that both print and braille copies can be produced to share with others.

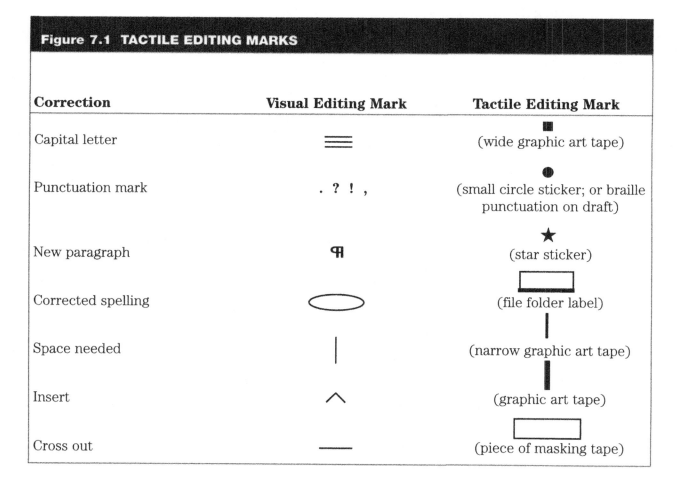

Figure 7.1 TACTILE EDITING MARKS

Correction	Visual Editing Mark	Tactile Editing Mark
Capital letter	≡	▪ (wide graphic art tape)
Punctuation mark	. ? ! ,	● (small circle sticker; or braille punctuation on draft)
New paragraph	¶	★ (star sticker)
Corrected spelling	⬭	▭ (file folder label)
Space needed	|	| (narrow graphic art tape)
Insert	∧	▮ (graphic art tape)
Cross out	—	▭ (piece of masking tape)

■ SUGGESTIONS FOR USING TACTILE EDITING MARKS

A simple system of tactile editing marks allows children who read and write in braille to have a written record of corrections to their writing. One such system is presented in Figure 7.1, but teachers can devise their own, as long as it is used consistently. Using tactile editing marks efficiently is a joint effort by the teacher and the student. The student takes the lead in finding errors, while the teacher prepares the editing marks. For example, when the student locates a spelling error, the teacher brailles the correct spelling onto a file folder label, with input from the student, and helps the student stick the label over the misspelled word. Keep the following points in mind when using tactile editing marks:

- Remind students to double- or triple-space their drafts to leave space for revision and editing changes.

- Devise your own tactile editing system that is easy for you and your student to use. Be consistent in your use of editing symbols.

- Indicate corrections by brailling directly on the draft or by using stick-on labels, dots, tape, or stars, which are readily available at office supply stores. Graphic art tape can be purchased in a variety of widths at large art and office supply stores, such as Pla-za (see Resources).

- Where space permits, stick the tactile editing mark exactly where it belongs in the line of braille, rather than above or below the line. This will ensure that the student notices it when brailling the final copy.

- Spelling corrections can be brailled on file folder labels and stuck over the misspelled words. Correct spelling can also be indicated above the word if there is not enough room on the original line.

- Use a wide piece of graphic art tape between two words to indicate that words have been inserted above the braille line.

- Stick a piece of masking tape over words or sentences to be deleted. Braille new text directly on the tape.

Publishing

- The student should write the final braille piece without major errors, either by copying from the teacher's version (for less experienced writers) or by copying from a draft with tactile editing marks (for more experienced writers).

- Make the student's final braille copy into a book, letting the student decide where pages should begin and end. The teacher may choose to rebraille the pages using the student's final copy as a guide, just as real publishers produce books from an author's manuscript (or, as in many general education classes, the teacher types children's final handwritten copies on the computer).

- Include a title page, dedication, and about-the-author section.

- Assist the student in making tactile pictures or a special cover. Students with usable vision sometimes enjoy drawing pictures.

- The student may want to publish the book in another medium by audiotaping it with sound effects.

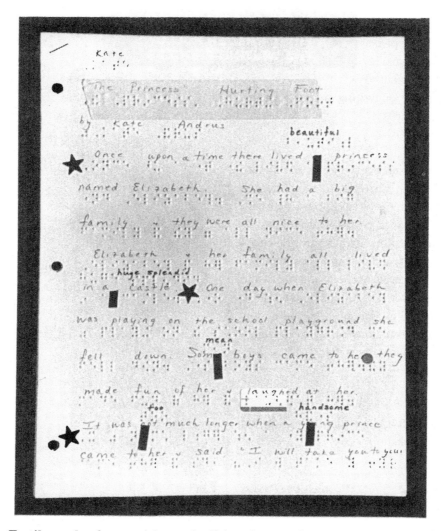

Tactile marks show revision and editing changes. The thick vertical pieces of graphic art tape indicate that adjectives have been inserted into the text. This second-grade author changed her title by placing a piece of masking tape over the original and brailling a new title on top. Editing also included paragraph indicators (stars) and a spelling change (file folder label).

■ Provide opportunities for the student to share his or her book with classmates and family members.

Using tactile marks to revise and edit braille text works best with short pieces typically written by younger children; this method becomes more cumbersome when the text is long and there are many changes to be made. Tactile marks provide young students with a concrete approach to manipulating their written text. This, in turn, builds a foundation for effective writing skills using a portable braille notetaker or a computer with synthetic speech by the middle to late elementary grades.

A TEACHER'S DIARY
A FIRST GRADER FOLLOWS THE WRITING PROCESS

Sharon is a mainstreamed first-grade student who speaks English as a second language. In the example presented here, she takes a piece of writing through all the stages of the writing process.

Planning

Sharon often relates how everyone in her family calls on her older sister Caroline to help them. I know already that Caroline spends part of every evening listening to Sharon read the braille books I send home. During Writers' Workshop one day I suggest that Sharon write a piece about all the work Caroline does, and Sharon is enthusiastic about the idea. We rehearse sentences out loud about each family member, including Happy, the new dog. Sharon thinks of the repeated phrase, "Caroline, Caroline, Caroline," which gives her story a predictable pattern.

Drafting

Sharon writes her draft independently during her first-grade Writers' Workshop:

When I am stoc
on a work I go

Caroline Caroline
Caroline

when Edward need
food he go

Caroline Caroline
Caroline

when mom
needs hep she go

Caroline Caroline
Caroline

When grandfather needs
noos papr he go

Caroline Caroline
Caroline

When dadddy wos
Happy to go down
he go

Caroline Caroline
Caroline

When Happy wos
to come out he go

m   m   m
••   ••   ••
•   •   •

Conferring/Revising

Sharon reads her draft to me without difficulty. I can certainly say that Caroline is a busy girl in her story! We talk about the need for a beginning (how will the reader know who Caroline is?) and an end. Sharon adds the beginning, "Caroline is my sister," and an ending, "Caroline does everything at home. Poor Caroline!"

I also have a couple of other questions. What kind of help does Mom need? Sharon inserts "with cleening" above the appropriate place in the sentence, and I add a thick vertical piece of graphic art tape between "hep" and "she" to show where the words belong. Sharon also adds the word "steyr" (stairs) after "down" in the sentence about Dad. Now Sharon's story has a beginning, middle, and end, and her message is clear.

Editing

Before we discuss mechanical errors together, I ask Sharon to edit her text independently by marking with a crayon wherever a capital letter or period is needed. She finds two missing capitals and five missing periods; we talk about the spelling of several important words and put them on her individualized spelling list for the week. I also teach Sharon to use commas between repeated words. The next day I do a focus lesson on quotation marks, which Sharon has encountered in her reading but never used in her writing. We use sentences from the Caroline story to illustrate where quotation marks belong.

Sharon reads her entire revised and edited story to me as I write it in correct grade 2 braille. I explain grammatical changes ("he go" becomes "he goes") and spelling corrections. Sharon has decided to put each person's sentence on a separate page of her book, so I braille a line at each page break to remind her to start on a new piece of paper. Sharon brailles her final copy independently by copying my corrected version. Now that she knows the story so well, she is alert to small details in spelling and punctuation. Perfection is her objective.

Publishing

Sharon helps to make the book's cover, title page, and simple tactile pictures. I braille the about-the-author information on the last page. For the first time we also include a dedication page. Sharon shares her published book with her family and proudly reads it to Caroline's class.

> *Caroline, Caroline, Caroline*
> This book is dedicated to Caroline.
> Thank you for helping me.
> Caroline is my sister.
> When I am stuck on a word I go, "Caroline, Caroline, Caroline."
> When Edward needs food he goes, "Caroline, Caroline, Caroline."
> When Mom needs help with cleaning she goes, "Caroline, Caroline, Caroline."
> When Grandfather needs a newspaper he goes, "Caroline, Caroline, Caroline."
> When Daddy wants Happy to go downstairs he goes, "Caroline, Caroline, Caroline."
> When Happy wants to come out he goes, "Mmm, mmm, mmm."
> Caroline does everything at home. Poor Caroline!

The steps of the writing process help children slow down and think about the message they are conveying to their readers. They learn that good writing takes time for everyone (including teachers and adult authors), but they also know that the end result will be worth the effort invested.

SUGGESTIONS FOR STUDENT-AUTHORED BOOKS

The bookmaking process at the preschool or early kindergarten level (described in Chapter 3) familiarizes young children with basic concepts related to books and helps them develop book-handling skills, such as finding the front cover and turning the pages from front to back one at a time. Student-authored books by developing writers in first and second grade often reflect weeks of hard work and represent the culmination of the writing process. As children hear and read more high-quality literature and share their published books with each other, they are motivated to try different kinds of writing. There is no limit to the types of books children make or the topics they choose to write about, but many of them fall into three broad categories. These include experience books, retellings, and specialty books.

A journal entry about a family or school event can become the first draft of an experience book like *Caroline, Caroline, Caroline.* Encourage children who have a lot of knowledge about a particular subject to write about it.

A retelling, or rewrite, involves the imitation of rhythms and patterns a child has heard or read elsewhere. Familiar poems, emergent reader books, or other children's literature provide the framework for the new piece of writing. For example, starting with the traditional rhyme (reprinted in Fowke, 1966)

> Jelly in the bowl
> Jelly in the bowl
> Wibble wobble wibble wobble
> Jelly in the bowl

one student composed these rewrites:

> Spaghetti on the plate
> Spaghetti on the plate
> Yum yum yum yum
> Spaghetti on the plate
>
> Andrew on the slide
> Andrew on the slide
> Whee whee whee whee
> Andrew on the slide

Similarly, after reading the emergent reader book, *Lions and Gorillas* (Nelson, 1989), a student was inspired to write an innovative version. The original contains the passage:

> There are lions in the jungle.
> There are lions at the zoo.
> There's a lion on my back porch,
> and I don't know what to do.

A collection of student-authored books includes retellings and experience stories.

The student's rewrite read:

> There are teachers at home.
> There are teachers at school.
> There's a teacher in the trash can,
> And I don't know what to do.

At a more advanced level, children may rewrite a book using new characters and events. For example, students in one first-grade class wrote their own versions of *The Very Hungry Caterpillar* (Carle, 1969), each child choosing a favorite animal and food while maintaining the structure provided by the days of the week.

The Very Hungry Puppy

One Sunday morning a little puppy was born.
On Monday she ate one pizza.
On Tuesday she ate two rice balls.
On Wednesday she ate three pretzels.
On Thursday she ate four pieces of bread.
On Friday she ate five goldfish.
On Saturday she ate chocolate cake, one cookie, one ice cream,
  one spaghetti, one macaroni, and one noodle.
That night she felt worse.
So on Sunday she ate doggy medicine and she was much better.

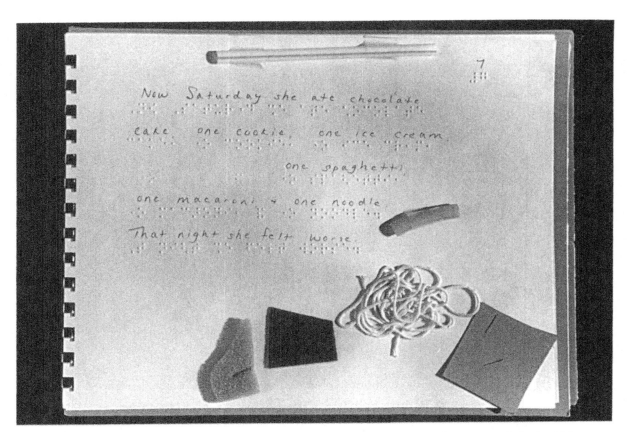

Retelling a story they have read gives children an opportunity to use their own ideas within a familiar framework. This page is from the book, *The Very Hungry Puppy,* a retelling of Eric Carle's *The Very Hungry Caterpillar.* Tactile illustrations show "chocolate cake, one cookie, one ice cream, one spaghetti, one macaroni, and one noodle."

Specialty books, which often feature a repetitive format related to a specific category or topic, provide a contrast to narrative-based books. Sometimes the structure provided by this type of text can motivate an otherwise reluctant writer. Specialty books may also be used to reinforce math concepts in a book format (as in the book of graphs suggested below). Some examples of specialty books are listed here; both teachers and students can come up with new topics.

- Book of lists: List foods, animals, clothing, vehicles, leisure activities, or objects shaped like circles or squares.
- Book of telephone numbers: Braille one name and telephone number per page and arrange in alphabetical order.
- Book of graphs: Use lines of full cells to represent numbers of items or objects being compared, such as the number of people in different families; the number of braillers and blackboards in a room; or the number of swings and slides outside.
- Book of instructions: Have the child give instructions on something he or she knows well, such as how to tie a shoe.

- Book about me: Include such information as the student's name, age, address, favorite foods, and family members.

SPELLING

Spelling, a major focus during the editing stage of the writing process, is a challenging subject area for many students who read braille. Not only must they learn the contracted form of the words they write on the braillewriter or notetaker, they must also memorize the conventional spelling of each word so that they will be able to use a computer with synthetic speech successfully. Students who are blind miss the incidental exposure to the written words that surround sighted students everywhere they look. The contracted nature of braille also limits readers' contact with the standard spelling patterns found in print materials. Despite these difficulties, students who read braille can become good spellers when given appropriate instruction and resources.

It is widely recognized that learning to spell is a developmental process (Fowler, Jackson, & McCallum, 1996). Students begin by writing random strings of letters that show no sound-symbol correspondence. During the next stages they rely first on consonants and then add long and short vowels to approximate standard spelling. As children progress, they spell increasing numbers of words conventionally and learn to space between words. In the author's experience, children who are blind follow the same sequence of steps in spelling development as their sighted peers.

Spelling instruction is most effective if it is integrated with the rest of the language arts program and the words studied are meaningful to the child. Words taught in isolation often do not transfer to children's own writing (Hudson & O'Toole, 1983).

SUGGESTIONS FOR TEACHERS

TEACHING SPELLING TO STUDENTS WHO READ BRAILLE

- Always spell contractions using the letters of the alphabet rather than pronouncing them as syllables (Godwin et al., 1995). For example, in spelling the word *long,* refer to the *o-n-g* contraction (saying each letter), rather than the */ong/* contraction.

- Include the contracted and the uncontracted form of words in spelling lists. Students should be expected to know both. If possible, teach conventional (uncontracted) spelling using a computer with synthetic speech or a notetaker with a QWERTY keyboard rather than a braillewriter. These are the writing tools on which students will actually use conventional spelling.

- Have students use the "look, say, cover, write, check" procedure to learn new words (Bolton & Snowball, 1993b). Teachers can easily adapt this method for students who read braille. Students say and spell the word while reading it, write it without referring back, and then check their work by comparing their written word to the original. (The "cover" step is not necessary for braille readers as long as they do not touch the original word while writing.) If the word is not correct, they try again. This method integrates oral language, reading, and writing and reinforces the formation of letters and contractions on the brailler. Simply spelling a word orally is not sufficient; it needs to be written.

- Teach and reinforce basic spelling patterns and rules. Call students' attention to spelling similarities among words whenever possible. Have students maintain an ongoing book of spelling patterns such as the *Words, Words, Words!* book described in Chapter 5. Bolton and Snowball's (1993a, 1993b) books are excellent resources for teaching spelling. Plan focus lessons to introduce and reinforce spelling strategies, especially if these are not included in the mainstream curriculum.

- Encourage students to try to spell problem words themselves before giving them the correct spelling. Observe the strategies they use. Do they look for the base word first? Apply the rules for adding a suffix? Segment the word and spell it syllable by syllable? Think of another word that rhymes?

- Make a personal braille dictionary for students to refer to while writing. Use a three-ring notebook and a set of 12 dividers with small tabs. Label the tabs of the dividers with alternate letters of the alphabet, starting with *a, c, e,* and ending with *w.* Label a blank piece of braille paper for each letter of the alphabet, and place each page after the appropriate divider, so that the *a* divider is followed by the pages for *a* and *b,* the *c* divider by the pages for *c* and *d,* and so on. The *w* divider will need four pages for *w, x, y,* and *z.* Help the student write the correct spelling of frequently used words on the appropriate pages of the dictionary. Words can be found quickly using the braille letters on the divider tabs, and new words can be added at any time.

- Discourage overreliance on invented spelling after kindergarten or first grade. Make note of words that students are consistently misspelling and teach the correct spelling, so that errors do not become a habit.

- Expect students to use conventional spelling if it is accessible. For example, when writing a reading response to a braille book, the student should refer to the book for the spelling of important names and places. Provide spelling resources such as a personal dictionary or specialized word list related to a particular piece of writing. National Braille Press produces *A Braille Spelling Dictionary for Beginning Writers* (Hurray, 1993), which includes an alphabetical listing of common words in grade 1 and grade 2 braille, a mini-thesaurus, and lists of words in categories such as months and geography.

- Teach students to spell a core group of high-frequency words correctly. These can be assembled from words that students use often in their personal writing and from published lists of commonly used words such as the Dolch (1942) basic sight word list (see Appendix B). It is also helpful to consult with the regular classroom teacher for a list of words that sighted children of the same grade level are expected to know how to spell. Some schools are developing lists of required words at each grade level—sometimes known as "no excuses words"!

- Focus on homophones—words that sound the same but are spelled differently, such as *their/there* and *blue/blew*. This is an area of particular weakness for many students that is not remediated with a computer spell checker.

Sometimes an individualized spelling program can be more beneficial than the regular spelling curriculum for a student who is learning braille. An individualized approach enables the child to master the additional demands of the braille code within the context of the total language arts program.

SUGGESTIONS FOR TEACHERS

AN INDIVIDUALIZED SPELLING PROGRAM

- Keep a running list of words that the student misspells as you transcribe the student's written work. Develop a weekly spelling list by scanning the misspelled words and choosing one or more contractions or spelling patterns to emphasize. Supplement the list with other words that fit the chosen spelling patterns and with unrelated words that appear frequently in the child's writing. Additional words may include family names, environmental words such as "McDonald's," or words from the student's reading.
- Ask the child to contribute several additional words to the list that he or she wants to learn to spell. They do not have to fit the target pattern.
- Have the child copy the list of words every evening for homework in both contracted and uncontracted braille, using the look, say, write, and check procedures. Although this is a rote activity, it ensures that the student actually looks at the words daily. Copying the words also reinforces spelling patterns and new contractions. Ask the child to read the list to you each day, and review the special characteristics of each word.
- Check the child's immediate retention with an informal written quiz once a week. However, true retention will be apparent when the words are spelled correctly in the child's everyday writing. Reinforce the student every time you see a spelling word written correctly in a piece of writing. Words that continue to be misspelled go back on the teacher's running list for later study.

A form that can be used to record weekly spelling lists is included in Figure 7.2, and a blank copy appears in Appendix B. This sample record shows a first grader's

Figure 7.2 SAMPLE COMPLETED SPELLING RECORD

Spelling Record Name: _Jessie_

Week: 2/9–2/13	2/17–2/20	2/23–2/27	3/2–3/6
Focus: Number words "all" spelling pattern "ff" contraction	Guinea pig writing	Silent w -self words	Time Short - form words Birthday vocabulary
1. twelve	guinea pig	Itself	3:30
2. fifteen	water	myself	10:55–11:20
3. eighteen	bottle	himself	afternoon
4. nineteen	alfalfa	yourself	tonight
5. call	fur	pretty	today
6. fall	nibble	these	tomorrow
7. puff, puffs	squeak	write, -ing	birthday
8. stuff, stuffed	drink	wreck	excited
9. Karen	bedding	wrong	giggle
10. Ms. Schroeder		McDonald's	present
11.			party
12.			
13.			
14.			
15.			
16.			
17.			
18.			
19.			

individualized spelling lists over a four-week period. The words in each list come from the student's own reading and writing, and some of them were suggested by the student. Each list targets one or more related groups of words, such as words for a writing piece about a guinea pig; a particular spelling pattern, such as "all"; or specific contractions, such as "f-f" or short-form words. Note that the number of words varies each week. Again, the child's score on the weekly spelling quiz is less important than spelling the words correctly in daily classroom writing activities.

SUMMARY

The many facets of the writing process contribute greatly to children's development of literacy in oral language, reading, and writing. By the time they publish a book, students have planned their piece, reread their work many times during the drafting and revision stages, edited their work carefully for mechanical errors, and discussed their writing with others throughout the process. Despite the time and effort involved in this type of writing, children maintain their motivation because they are learning skills in a meaningful context.

CHAPTER 8 Teaching Braille to Students with Multiple Disabilities

Teachers of students with visual impairments are encountering an increasing number of children with other disabilities in addition to their blindness. These disabilities may be relatively easy to identify, such as deaf-blindness, moderate to severe mental retardation, or physical limitations; or they may manifest themselves in more subtle forms, such as suspected learning disabilities or emotional concerns. It is beyond the scope of this book to address strategies for teaching braille to all students who have multiple disabilities. For further information, the reader may refer to the chapter on "Teaching Braille to Students with Special Needs" (D'Andrea, 1997) in *Instructional Strategies for Braille Literacy* (Wormsley & D'Andrea, 1997), which offers many excellent suggestions for working with students who have physical, learning, or intellectual disabilities or who are deaf-blind. Teachers needing strategies specifically related to children with deaf-blindness will find *Hand in Hand: Essentials of Communication and Orientation and Mobility for Your Students Who Are Deaf-Blind* (Huebner, Prickett, Welch, & Joffee, 1995) extremely helpful. For guidance in assessing and teaching children with learning disabilities and visual impairments, "The Student with a Visual Disability and a Learning Disability" (Erin & Koenig, 1997) is recommended.

This chapter focuses specifically on students who have cognitive disabilities in addition to their visual impairment, a population with which the author has significant firsthand experience. The case study of Eddie, presented in this chapter and Chapter 9, shows how one student with very limited intellectual ability was able to acquire basic literacy skills, which reinforced significant gains in other developmental areas. Many of the reading and writing activities described earlier in this book have been used successfully with students who have mild to moderate retardation. This chapter outlines the prerequisite skills a student must have to be able to learn braille and offers suggestions for modifying instruction for this population. Chapter 10 presents options for assessing the literacy development of students with cognitive disabilities.

CANDIDATES FOR BRAILLE INSTRUCTION

For many years students with significant intellectual disabilities in addition to their blindness were not considered to be candidates for braille instruction. Recently, however, educators have begun to question this assumption (Rex et al., 1994). *The Perkins Activity and Resource Guide* (Heydt, Clark, Cushman, Edwards, & Allon, 1992) and *Learning Media Assessment of Students with Visual Impairments* (Koenig & Holbrook, 1995) explore the possibility of functional braille literacy for certain students with intellectual and other disabilities. Functional reading, as opposed to conventional reading, is directly related to an individual student's needs and is content specific (Koenig & Holbrook, 1995). The goal of functional literacy instruction is to enable a particular student to use basic reading and writing skills for specific tasks at home, at school, or in the community. Thus, the reading vocabulary taught to one student may be very different from that taught to another. A more detailed discussion of functional braille literacy for students with intellectual disabilities can be found in *Instructional Strategies for Braille Literacy* (Wormsley & D'Andrea, 1997).

Students who are capable of achieving functional braille literacy at some level and who will be able to use their skills to enhance their independence benefit from braille instruction in other ways as well. Among these advantages are the following:

- Braille instruction provides structure to the educational program and permits the student to participate in academic activities with sighted classmates. Daily braille-related activities may include marking the date on a calendar, reading a schedule, or completing sorting and matching tasks with braille letters, words, and numbers.

- Integrating listening and speaking with reading and writing braille reinforces attending, listening, and oral language skills. Materials and activities that focus on a child's own interests and experiences are ideally suited to promoting oral language development.

- Braille-related activities help develop job-related skills for the future. Although elementary students may be too young for formal vocational training, learning to read braille improves their understanding of positional concepts; develops efficient scanning and tracking patterns; and teaches them to complete sorting, matching, and sequencing tasks independently.

Both Heydt et al. (1992) and Koenig and Holbrook (1995) emphasize that the educational team must use a variety of assessment tools to determine whether braille should be included in a particular student's educational program. Not all students with cognitive disabilities are appropriate candidates for braille instruction. *The Perkins Activity and Resource Guide* (Heydt et al., 1992) lists three prerequisite skills that the student should have for learning braille:

1. a grasp of basic concepts, such as same and different and positional concepts

2. good tactile discrimination skills

3. language to understand and express symbolic thought—for example, the ability to understand that an object or tactile symbol can represent a real person, place, or event

Additional behaviors for educational team members to look for when assessing a student's readiness to learn braille are listed in checklist form in "Indicators of

---

Figure 8.1 CHECKLIST FOR ASSESSING READINESS TO LEARN BRAILLE

Indicators of Readiness for a Functional Literacy Program

Student _____

Date _____ Evaluator _____

Yes	No	No Opportunity	Behavior
___	___	___	Attends to and responds meaningfully when others read.
___	___	___	Anticipates activities and events.
___	___	___	Differentiates sounds and spoken words, gestures, or signs.
___	___	___	Attaches meaning to sound or spoken words, gestures, or signs.
___	___	___	Differentiates objects visually and/or tactually.
___	___	___	Demonstrates an association of pictures or objects with stories or books.
___	___	___	Identifies objects visually and/or tactually.
___	___	___	Associates signs in the home or community with important events (such as the golden arches mean "time to eat").
___	___	___	Chooses independently to examine books, letters, and/or symbols.
___	___	___	Notes likenesses and differences in words when presented in print or braille.
___	___	___	Follows simple directions of two or three steps.
___	___	___	Generalizes directional concepts (such as top, bottom).
___	___	___	Generalizes the ability to sequence a series of objects, activities, or events.
___	___	___	Generalizes the use of primitive symbolic communications systems such as real objects or miniatures.
___	___	___	Generalizes the use of abstract symbolic communication.
___	___	___	Initiates interactive communication through systems such as sign, gestures, or augmentative communication devices.
___	___	___	Recognizes that words in print or braille have meaning.
___	___	___	Recognizes name in print or braille.

Source: Reprinted with permission from Alan J. Koenig and M. Cay Holbrook, *Learning Media Assessment of Students with Visual Impairments*, 2nd ed. (Austin: Texas School for the Blind and Visually Impaired, 1995), p. 193.

Readiness for a Functional Literacy Program" (see Figure 8.1; this form also appears in Appendix B). The team should also consider whether learning braille is an educational priority, given the student's needs in other areas.

Assessing a student's abilities in these three areas requires time, patience, and careful observation. Prerequisite skills may have to be taught over a period of several weeks or months, and the student's potential as a braille reader evaluated on an ongoing basis. The case study of Eddie in the following chapter illustrates the assessment of a student with significant cognitive disabilities. Although Eddie initially demonstrated some prerequisite skills, such as a grasp of basic concepts and simple symbolic language, it took several months before he was able to make even gross discriminations among braille characters.

If braille is included in the student's Individual Educational Program (IEP), the educational team must allot sufficient instructional time each day to enable students to achieve the desired level of proficiency. It is unlikely that children who practice braille only two or three times a week will master any useful reading or writing skills. Under ideal circumstances, braille activities should be integrated with lessons throughout the day, even when the itinerant teacher is not there. Students with cognitive disabilities benefit from "braille immersion" (see Chapter 2), just as do their counterparts who use braille in regular education classes.

SUGGESTIONS FOR MODIFYING BRAILLE INSTRUCTION

In general, students with cognitive disabilities learn braille following the same basic sequence of instruction as students in regular academic programs. They also require the same time commitment from a teacher of students with visual impairments. Daily individual instruction is necessary to ensure that the student has adequate opportunity to reach a functional level in braille reading and writing. Although instruction will be tailored to the student's needs and abilities, a number of general strategies for working with children who have cognitive disabilities may be helpful when teaching a modified academic program in braille. Most of these strategies are illustrated in the account of Eddie's first year of braille instruction in Chapter 9.

SUGGESTIONS FOR TEACHERS

MODIFYING INSTRUCTION FOR CHILDREN WITH COGNITIVE DISABILITIES

- Set clearly defined, realistic objectives. The IEP team needs to consider both short-term and long-term goals in planning braille instruction. Will it be realistic for the student to label food or clothing items in braille? Will he or she be able to use braille numbers, letters, or words to work more efficiently in a vocational setting? The sequence of instruction should reflect a steady progression toward these specific individualized objectives.

- Make literacy relevant. Students with cognitive disabilities may require a long time to achieve even functional literacy in braille. Give students many opportunities to tactilely observe the teacher or others reading and writing braille in a variety of contexts so they begin to understand the ultimate goal. As soon as possible, have them use braille for very simple tasks, such as reading their names on personal belongings, recognizing key words on a daily schedule by decoding the first letter (*l* for lunch), or reading a telephone number if the digits are widely spaced. Incorporate meaningful activities into the student's daily program, such as bookmaking, teacher-made braille stories, and journal writing (see Chapters 4, 5, and 6).

- Pair objects or simple tactile pictures with braille. Even before students are able to recognize any braille letters or words, they will be able to "read" a daily schedule (see the photograph of schedule cards in Chapter 5) or a simple teacher-made book if a familiar object or tactile picture is placed next to each word—just as young sighted children typically start to read by using pictures as clues to the text. Have students touch the object first and then the braille word. Praise them for "great reading!" Gradually decrease reliance on the object cues as the student's braille skills improve.

- Focus on skill development. Students may need more tasks from the skill-oriented half of the language arts continuum to learn letters, contractions, and words. These can include sorting, matching, and completing short worksheets (see the beginning reading activities described in Chapter 5). It is not always necessary for students to master every skill at the readiness level before moving on to reading and writing. Some students who never achieve efficient tracking movements or totally accurate character recognition may still be able to use braille for simple functional tasks.

- Use task analysis. Break down complex tasks, such as marking answers on a worksheet, into small, sequential steps. Present only as much information as students can handle at one time. (An example of task analysis is presented in the following section.) Success, even in small increments, is essential to maintain students' motivation to continue with braille instruction.

- Offer more repetition. It may be necessary to repeat the same activity a number of times until students have learned a new word or mastered a new skill. If they do not achieve success after reasonable repetition and task analysis, however, simplify the activity further or set it aside and return to it after several weeks or months.

- Consider alternative modes of instruction. Consider using grade 1 braille, jumbo braille, or double spacing between letters if these techniques make it easier for the child to reach a specific communication goal (Heydt et al., 1992). Be aware, however, that the relearning involved in switching from grade 1 to grade 2 braille may be difficult for many students with cognitive disabilities (Swenson & Norrish, 1994).

■ Emphasize oral language. Use the simplest sentences as springboards to conversation. When a student reads the braille sentence, "I can go," discuss where, when, why, and with whom. Make listening and responding to stories, messages, and directions a part of daily language arts instruction.

■ Involve other school staff. Students' exposure to braille should extend beyond the individual lesson with the itinerant teacher. Offer workshops in braille to interested classroom teachers and assistants so that they can monitor simple reading and writing activities throughout the day.

■ Encourage parental support. All students progress faster when parents become involved in their learning. If possible, place a braillewriter in the student's home and send short daily homework assignments for parents to work on with their child. (See also the section on working with parents in "Guidelines for Collaboration" in Chapter 2.)

EXAMPLES OF MODIFIED INSTRUCTION

As noted earlier, many of the reading and writing activities presented in Chapters 4, 5, 6, and 7 are appropriate for students with cognitive disabilities. With daily instruction in braille, these children can learn to complete skill-oriented tasks involving matching, sorting, and sequencing independently. They also benefit from using their literacy skills in meaning-oriented activities such as reading a calendar, composing a story, or discussing the events on a daily braille schedule.

Adapting a Skill-Oriented Activity Using Task Analysis

Teaching a child with multiple disabilities to complete an activity independently often requires detailed task analysis. Even though discriminating braille characters on a worksheet may be a short-term objective for a particular student, it can take many months to master. In this case, the IEP team has decided that the long-term objectives of using efficient tracking and scanning patterns, improving independent work skills, and refining tactile discrimination justify the time spent learning to do this activity.

In the example offered here, the task of marking answers on a two-line worksheet with pushpins is broken down into a carefully planned sequence of eight steps. (See Chapter 5, "Beginning Reading Activities," for more worksheet ideas.) Students with additional disabilities may need to learn how to manipulate pushpins, work in a top-to-bottom, left-to-right sequence, and use two hands simultaneously for different tasks before attempting a formal worksheet. To develop these prerequisite skills, they can complete a sequence of pinning activities. These steps can also be followed using loops of masking tape or magnets on a cookie sheet instead of pins.

1. Stick pins randomly on the bulletin board.

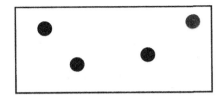

2. Stick pins randomly on a piece of tape stretched horizontally across the middle of the bulletin board.

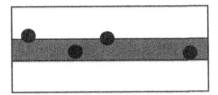

3. Stick pins left to right across the piece of tape, using one hand to keep the place and one to find a new pin.

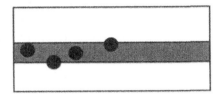

4. Stick one pin in each of several fuzzy felt circles, working from left to right on a simple one-line worksheet.

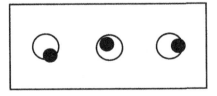

5. Stick one pin in each of several brailled full cells, working from left to right on a simple one-line worksheet.

Directions: Pin all the full cells.

6. Complete a one-line worksheet with a single word or letter, pinning every shape from left to right.

Directions: Pin "like."

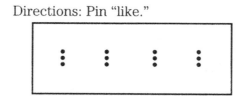

7. Complete a one-line worksheet with more than one braille shape—a target word or letter and one or more distractors to skip over.

Directions: Pin "like," not "you."

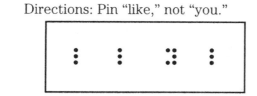

8. Complete a two-line worksheet with widely spaced top and bottom lines.

Directions: Pin "like."

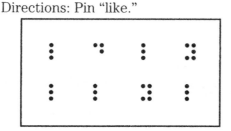

Learning a task such as completing a tactile discrimination worksheet independently may require a significant period of time for a student with multiple disabilities. When the task is presented in small increments, students receive frequent positive feedback as they master each step. They also need to understand, however, that the braille numbers, letters, and words they are learning in skill-oriented exercises have a real purpose. Balancing their literacy program with activities from the meaning-oriented end of the language arts continuum can help students connect braille to their own lives.

Adapting a Meaning-Oriented Activity: The Writing Process

Although students with cognitive disabilities may not work as independently as other students during the writing process, they still benefit from the opportunity to use their braille skills in meaningful contexts. When working with a student whose braille reading and writing skills are limited, consider the following adaptations.

ADAPTING THE WRITING PROCESS

- Rely heavily on oral language during all stages of the process. Students can only write ideas that they are able to verbalize.

- Use a guided-writing approach during the drafting stage (see Chapter 6). Assist the student as needed with spacing, letter formation, and invented spelling.

- Suggest a patterned or repetitive sentence structure to promote fluency.

- Have the student write for a short time every day.

- Review the previous days' work before beginning new writing.

- Do not expect an emergent-level student to produce a perfect final copy. However, with practice, the student should be able to read a final copy brailled by the teacher.

- As the student's skills improve, ask the student to copy one or more sentences in standard grade 1 or grade 2 braille, depending on which is being taught.

In the following example, a student with cognitive disabilities uses his braille skills to write a story about people he knows.

A TEACHER'S DIARY
A STUDENT WITH MULTIPLE DISABILITIES FOLLOWS THE WRITING PROCESS

Nine-year-old Eddie has severe cognitive and physical disabilities. He has been learning grade 2 braille for a year and a half. Eddie knows how to write about 12 letters and contractions on the braillewriter and has a good grasp of sound-symbol relationships for most consonants.

Planning

Eddie has recently learned to read and write the contraction for *people* (the letter *p*) and is starting to recognize the names of people in his family. I introduce the idea of making a "people book," and we talk about each person who might be included.

Drafting

Eddie chooses one person to write about each day during a guided-writing lesson. I assist him with hearing consonant sounds, writing unfamiliar letters, and spacing. A repeated sentence structure (such as "I like . . ." or "I can . . .") helps his writing fluency. After five days, Eddie's draft looks like this:

I   like   Dad

I   can   call   Dad

I   like   Antie

I   can   get   lunch

with   Antie

I   like   Grma

I   can   play   with   Grma

I   can   hg   Grma

I   like   Mcl

I   can   play   with   Mcl

I   can   love   Mcl

I   like   Mssn

I   can   add   with   Mssn

I   can   play   with   Mssn

Conferring/Publishing

Each day Eddie reads all pages of his draft and adds a new one. To publish the book, I write the correct grade 2 braille text on new sheets, and Eddie helps to make the pictures, the title, and the title page. After it is completed, Eddie reads his new book many times to family, teachers, and classmates:

I Like People

I like Dad
I can call Dad
I like Auntie
I can get lunch with Auntie
I like Grandma
I can play with Grandma
I can hug Grandma
I like Michael
I can play with Michael
I can love Michael
I like Ms. Swenson
I can add with Ms. Swenson
I can play with Ms. Swenson

During the process of writing his book, Eddie practiced oral language, tracking, reading, and writing skills in a meaningful context. Sharing his completed book with others also reinforced social skills with both peers and adults.

SUMMARY

Certain students with cognitive disabilities can master functional braille skills when provided with carefully sequenced, daily instruction. Once the IEP team has determined specific short- and long-term objectives for each student, the teacher can break down the steps needed to achieve each objective and pace instruction so that the child can be successful with each small increment of learning. This process necessitates consistent, daily instruction from a teacher who knows braille.

Although they may require more repetition and a slower pace than learners with normal ability, students with cognitive disabilities still benefit from a balance of skill-oriented and meaning-oriented tasks designed to meet their individual needs. When functional braille instruction is integrated into a student's total program, it can facilitate the development of prevocational, oral language, fine motor, and social skills.

CHAPTER 9 Case Studies: Two Beginning Braille Readers

Several years ago I was fortunate to have two beginning braille readers at the same school on my itinerant caseload. Sharon and Eddie could not have been more different. Sharon was a fully mainstreamed kindergartner on grade level with her sighted classmates. Eddie had significant cognitive and physical disabilities, with limited school experience. Working with these two students, one after the other, every day over a two-year period, was a fascinating experience. Despite the wide disparity in their cognitive abilities, their learning was similar in several ways. Both students followed the same sequence of steps in learning braille, and I found that many of the activities I had used earlier with Sharon in preschool could be modified for Eddie so that they were age appropriate. Both children responded well to a meaning-oriented focus, although Eddie also required a significant amount of skill work and repetition. Finally, both benefited from the willingness of school personnel to reinforce braille skills during the part of the day when I was not there.

The anecdotal records presented here are taken from my notes during the first year that I worked with both Sharon and Eddie. They illustrate many of the techniques, activities, and materials described earlier in this book, as well as the frustrations and successes of real-life teaching.

SHARON

Sharon is a totally blind 6-year-old whose family speaks Korean at home. She has a bubbly personality and excellent interpersonal skills. Although her receptive and expressive English language skills are adequate for most situations, Sharon still displays some difficulty with vocabulary and grammar. However, she has no disabilities other than her blindness.

At the age of 3, Sharon began attending a noncategorical special education preschool class, where she received itinerant services. Because her birthday fell three days after the entry cutoff date for kindergarten, she had the equivalent of an extra year in preschool when she was 5. This year served as a transition between preschool and regular kindergarten. Although still technically a preschooler, Sharon received an hour of itinerant services each day, with an emphasis on braille literacy, and had frequent opportunities to participate in selected mainstream kindergarten activities at her school. As a result, she arrived in kindergarten the following year well prepared to learn and play with her sighted peers.

Sharon participated fully in all aspects of the kindergarten curriculum. As her itinerant teacher, I worked directly with Sharon for one hour during the three-hour kindergarten day, sometimes in the classroom, sometimes in our small room across the hall. Pullout sessions were designed to reinforce, supplement, or enrich the regular education program by providing individual instruction in braille.

The comments about Sharon are taken from anecdotal records related to her progress in braille literacy skills. All Sharon's writing samples were completed independently, without a teacher's guidance, unless indicated otherwise.

A TEACHER'S DIARY
SHARON'S KINDERGARTEN YEAR

September: During the first week, I assess what Sharon remembers from last year. She can recognize 23 alphabet letters in isolation and write 20 of them; attending summer school for four weeks certainly helped her retention! About half the other children know many of their letters, so Sharon is right on track. She is less sure of the family names that she learned last year, but recalls some contractions (such as *go* and *with*) as we begin to read simple materials. We use a braille copy of the kindergarten's daily message to find a sentence, word, letter, and contraction. These are essential concepts that Sharon will need as a foundation for other literacy activities. I also braille a small copy of *Joshua James Likes Trucks* (Petrie, 1982), the first "big book" that the teacher reads to the class, and include some simple tactile pictures. The book is too difficult for Sharon to learn to read independently right now, so we read it together and talk about the parts of a book: the front cover, back cover, and title page.

The children in Sharon's kindergarten class write nearly every day, with Mondays reserved for journals. Sharon writes her first independent journal entry about a guinea pig:

gpg

At the bottom of the page I braille the "book spelling" of guinea pig, just as the kindergarten teacher writes the conventional spelling for the other children's entries. Sharon wants to color a picture using her scented crayons, and I place a piece of sandpaper under her paper to provide some texture. She starts writing braille spontaneously at home on her brailler—pages and pages of letters, which she proudly brings in to show me.

October: This month the class learns color words while reading *Brown Bear, Brown Bear, What Do You See?* (Martin, 1983) Sharon has her own braille copy of *Brown Bear* and color word flash cards in her word box. Although she only needs to look at the first letter to read *red* and *green,* her fingers slow down when she comes to *blue, black,* and *brown.* Suddenly, she realizes that she has to consider middle and ending letters as well.

Sharon falls in love with the book *We're Going on a Bear Hunt* (Rosen, 1989), which her kindergarten teacher reads to the class. She can't wait to check it out on library day, and I read it to her again, spending time describing the pictures and explaining vocabulary. I find that because of her blindness and bilingual background, Sharon does not always completely understand books that are read to the large group of kindergartners. There is enormous value in rereading books together in a relaxed atmosphere, where our dialogue helps to build Sharon's concepts and English vocabulary. It is one of our favorite activities.

I give Sharon a plastic spider for Halloween. Later that morning she writes in her journal:

Anna   g   m   aspz

(Anna gave me a surprise.)

In two months, Sharon has progressed from writing a single word to writing a short sentence using beginning, middle, and ending consonant sounds in the word *surprise.*

November: One of the big books Sharon's teacher reads to the class this month, *Just Like Me* (Neasi, 1984), provides the inspiration for a retelling that Sharon writes and publishes over the course of several weeks. In *Just Like Me*, a little girl describes ways in which she and her twin sister are the same and different. Sharon and I take turns writing, using language patterns from the original book. I write:

Sharon likes chocolate. Just like me!
Sharon has hearts [a reference to her barrettes] in her hair. Not like me!

Sharon writes:

Crlne   ls   tktks

just   like   me!

mi   ser   sezs   ld

not   like   me!

(Caroline likes Tic Tacs. Just like me!
My sister sneezes loud. Not like me!)

Sharon writes each sentence at the top of the page using guided writing; she writes in invented spelling as I help her hear the sounds and remind her to space. Later I write the sentence again at the bottom of the page in conventional spelling. We complete the book with a title page, an about-the-author

section, front and back covers, and tactile pictures, including a box of Tic Tacs on the front. It's a real temptation for both of us to eat a Tic Tac every time the book is read!

Sharon reads her book to family members, teachers, and classmates. Because she has the text memorized, her fingers fly across the page without really "seeing" the words that are there. I ask her to slow down and match her voice to the braille words. The transition from imitating braille reading using memorized text (an emergent reading behavior) to developing a voice-to-braille match is difficult for Sharon because it is so easy for her to memorize. I insist, however, and her fingers begin to move more deliberately from word to word.

December: We continue to work on voice-to-braille match using *Five Little Monkeys,* a poem the kindergartners are reading to learn their number words. In a writing assessment administered to all the kindergartners, Sharon demonstrates consistent use of beginning and ending consonant sounds and the short *a* sound in her invented spelling; however, she often fails to space between words. Her teacher and I target spacing as a goal for the second quarter, along with more short vowel sounds.

January: Sharon and I talk about the importance of listening for all the sounds in a word when writing with invented spelling. Several of the books her teacher reads to the class help Sharon add new sounds to her repertoire: the short *o* sound from *Mop Top* (Freeman, 1955), and the short *i* sound from *Mrs. Wishy-Washy* (Cowley, 1990). Sharon hears the short *i* sound three times when she labels a tactile picture of Mrs. Wishy-Washy and her pig:

msiwish   wsh   and   pig.

Sharon is increasingly aware of punctuation. She is starting to recognize periods, commas, question marks, and exclamation marks in her reading, and often puts a period at the end of her own writing.

I note that Sharon is having difficulty with reversed letters, especially *d/f, w/r,* and *e/i.* Although some reversals are normal at this age for many blind and sighted children, Sharon does have more problems than many other students I have taught. A quick worksheet check indicates that Sharon is able to discriminate *d* from *f* and *w* from *r* when asked to find the shape that is different in a group of four; her problem is remembering which shape means which letter. The *e/i* pair is significantly more difficult. Sharon is not able to discriminate a different letter (*e* or *i*) from three of the other letter in a group of four, but I think this will develop with maturity. We focus on one problem letter at a time, using the Swing Cell, talking about the unique shape of each, and practicing with worksheets and words from her reading. I place an alphabet strip along the edge of the table where Sharon sits in kindergarten so that she can check the orientation of the letters as she reads or before she writes.

February: This month the kindergartners are studying the five senses. During the week devoted to touch, a friend of mine, Donna Pastore, visits the kindergarten class with her guide dog. I have Sharon place her hands on Donna's while Donna reads so that Sharon can feel the tracking pattern that she uses. In the weeks after Donna's visit, Sharon practices tracking "like Ms. Pastore," using first the Mangold materials (S. Mangold, 1977), then some of her own writing.

Like the other kindergartners, Sharon is developing a sight-word vocabulary that enables her to read simple messages without hearing the teacher read them first. She can recognize words like *is*, *it*, *will*, *have*, and *see*, and use beginning sounds and context clues to identify longer words like *house*. Sharon is also using more conventional spelling and braille contractions in her writing. This is evident in one of her February journals, in which she writes about hitting a tennis ball to her brother during a ball game. (Grammatical errors are related to her bilingual background.)

we play awt sod.
my brodr thod
z bow

I thow it. with
the tns rakt

(We play outside. My brother throwed the ball. I throw it with the tennis racket.)

March: In March I decide to teach Sharon how to dial the telephone, and discover that she learned long ago from her brother and sister. We use a small three-ring notebook to make a telephone book of important numbers (including time and weather), sequencing the pages in alphabetical order by each person's name. Sharon is so excited to have her own telephone book that she goes home and calls everyone in it!

Sharon is developing an interest in spelling patterns. We have talked frequently about how the /k/ sound at the end of words like *snack* on her schedule is often spelled with a *ck*. She remembers this when writing *pick* and *stick* in her journal about a calm March day (a "lamb day").

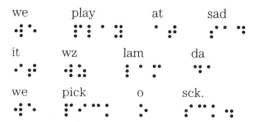

we play at sad
it wz lam da
we pick o sck.

(We play outside. It was lamb day. We pick up sticks.)

April: Sharon's mobility teacher initiates a book project this month. On one lesson they go in search of Sharon's sister, Caroline, and finally find her after traveling to four different places in the school. The mobility instructor brailles a simple book for Sharon based on this experience, using a predictable sentence pattern:

Title: Where is Caroline?

p. 1: We went to the cafeteria. Caroline was not there.

p. 2: We went to the playground. Caroline was not there.

p. 3: We went to Caroline's classroom. Caroline was not there.

p. 4: We went to the front door.

p. 5: I felt a hand touch my face. It was Caroline's hand.

p. 6: I love my sister very much!

Sharon puts herself in charge of making the pictures for each page using materials from my art box. She fills the playground page with self-adhesive dots to represent children, proposes a large laminated square to show the empty classroom, and painstakingly cuts five separate fingers and a circle for Caroline's hand. Sharon reads *Where is Caroline?* to her sister's class using efficient tracking movements and a perfect voice-to-braille match. She is so proud of her new book!

Sharon's teacher creates small individual "word banks" for the students to help them learn the conventional spelling of words they use often in their journals. I bind ten index cards together with a plastic binder to make a similar book for Sharon with one braille word on each page. Sharon requests the words *outside, went,* and *Daddy* to start with, and soon her book is in need of more pages. I am impressed with how conscientiously she uses her word bank during journal writing. She seems to feel a special attachment to these words, since they come directly from her own writing.

May: The kindergarten students begin to read emergent reader books from the Storybox series, published by the Wright Group (see Resources). They choose books that interest them from a special basket, take them home for the evening, and keep a written log of the books they have read to an adult. I stick self-adhesive braille labels over the text in about 20 of the books, so that Sharon has a choice of reading material. Her task is much more difficult than that of her classmates, because she cannot rely on picture clues to decode the text. We read each book together before it goes home, and I emphasize phonics and context clues. Sharon reads a total of 14 books before the end of the year. I observe her word-identification strategies each time she comes to a word she has forgotten; invariably she makes the beginning sound and uses context to come up with a plausible word—usually the right one!

Sharon writes in her journal with confidence and enthusiasm. She never has difficulty deciding on a topic. One of her last journal entries includes a long sentence with the word *went* (including the lower sign) correctly copied from her word bank:

I   went   to   the   bute

shop   to   kaprm.

(I went to the beauty shop to get a perm.)

A final assessment indicates that Sharon can write consonant-vowel-consonant words containing short a, i, o, and u sounds, space correctly between words in a dictated sentence, and use a period at the end of a sentence.

Because she entered kindergarten with strong literacy skills, Sharon was able to participate fully in the mainstream language arts program from the first day. Her growth as a reader and writer resulted almost exclusively from activities toward the meaning-oriented end of the language arts continuum; she learned sight words, phonics, braille contractions, and writing skills through using language in meaningful contexts, rather than from worksheets or drills. Sharon ended her year on grade level with her classmates and ready for the increased demands of first grade.

Eddie, my other student at Sharon's school, also received daily instruction in braille, although on a much different level because of his multiple disabilities. Sometimes I overlapped Sharon's and Eddie's lessons for five or ten minutes so that they could read their student-authored books to each other or demonstrate a new skill.

Despite the disparity in their abilities, they enjoyed each other's company and ben-efited from interacting regularly with another child who was learning braille.

EDDIE

Eddie, a student from abroad who attends a program for children with physical dis-abilities, became totally blind as a result of a massive seizure at the age of 6. When he began school in the United States at the age of 8, about a year and a half after his seizure, Eddie exhibited multiple learning difficulties, including cognitive deficits, orthopedic impairments, speech and language delays, significant short-term memo-ry problems, petit mal seizures, and behavioral outbursts. His limited preschool experience had left him with a few rote skills, such as the ability to recite the alpha-bet and count to 20, but no real exposure to books or other school materials. Eddie spoke English, although his conversation skills and vocabulary were limited. He had few self-help skills and used a wheelchair for mobility.

Despite this array of special needs, Eddie demonstrated a number of strengths that indicated that he might have the potential to become a functional braille read-er. In addition to his basic language skills, he had a good grasp of important concepts, including laterality and directionality. During the first few weeks of instruction, he quickly learned to discriminate raised shapes of varying sizes and textures. Eddie was very motivated to work, as long as tasks were presented in small enough increments to avoid frustration. He also enjoyed the attention of teachers and classmates and displayed a delightful sense of humor.

A team of teachers and therapists provided Eddie with a highly individualized program during his first year of school in the United States. He received an hour of instruction from the itinerant teacher each day, with follow-up from an assistant who had extensive experience working in the physical disabilities program and was excited about learning braille along with Eddie. Teaching Eddie braille required a great deal of trial and error. His short-term memory problems, language deficits, and lack of literacy experiences presented particular challenges. Throughout the year we forged ahead with tentative goals and objectives, regrouped when learning did not occur, and celebrated the successes that Eddie worked so hard to achieve.

As we developed a better understanding of Eddie's learning style and potential, we adjusted long- and short-term goals. Long-term literacy objectives for Eddie included such skills as reading telephone numbers, labeling belongings and food containers, and following simple written directions. It was also felt that the ability to read and write braille would benefit him in a sheltered workshop setting, where written clues might help him compensate for his poor short-term memory. Short-term goals related mainly to the school setting, such as the ability to recognize his name, read a braille schedule, use a calendar, and work independently on sorting, matching, and sequencing tasks.

Eddie made significant gains in all developmental areas during his first year in school. The time available for instruction increased as he learned to control his behavior. The following anecdotal records relate primarily to Eddie's progress in literacy skills.

Summer School: Eddie attends a self-contained program for students with physical disabilities. Frequent episodes of poor behavior—biting, pinching, hitting, screaming, and throwing objects—interfere with his learning. Initially Eddie has no interest in exploring the pages of books with tactile shapes or pictures; it is not certain that he even knows how to use a book. He also resists tracking textured lines with a teacher's guidance. By the end of the four-week summer session, however, Eddie has one favorite book that his itinerant teacher has created from three musical greeting cards. Each time he turns a page, he hears a new song.

September: Eddie begins the school year with a new team of teachers in a different building. He and I meet first thing every morning to talk about his schedule and hang his tactile schedule cards in sequence. Eddie quickly grasps the routine, asking to do the schedule every morning and remembering to find both the object and the corresponding braille word on each schedule card before hanging it on the board. We also start to talk about beginning sounds as we discuss each activity in his day (for example, lunch starts with the letter *l*). Phonics turns out to be an area of strength for Eddie, and he soon learns the beginning consonant sounds of all his schedule words.

Eddie helps to make his first book, a texture book that he calls *My Finger Book*. We talk about how people and books both have names. Because of Eddie's limited experience with books, the cover is a standard shape—a square—rather than the hand shape that I usually use with my students, but a felt cutout of a hand is stuck to the front. Eddie can place his own hand over the cover picture and name all the fingers. We read the book every day, often to an audience. For the first time Eddie is turning the pages of a book and finding the tactile pictures independently. He "reads" the accompanying braille words with guidance. New vocabulary, such as

A TEACHER'S DIARY
EDDIE'S FIRST YEAR OF BRAILLE INSTRUCTION

"squishy" (a tactile picture with a real sponge), is difficult for him to remember. His favorite page is "tickling" (a tactile picture of a feather), which makes him pretend to sneeze when he tickles his nose with a feather.

I write a one-sentence message on the braillewriter each day—for example, "Eddie will have music today"—verbalizing as I press the braillewriter keys. Eddie does not object to placing his hands on mine as I write the message and read it back. He "scribbles" on the braillewriter for a few minutes when it is his turn to write, but does not say the words as he writes.

October: A braille calendar becomes a part of our daily lesson, along with the schedule board and the message. Eddie needs help in finding the month, tracking across the days of the week (reciting "Sunday starts with S, Monday starts with M, . . ."), and sticking the day's number in the correct place. He loves the routine, however, and becomes more independent over the next few months.

We begin some very basic "formal" braille instruction this month. I show Eddie how to track wide textured lines, using two hands, with most of his fingers down. Interest is added by inserting his name or a fuzzy felt shape somewhere in the line. I also introduce the word *a*. Eddie sorts flash cards for *a* and *Eddie* and explains, "*a* is one dot and Eddie is lots of dots." It is a gross discrimination, but I am pleased that he can verbalize the difference. Eddie is able to sort eight cards accurately, with supervision to make sure the cards are turned the right way. I continue to model braille writing every day. When it is Eddie's turn to write, I have him do some short drills for the left and right hands separately to encourage him to keep his fingers on the correct keys.

Eddie makes two books this month. The first, a counting book, is a very successful joint effort. Eddie thoroughly enjoys stapling, gluing, punching holes, and manipulating fasteners to make pictures on each page. As with *My Finger Book,* Eddie is able to read his counting book independently, counting the objects on each page and finding the corresponding braille number. The second book, about the season of fall, contains leaves, sticks, pine needles, and bark that he has collected outside during walks with an instructional assistant. This book is less successful, possibly because these nature objects are less a part of his experience than shapes, textures, and numbers. This month Eddie also begins to explore the pages of the *Touch and Tell* (1969) set of reading readiness books from the American Printing House for the Blind, which talk about shapes and sizes.

November: After working on the concept of same and different with objects, Eddie is ready for his first tactile worksheet. I stick a row of three large felt circles and one felt triangle to a sheet of paper, show Eddie how to "read" the shapes from left to right, and help him mark the one that is different with a loop of masking tape. We repeat variations of this activity every day until he can complete a sheet independently.

Eddie's success in discriminating his name from the word *a* inspires me to introduce the word *go.* To my surprise, Eddie has great difficulty remembering the name of this new shape, confusing it with *a,* even though he can tell me that there is more than one dot under his finger. The problem appears to relate to word retrieval rather than tactile discrimination. We remove the *a* flash cards from Eddie's work and use the word *go* constantly in meaningful sentences as we do flash card drills and simple reading activities. By the end of the month we are able to reintroduce *a,* and Eddie has a braille reading vocabulary of three words: *a, go,* and *Eddie.* He is also able to recognize 14 beginning consonant sounds.

Eddie is starting to write full cells on the braillewriter, so I make a full cell flash card, too. He is quick to see that a full cell looks a lot like *go,* and I am careful never to use these two shapes together in the same activity.

December: Eddie has been enjoying finger plays and songs, but does not have the language skills or experiential background to understand books that are read to him. I feel that he needs more exposure

to oral literature. Eddie's assistant and I begin a daily story time, telling Eddie a familiar repetitive story and encouraging him to join in once he is familiar with the language patterns. Our first two stories are *The Three Billy Goats Gruff* and *The Gingerbread Boy.* We tell these two stories over and over again, using simple props (such as a gingerbread boy cookie cutter) and sound effects ("trip, trap; trip, trap"). Eddie loves them and makes a marvelous troll voice!

Braille instruction hits some roadblocks this month. I am trying to get Eddie to turn his flash cards the right way around by feeling for the cutoff edge at the upper-right-hand corner; the goal is to make sorting an independent activity. However, the turning step is just one too many in the series of steps involved in sorting:

Take only one card out of the basket.

Turn it around.

Read it.

Look for the correct tray.

Place it in the tray.

I'd never thought of sorting as such a complicated activity! Eddie is also having difficulty marking full cells with a pin, a prerequisite skill for completing worksheets. I cannot see this becoming an independent activity for a long time. Finally, although he can recognize *Eddie* and *go* in isolation with 100 percent accuracy, he cannot read simple phrase cards such as "go go go," "go Eddie," and "go Eddie go." He says too many words or not enough; there is no voice-to-braille match.

We are having a little more success with writing full cells. I've added tactile clues to the braillewriter keys to make it easier for Eddie to keep his fingers on the correct keys. There is sandpaper on keys 3 and 6 ("rough"), nothing on keys 2 and 5 ("smooth"), and stick-on felt on keys 1 and 4 ("fuzzy").

January: I return to school after the break with a new strategy to teach the pinning skill that is so important for independent completion of braille worksheets. Remembering how well Eddie had done in November with his simple "same/different" worksheets made with stick-on felt shapes, I devise a variation to use as a pinning exercise. These long, rectangular worksheets have four large identical felt shapes in a row, one per page. Eddie "reads" the shapes from left to right, then marks each with a pin in that order. This is much more successful. Eddie can complete the sheets independently and is very proud of his ability to use the pins. I plan to reduce the size of the shapes and increase their number gradually before returning to braille characters.

Eddie's newest word, *can*, introduced in mid-December, just is not sticking. Even though we use *can* constantly in meaningful contexts, just as we did for *go*, Eddie can't remember it—there doesn't seem to be a hook in his brain to hang it on. We abandon *can* and introduce *like* with almost instant success. There are lots of people and things Eddie likes! By the end of January, Eddie knows four braille words: *a*, *go*, *Eddie*, and *like*. He can also recognize 18 beginning consonant sounds.

Eddie is now placing his fingers on the braillewriter keys and writing full cells independently. He sometimes verbalizes a sentence as he writes his full cells, indicating that he understands that spoken words can be written as braille dots. We have started short finger-isolation drills. It is difficult for Eddie to press only one key at a time.

Our most recent story-time selection is *Goldilocks and the Three Bears*. Eddie has also helped to make another book called *go Eddie*, which has a tactile picture of a work or play activity on each page, including a braille flash card, a circle puzzle piece, and two coins used in money sorting. The braille text is the same on every page: "go Eddie," imitating a chant that the teaching assistant made up to reinforce good work.

February: "Mr. Nobody," a group of five unspaced full cells, is added to Eddie's words. The purpose is to see if Eddie can discriminate his own name from a "word" of similar length and begin to recognize that many words have "lots of dots." Eddie learns this new word quickly (he finds it funny) and is able to pin a line of Mr. Nobodies from left to right independently. An attempt to introduce *Dad*, however, is unsuccessful. Eddie's other new word this month is *I*.

We focus a lot on developing a voice-to-braille match, using meaningful sentences and phrases composed of the six braille words Eddie knows, such as "I go," "I like Mr. Nobody," "I like Eddie," and "go go Eddie." Every reading session includes oral discussion about places Eddie likes to go, people Eddie likes, and people who like Eddie. Eddie is also making progress in braille writing. He can press each key in isolation and write a line of full cells with spaces between.

I bring in some straw, a bag of sticks, and a brick as props for telling *The Three Little Pigs*.

March: Eddie finally has voice-to-braille match! He can read three-word phrases and sentences on his flash cards accurately when the words are widely spaced from one another. New words this month are *you* and *can*; the latter was abandoned in January, but now seems much easier. Eddie practices identifying these words on pinning worksheets, which include distractors for the first time. When directed to pin the word *you*, Eddie knows to skip over any other words in the line and not pin them. The two new words greatly increase the number of sentences Eddie can read. We make another book, *Eddie can go*, which has a tactile picture from one of his schedule cards on each page and the words "Eddie can go" underneath.

Tracking becomes an issue this month as I introduce two-line "stories" with a sentence at the top of the paper and one at the bottom. Up until this point Eddie has only dealt with one line at a time. We begin brief daily tracking drills using a sheet of braille paper with a top, middle, and bottom line of full cells. Eddie verbalizes "all the way to the end, come back, down to the next line" as his fingers move from line to line.

We are at a crossroads in braille writing. Eddie can write full cells and demonstrate finger isolation. He understands that letters and words can be written using the braillewriter, and he has written a few easy words such as *go*, *a*, and *like*. Normally I would teach students to write their names at this point, but the *e-d* contraction is so difficult that I hesitate. Finally I decide to give it a try, and we practice for short periods every day. It is a struggle for Eddie to get his right middle finger down below key number 5 "out of the way," but he is very motivated. By the end of the month, he can write *e-d,* and we are ready to add the capital sign.

April: One of Eddie's most significant achievements this year has been his progression from a wheelchair to a walker to walking with one hand trailing the wall. Last month he was strong enough to use some of the playground equipment for the first time with two adults assisting.

On the playground Eddie loves the slide, "jumping bridge," and "horse" (a long tube that jiggles up and down when sat on), and these become the subject of *Eddie's Playground Book,* which is created over a two-week period in April. We take the finished book to the playground with Eddie to be sure that he relates the tactile pictures to the real playground equipment. Reading the braille sentences on each page is challenging for Eddie because they include words that are not part of his core vocabulary, but that must be inferred from the pictures. For example, in the sentence "Eddie can go on the slide," Eddie must use the picture clue and his memory to read "on the slide." He reads his new book over and over again to many people, never quite perfectly, but with a real understanding of how a book's pictures and words convey important information.

Eddie continues to work on writing his name, saying "capital E-d, . . . regular d," as he painstakingly arranges his fingers on the keys. I use finger names and key textures rather than numbers to remind him which fingers to use, for example, "Put right pointer on the fuzzy key."

May: Attempts to teach Eddie two new words—first *we* and then *do*—are not producing consistent results. There seems to be a language problem with *we* (he keeps confusing it with *you*) and a tactile discrimination problem with *do* (it is too much like *go*). Since it is so near the end of the school year, I decide to focus on reinforcing the seven words that Eddie does know (*a, go, like, Eddie, can, I,* and *you*) and direct more energy toward writing.

Eddie is now able to write *Dad* with only verbal prompts and is making excellent progress with his name. My excitement about his writing must be contagious, because he asks to write first during each lesson, right after we finish the calendar. Eddie has also discovered invented spelling after listening to me model it in the daily message for so many months. He enjoys writing the names of favorite people, sounding out each word and letting me help him with the finger positions for the letters he doesn't know. Auntie is written *Ate,* and brother Michael is *Mkl.*

June: Eddie writes his name by himself!

On the surface, the seven short braille words that Eddie learned to read during the year may seem insignificant; however, they represent a vast array of new skills and concepts for a child with severe disabilities and no real prior school experience. Through his braille instruction, Eddie gained an understanding of books and the reading process, expanded his oral language abilities, improved his fine motor skills, and developed the ability to work systematically and independently on simple matching and sorting tasks.

Although many of the activities were taken from the traditional skills-oriented end of the language arts continuum (worksheets, tracking drills, writing exercises), Eddie definitely benefited from the meaning-oriented aspects of his program as well. Knowing only a few words and letters, he was nevertheless able to read and write about friends, family members, and personal experiences at a very basic level. These types of activities were extremely motivating for him and gave him a reason to persevere with the difficult task of learning braille.

SUMMARY

Sharon and Eddie's braille instruction represents two different ends of the literacy learning continuum. Sharon followed a conventional literacy program based on the mainstream curriculum with adaptations. Eddie required a highly individualized functional literacy program designed to prepare him to use braille in very specific contexts. Despite these differences, however, instruction was guided by ongoing assessment in both cases. Constant reevaluation of each child's progress was a key factor in determining what to teach next. Chapter 10 discusses types of commercial and teacher-made assessment measures, as well as a proposed assessment schedule, that will assist teachers in evaluating their students' progress and the results of their own instructional strategies.

CHAPTER 10 Assessment

The purpose of language arts assessment is to facilitate the learner's continued growth in literacy skills. A well-designed assessment plan is multifaceted, ongoing, and has a direct impact on instruction. It includes a variety of instruments administered at regular intervals: daily, weekly, or at specific points in the school year. Results of assessments enable the teacher to set goals with the student, plan instruction, and evaluate progress.

Traditional basal reading programs supply teachers with end-of-the-book tests that measure students' mastery of the vocabulary and skills taught at a particular level. Often these tests have a multiple-choice format and address a relatively narrow range of literary behaviors. Most focus on the product ("the right answer"), rather than the process of reading, and provide no information about a student's writing ability.

Formal assessment measures, such as standardized tests, are also of limited value to the teacher. These measure skills in isolation that often have little relevance to actual classroom instruction (Rex, Koenig, Wormsley, & Baker, 1994). Because the majority of formal assessments are designed for sighted students, they require significant adaptation for students who read braille. As a result, their validity and reliability are affected, and scores must be interpreted with caution. In contrast, informal assessment measures, such as observation logs, checklists, reading inventories, writing samples, and students' self-evaluations, are closely aligned with classroom instruction. Teachers can use the results of these measures to plan and revise lessons so that maximum learning occurs.

Teachers who rely primarily on children's literature and students' writing to teach language arts can devise their own assessment procedures using materials from many different sources, some of which are described in this chapter. The assessment of a young student's braille skills (such as tracking or recognition of contractions) must be integrated with the assessment of general literacy behaviors (such as decoding skills and comprehension). This can be achieved by using a broad range of assessment tools, including both those designed specifically for braille readers and informal instruments intended for print readers. In this way, reading and writing, not simply braille, become the primary focus of instruction and evaluation.

ASSESSMENT TOOLS

Commercially Available Assessments for Students Who Read Braille

Several assessment instruments are available commercially that are specifically designed to measure progress in reading and writing braille. With the exception of the Assessment of Braille Literacy Skills (ABLS), they tend to focus on skills unique to braille and do not address overall literacy learning. These measures are best used in conjunction with other types of informal assessments commonly found in general education programs in order to gain a complete picture of a student's literacy level.

- *Assessment of Braille Literacy Skills* (ABLS) (Koenig & Farrenkopf, 1994–1995). The ABLS is a checklist that focuses on a student's mastery of braille skills within a literacy framework. It assesses both knowledge of the braille code and reading and writing behaviors in braille. The ABLS contains three sections: Emergent Literacy, Academic Literacy, and Functional Literacy. It can be used on an ongoing basis with students of all ages, including those with multiple disabilities. The Grade 2 Braille checklist is particularly useful as a continuous record of the contractions and short-form words that a student knows (see Figure 10.1). The teacher can use a check mark after each word or contraction that the student can recognize consistently, as suggested, or write the date that each is mastered. As an alternative, each contraction or word can be checked as it is introduced and circled when the student demonstrates mastery. A quick glance at the checklist can help a teacher plan which contractions to preview before a reading assignment. Although the checklist is designed to show progress in reading grade 2 braille, a second copy can also be completed to show progress in writing.

- *Minnesota Braille Skills Inventory* (MBSI) (Godwin et al., 1995). The MBSI assesses a student's knowledge of isolated braille code symbols in six different areas: literary, basic Nemeth (mathematics and science), advanced Nemeth, computer, music, and dictionary/foreign language. It is not intended to provide information about how a student actually uses braille to read or write.

- *Assessment Tools for Teacher Use* (Sewell, 1997). These assessment tools consist of informal checklists designed to assess progress in many different academic areas, including braille instruction. Among the many checklists are ones that measure students' ability to recognize braille contractions and skills in operating the braillewriter, keyboarding, and using an electronic braille notetaker. (This publication is sold as part of a four-part Assessment Kit by the Texas School for the Blind and Visually Impaired; see Resources.)

Grade 2 Braille—Oral Reading

Over a period of readings, monitor the student's level of braille reading using the following list of contractions and short-form words. Place a check mark next to those that the student is able to identify consistently.

about	beneath	dis	him	necessary	receiving	tion
above	beside	do	himself	neither	rejoice	to
according	between	ea	his	ness	rejoicing	today
across	beyond	ed	immediate	not	right	together
after	ble	either	in	o'clock	said	tomorrow
afternoon	blind	en	ing	of	sh	tonight
afterward	braille	ence	into	one	shall	under
again	but	enough	it	oneself	should	upon
against	by	er	its	ong	sion	us
ally	can	ever	itself	ou	so	very
almost	cannot	every	ity	ought	some	was
already	cc	father	just	ound	spirit	were
also	ch	ff	know	ount	st	wh
although	character	first	knowledge	ourselves	still	where
altogether	child	for	less	out	such	which
always	children	friend	letter	ow	th	whose
ance	com	from	like	paid	that	will
and	con	ful	little	part	the	with
ar	conceive	gg	lord	people	their	word
as	conceiving	gh	many	perceive	themselves	work
ation	could	go	ment	perceiving	there	world
bb	day	good	more	perhaps	these	would
be	dd	great	mother	question	this	you
because	deceive	had	much	quick	those	young
before	deceiving	have	must	quite	through	your
behind	declare	here	myself	rather	thyself	yourself
below	declaring	herself	name	receive	time	yourselves

Comments:

Source: Reprinted with permission from A. J. Koenig and C. Farrenkopf, *Assessment of Braille Literacy Skills* (Houston, TX: Region IV Education Service Center, 1994–95).

- *Informal Assessment of Developmental Skills for Visually Handicapped Students* (Swallow, Mangold, & Mangold, 1978). This book includes a wide variety of checklists relating to the unique needs of children with visual impairments. Within the cluster of academic assessments are checklists designed to measure progress in braille reading and writing, use of the slate and stylus, writing script, and listening skills.

In addition to these instruments, the chapter on assessment (Layton, 1997) from *Instructional Strategies for Braille Literacy* (Wormsley & D'Andrea, 1997) offers a variety of assessment checklists and other forms that may be copied for educational use. Among them are a reading interest inventory, a braille assessment checklist for persons with multiple disabilities, a sequence of braillewriter skills, self-assessment forms for reading and writing, and record sheets for analysis of students' reading errors (miscues).

Informal Assessment Measures

A variety of informal assessment measures that are often used in general education classes are equally applicable to assessment of braille skills. They provide the teacher with detailed, in-depth information about a student's progress that can be applied to modify instruction, as needed. A number of such measures are listed here.

Anecdotal Records

Anecdotal records—dated observational notes—document progress in literacy skills. Observation provides an ideal opportunity to analyze the processes a student uses during reading and writing activities, not just the final products. A teacher's notes may include information about reading strategies, development of oral vocabulary, use of grade 2 braille contractions, tracking movements, or other strengths and weaknesses. Records from reading and writing conferences also form part of the anecdotal records.

Lists

Both teachers and students use lists to record detailed information related to literacy activities. For example, students may update daily reading or writing logs, and teachers may maintain records of individualized spelling lists. The teacher or the student may keep an ongoing "strategies list" of successfully demonstrated reading and writing behaviors.

Work Folders

A work folder contains a collection of one student's work over an extended period of time. The papers are usually organized chronologically, such as the entries in a student's journal for the year. Teachers generally maintain control of the work folder, although a student may look at earlier work samples from time to time to compare past and present performance.

Portfolios

Portfolios contain a sampling of a student's work that is designed to show academic progress and achievement. Unlike work folders, they contain items selected on a regular basis by the student or by the student and teacher together according to specific criteria. A portfolio may include samples of creative writing showing the entire writing process, reading responses, oral reading tapes, learning log entries from other subject areas, a photocopied page from a book the student has read, or reading logs. Both the teacher and the student attach a short note to each item explaining why it was included. Proponents of portfolio collections advocate conferences and regular goal setting to develop students' skills in self-assessment (Clemmons, Laase, Cooper, Areglado, & Dill, 1993). Routman (1991), however, cautions that the creation of portfolios places significant responsibility on students and requires skilled management from teachers.

Quantitative Measures

Many teachers gather quantitative data on students' performance at regular intervals. Whereas qualitative instruments provide narrative or anecdotal information that may be obtained through observation, analysis of reading and writing assignments, or interviews, quantitative information usually consists of a numerical score, percentage, or grade level that can be compared to past or expected performance. An assessment measure that provides quantitative data, such as an informal reading inventory, may also provide qualitative information as the teacher observes the child's work habits and problem-solving strategies. Among the types of quantitative data on students' braille reading that teachers' may find useful are these:

- The percentage of words a student can recognize in isolation from the Dolch Basic Sight Vocabulary (Dolch, 1942)—a list of the 220 words most commonly encountered in elementary reading materials. (The complete list is found in Appendix B. These Dolch words are also available on a set of braille flash cards from the American Printing House for the Blind; see the Resources section.) Students should recognize all these words automatically by the time they reach third grade (Maggart & Zintz, 1990).

- Silent and oral braille reading speeds. (See Layton, 1997, pp. 259–261, for details on how to calculate these.)

- Informal reading inventories, consisting of a series of graded word lists and reading passages that help the teacher determine a student's independent, instructional, and frustration reading levels. (These are, respectively, the level of material that a student can read fluently, is challenged by, and experiences extreme frustration with; see Layton, 1997, p. 258.) One source of such inventories, the *Basic Reading Inventory: Pre-Primer Through Grade Twelve and Early Literacy Assessments* (Johns, 1997) is available in regular print, large print, and braille as part of the four-part Assessment Kit from the Texas School for the Blind and Visually Impaired (see the Resources section).

- A running record of the child's miscues. Detailed instructions for analyzing a student's reading miscues during the administration of an informal reading inventory are provided in Chapter 7 of *Instructional Strategies for Braille Literacy* (Layton, 1997).

Checklists

Checklists help to focus a teacher's attention on specific strategies that students must acquire to read and write successfully. However, overreliance on checklists may limit a teacher's awareness of an individual child's unique approach to learning. Checklist information should be used in conjunction with other measures, such as anecdotal records and work samples, to provide a complete picture of a child's learning.

Student Self-Assessment

Students' attitudes toward reading and writing affect their academic progress. Providing opportunities for students to participate in their own assessment, such as completing short written surveys of reading habits and preferences, setting goals, filling out self-evaluation forms, and taking part in individual student conferences, gives students a voice in their learning and helps teachers plan activities that match children's interests and needs. Several self-assessment forms are included in Chapter 7 of *Instructional Strategies for Braille Literacy* (Layton, 1997).

Teacher-Designed Assessments

Teachers can adapt assessment instruments used in regular classes with sighted students or design their own to meet specific needs. The examples provided here are of both types. They can be used as is, be modified as needed, or serve as samples for teachers who are creating their own tools. Blank copies of the forms described on the following pages are included in Appendix B. They are presented roughly in the order in which the teacher would introduce them; the Planned Objectives and Anecdotal Record Sheet and the Task List would be used with students at any level.

Planned Objectives and Anecdotal Record Sheet

The Planned Objectives and Anecdotal Record Sheet form normally covers a two-week period, although only one week is shown in Figure 10.2. It is used to list weekly objectives and record daily anecdotal information related to them. Notes can be continued on the back if more space is needed. The example given here lists objectives and anecdotal records for Sharon, the mainstreamed student discussed in Chapter 9, who is now in first grade. The *Caroline* book referred to on this form was used to illustrate the writing process in Chapter 7.

Task List

An itinerant teacher may leave one or more literacy-related activities for a student to complete in class, either independently or with supervision from the regular teacher. Using the Task List form (see Figure 10.3), the itinerant teacher can list the student's activities for the week down the left side and ask the classroom teacher or assistant to indicate in the appropriate rectangle how successful the student was with each task, using the codes *I* (completed independently), *A* (completed almost independently—with minimal assistance), or *H* (completed with help). Brief comments related to the student's performance may also be included, as well as

Figure 10.2 SAMPLE COMPLETED PLANNED OBJECTIVES AND ANECDOTAL RECORD SHEET

Name: Sharon

Week of: 4/29–5/3

Planned Objectives/Activities

1. Spelling: spell "wa" words and words from the Caroline book

2. Caroline book: self-edit for capital letters and periods; begin final copy if time

3. Tracking: use more efficient hand movements with familiar materials

4. Home reading: finish "Snow White"; work on strategy of skipping and returning to unknown word

5. Keyboarding: lesson 7 ("b" and "n")

Anecdotal Records/Comments

4/29: Caroline book—self-editing with crayon: found 2 missing capitals and 5 missing periods; added "cleaning," "help," "poor," and "paper" to spelling list for the week (words from Caroline book)

4/30: Caroline book—talked about commas needed between repeated words ("Caroline, Caroline, Caroline")

Remembered she had used commas in list of food items in Very Hungry Puppy book

5/1: "Snow White"—good independent hand movements on beginning pages, which are almost memorized

5/2: spelled "want" and "water" correctly in journal entry about swimming pool

---

information such as the number of correct responses in a certain number of attempts at a task (for example, +9/12, means 9 correct responses out of 12 tries). This form is particularly useful for students following a functional literacy program who may require an individualized set of work activities for a portion of the day when classmates are working on visual tasks. The example shown here lists two days of activities for Eddie, the 9-year-old student enrolled in a special program who was discussed in Chapter 9 and is now in his second year of braille instruction; however, the full form presented in Appendix B gives space for the entire week.

Figure 10.3 SAMPLE COMPLETED TASK LIST

Task List

Name: Eddie   Week of: 3/25–3/29

Task	Monday	Tuesday
1. Read calendar and schedule	A	Read schedule perfectly second try; found the "p" in "PE"
2. Sort "people" vs. "play" vs. "pill" flash cards	+9/12 tries missed "pill" 2 times	+10/12 tries
3. Pin new word "people" on worksheet	+6/8 tries	OK—I
4. Read sentences and stories	H; had trouble remembering "people"	H; but better today with "people"
5. Sequence numbers 1–10 on Velcro board		A (took almost 15 minutes)
6. Match family names on Velcro board	I	

I = Completed *independently;* **A** = Completed *almost* independently—with minimal assistance; **H** = Completed with *help*

Beginning Braille Alphabet Skills Checklist

The Beginning Braille Alphabet Skills Checklist can be used for ongoing assessment of a beginning reader's progress by recording the date on which each letter, word, number, or sound is introduced or mastered. Depending on the instructional approach, the student may learn common whole-word contractions before isolated letters of the alphabet, as in the example of Joshua included here (see Figure 10.4). Other words that the child is learning can be listed at the bottom of the form. An easy way to check for letter-sound recognition is to say words beginning with different letters of the alphabet in random order and ask the child to identify the beginning letter. Or, say the letter and ask the child to supply a word beginning with the sound made by that letter. Write the date of assessment at the top of the Recognizes Sound column and check off the letter sounds the student knows.

Figure 10.4   SAMPLE COMPLETED BRAILLE ALPHABET SKILLS CHECKLIST

Beginning Braille Alphabet Skills Checklist

Name: Joshua

Letter	Identifies Letter	Reads Whole-Word Contraction	Writes Letter or Contraction	Recognizes Sound 9/20	10/25
a	9/13		9/13		
b		but 10/11	10/11	✓	✓
c	10/26	can 9/27	9/30		✓
d		do 10/8	10/13	✓	✓
e		every			
f		from		✓	✓
g		go 9/23	9/24		✓
h		have 10/26	11/1		
i		I 10/6	10/11		
j	9/20	just	9/20	✓	✓
k		knowledge			
l	9/13	like 9/13	9/13		✓
m	11/15	more		✓	✓
n		not 10/18			✓
o					
p		people		✓	✓
q		quite			
r		rather			✓
s		so			✓
t		that		✓	✓
u		us			
v		very			✓
w		will 11/3			✓
x		it			
y		you 10/1	10/12		
z		as			✓
				7	16
0			**Other words:**		
1	11/5		Joshua 9/13		
2	11/9		Mommy 9/22		
3			Daddy 10/4		
4			Carey 10/26		
5			get 11/4		
6			microphone 11/15		
7			lunch 11/18		
8					
9					
10					

Tactile Sight Words and Familiar Names

Like a print sight word, a tactile sight word is one that a child recognizes instantly, without having to apply decoding strategies. Students learn these words in step 1 of the sequential reading approach described in Chapter 4. The vocabulary list on this checklist of Tactile Sight Words and Familiar Names includes many single-letter whole-word signs and common contracted words in grade 2 braille (see Figure 10.5). The words do not necessarily need to be learned in order, as long as those with similar or reversed configurations (such as *not* and *the* or *and* and *you*) are not introduced too close together in time. Nor does a student need to master the entire list before moving on to step 2 (learning the letters of the alphabet) and step 3 (reading emergent reader books). Space is provided for the teacher to note other words that the student has learned, such as the names of family members and classmates. This checklist is a handy reference for teachers as they write controlled-vocabulary stories to help children practice reading new words. (See Chapter 5 for samples of controlled-vocabulary stories.)

Figure 10.5 SAMPLE COMPLETED TACTILE SIGHT WORD CHECKLIST

Tactile Sight Words and Familiar Names

Name: Joshua

Write the date that the child learns to read each of the words below in grade 2 braille.

go 9/23	you 10/1	can 9/27
I 10/6	we _____	like 9/13
have 10/26	the _____	a 9/13
do 10/8	but 10/11	just _____
that _____	people _____	not 10/18
me _____	to (uncontracted) _____	and _____
with _____	get 11/4	will 11/3
for _____	it _____	in _____

Other tactile sight words and names

Joshua 9/13	microphone 11/15	
Mommy 9/22	lunch 11/18	
Daddy 10/4		
Carey 10/26		

Source: Adapted from Hilda Caton, Eleanor Pester, and Eddy J. Bradley, *Go and Do* (Louisville, KY: American Printing House for the Blind, 1982).

Braille Oral Reading Individual Checklist

The Braille Oral Reading Individual Checklist, as well as the two that follow, have been adapted from ones used with print readers. This checklist can be completed on a periodic basis as the student reads a book aloud (see Figure 10.6). The book may be familiar or one that the student has not seen before, depending on the objective of the assessment. Results may be compared over time to evaluate the student's progress.

Figure 10.6 SAMPLE COMPLETED BRAILLE ORAL READING CHECKLIST

Braille Oral Reading Individual Checklist

Name: Carlos

Book Read: Shoo!

Date: 3/16

	Check	Comments
Reads familiar material fluently with appropriate expression	✓	
Matches one spoken word to each braille word	✓	Yes, consistently
Uses efficient tracking movements	✓	Two hands together without separating
Self-corrects to preserve meaning	✓	Changed "wet" to "went"
Takes risks in pronunciation	✓	Read "came" as "cam," then "came"
Recognizes braille contractions	✓	
Observes punctuation	✓	
Notices when reading does not make sense	✓	"wet/went" correction
When confronting unfamiliar words:		
• rereads the sentence	✓	
• uses context clues	✓	
• skips unknown words, reads on, returns to word		
• uses phonics clues	✓	Decoded "duck" & "pig"
• substitutes words that make sense (*little* for *small*)		

Source: Adapted with permission from D. Fowler and S. McCallum, *Primary Purposes Language Arts Resource Guide: Assessing* (Fairfax, VA: Fairfax County Public Schools, 1995).

Early Braille Writing Development Checklist

The Early Braille Writing Development Checklist can be completed every three or four weeks to document a student's progress in beginning writing skills on the braillewriter. The skills listed will develop over a period of one to two years, usually from late preschool through the end of first grade. The example given here shows Rebecca's progress during her kindergarten year (see Figure 10.7).

Figure 10.7 SAMPLE COMPLETED EARLY BRAILLE WRITING DEVELOPMENT CHECKLIST

Early Braille Writing Development Checklist

Name: Rebecca

Directions: Date entries every 3 or 4 weeks. Comment on the child's progress.

	Date	Comments
Imitates writing behavior by randomly pressing keys and speaking message	9/97	Chooses as a free time activity
Writes a line of full cells	9/97	Can do independently
Isolates fingers, pressing one key at a time	10/97	All except finger 3 (11/97—all)
Inserts paper into the brailler	12/97	Successful 2/3 tries
Writes random letters	10/97	"r," "a," and "l"
Uses letter-sound relationships to write words (temporary spelling)	11/97	During guided writing
Uses grade 2 braille contractions	2/98	Yes; see ABLS checklist
Leaves spaces between words	4/98	About 80% of the time
Uses some conventional spelling	4/98	Using word bank of favorite words
Reads writing to others	12/97	Good voice-to-braille match!
Organizes writing in time order	6/98	Field day story
Organizes writing around a topic or event	6/98	Field day, birthday, new dog
Uses capital sign at the beginning of a sentence		
Uses end punctuation		
Marks words not spelled correctly		
Uses more conventional spelling than approximations		
Other:		

Source: Adapted with permission from D. Fowler and S. McCallum, *Primary Purposes Language Arts Resource Guide: Assessing* (Fairfax, VA: Fairfax County Public Schools, 1995).

Braille Writing Assessment Checklist

The Braille Writing Assessment checklist provides information about a student's ability to plan, revise, and edit written work. It is completed while a student is taking a piece of writing through the writing process. This example shows the strategies that Albert, a first-grade student, used when writing his guinea pig book (see Figure 10.8).

Figure 10.8 SAMPLE COMPLETED BRAILLE WRITING ASSESSMENT CHECKLIST

Braille Writing Assessment

Name: Albert

Date: 12/16

Title: My Guinea Pig

Student plans writing by:	Check	Comments
• discussing with others	✓	Held guinea pig during discussion
• orally rehearsing sentences	✓	Very helpful!
• reading		
• brailling a sample list or outline	✓	Listed 5 key words with help
• other		
Student revises writing by:		
• rereading to see if it makes sense	✓	
• checking for a beginning and an end		
• adding information	✓	Added sentence about water bottle
• deleting or substituting information	✓	Deleted 1 of 2 sentences that said the same thing
• reorganizing ideas		
• carefully choosing the best word	✓	Changed "eat" to "nibble"
• other		
Student edits writing by using:		
• capital letters (sentence beginnings)	✓	No errors
• capital letters (proper nouns)		
• end punctuation	✓	Added 2 periods
• commas in a series		
• conventional spelling/grade 2 braille	✓	Marked 4/6 spelling errors with a crayon
• apostrophes (contractions/possessions)		
• other		

Source: Adapted with permission from D. Fowler and S. McCallum, *Primary Purposes Language Arts Resource Guide: Assessing* (Fairfax, VA: Fairfax County Public Schools, 1995).

PLANNING AN ASSESSMENT SCHEDULE

Regular collection of data at specified intervals helps to provide an in-depth picture of a student's progress. Samples of assessment measures and a possible time line are suggested in the accompanying tables (see Tables 10.1, 10.2, and 10.3). No teacher will use all of these assessments with a single student, nor will the suggested time intervals be appropriate in every situation. In deciding what, when, and how to assess, teachers select measures that provide a balance of information that is useful for instruction and for reporting a particular student's progress. They need to know how well the student is progressing in specific braille-related skills as well as how successful he or she is in meeting school system performance requirements for language arts. Teachers of students in mainstreamed classes can plan their assessments within the framework of regular classroom procedures, especially as they will probably work with the mainstream teacher using general education assessments. As part of this collaboration, they may transcribe assessment materi-

Table 10.1 SCHEDULE OF BRAILLE READING AND WRITING FOR A TYPICAL STUDENT

Frequency of Assessment			
Daily or Weekly	**Monthly**	**Quarterly**	**Longer Intervals (e.g., 2–3 times per year)**

Teacher's anecdotal records
 	
Student-kept records (e.g. reading and writing logs)
 	
Ongoing checklists:
  Beginning Braille Alphabet Skills Checklist
 	
  Tactile Sight Word List
 	
  Grade 2 Braille Checklist
 	
Spelling records (e.g. individualized spelling lists)
 	
Notebook of dated journal entries
	Other reading and writing checklists:
	  Braille Oral Reading Individual Checklist
	
	  Early Braille Writing Development Checklist
	
	  Braille Writing Assessment
	
	Writing samples:
	  reading responses
	
	  learning logs
	
	  retelling of a passage heard or read
	
	  creative writing
		Records of student's goal-setting and self-evaluation, and student-teacher conferences
		
		Portfolio samples
		
		Assessment of Braille Literacy Skills checklists
		
		List of reading and/or writing behaviors consistently demonstrated by the child (as summarized from anecdotal records and work samples; may be maintained by the teacher, student, or both)
			Informal reading inventory to determine independent, instructional, and frustration reading levels
			
			Recognition of Dolch words in isolation (percentage)
			
			Oral and silent braille reading speeds
			
			Written response to specific prompt or assigned topic

Table 10.2 ASSESSMENT SCHEDULE FOR SHARON, A MAINSTREAMED KINDERGARTNER

Frequency of Assessment		
Daily/Weekly	**Monthly**	**Quarterly**

Planned Objectives and Anecdotal Records sheet
 	
Beginning Braille Alphabet Skills Checklist
 	
Tactile Sight Word List
 	
Grade 2 Braille—Oral Reading Checklist
 	
Notebook of journal writing entries
 	
List of books read (teacher's list for first part of year; student's list for last quarter)
	Writing samples (other than journal entries) with teacher notes attached
	
	Braille Oral Reading Individual Checklist
	
	Early Braille Writing Development Checklist
		Checklists from *Assessment of Braille Literacy Skills*
		
		Mainstream kindergarten assessments administered with the kindergarten teacher:
		
		  book-handling skills
		
		  concept of letter, contraction, and word
		
		  voice-to-braille match
		
		  knowledge of letters and sounds
		
		  early writing skills
		
		  phonemic awareness
		
		Self-assessment discussion and braille list: What have I learned? What do I want to learn?

Table 10.3 ASSESSMENT SCHEDULE FOR EDDIE, A PRIMARY STUDENT WITH MULTIPLE DISABILITIES

Frequency of Assessment	
Daily/Weekly	**Monthly/Quarterly**
Planned Objectives and Anecdotal Records sheet Beginning Braille Alphabet Skills Checklist Tactile Sight Word List Grade 2 Braille—Oral Reading Checklist Weekly task lists of performance on literacy tasks in his special education classroom Dated samples of guided writing and controlled-vocabulary stories	Checklists from *Assessment of Braille Literacy Skills* List of reading and writing behaviors consistently demonstrated, as summarized from anecdotal records and checklists (sent home with report card)

als into braille and administer them together with the classroom teacher, as described in "A Morning in the Mainstream" in Chapter 2.

The assessment schedule illustrated in Table 10.1 is suggested for a "typical" student. Actual schedules used for Sharon (when she was in kindergarten) and for Eddie, the students presented in Chapter 9, are provided in Tables 10.2 and 10.3 to show how the typical schedule might be adjusted to meet the needs of a particular individual.

SUMMARY

A variety of ongoing and periodic assessments provides a comprehensive picture of a student's progress in language arts. Although there are only a limited number of instruments specifically designed for learners who read braille, assessment procedures used in the general education classroom are often applicable to braille reading and writing with only slight modifications. Students in mainstream classes benefit from collaborative evaluation by the classroom teacher and the itinerant or resource teacher, each contributing input in his or her area of expertise.

CHAPTER 11 Braille Literacy for Sighted Classmates

Integrating a student who is blind or visually impaired into a regular classroom setting is sometimes easier to achieve academically than socially. Providing opportunities to develop classmates' understanding of a blind student's disability and special skills helps to establish a more comfortable classroom environment for all. Moreover, in the process of sharing his or her knowledge of braille, the student practices social skills, gains self-esteem and makes a unique contribution to classroom learning.

Sighted students of all ages are fascinated by braille. Making a classroom presentation about braille with a child who is blind or visually impaired is a natural way to satisfy classmates' curiosity and increase their understanding of how compensatory skills enable people who are blind or visually impaired to function independently.

Plan the presentation ahead of time with your student if you will be speaking together. Determine how much guidance the student will need from you and which specific skills or devices he or she would like to demonstrate. Assemble a collection of "hands-on" items to leave in the regular education classroom for a week or so after your talk (see "Readings for Students about Blindness" in the Resources section). Braille charts and worksheets are included in Appendix C and may be copied for use in presentations to students.

STRUCTURING THE "BRAILLE TALK"

Most teachers of students who are visually impaired are called on to talk about braille at some point in their careers. The suggestions offered here can supplement an existing talk or serve as the basis for a new one. A variety of questions to stimulate discussion are offered, along with hands-on materials and follow-up activities, to challenge students' thinking skills and help them to remember the new concepts. Another excellent resource, *Classroom Collaboration* (Hudson, 1997), provides further suggestions for braille awareness activities suited to elementary school audiences and includes worksheets that may be photocopied. The format of the presentation will vary, depending on whether the teacher is speaking with a student or alone. Be sure to allow time for the sighted students to ask their own questions either during the presentation or at the end.

Introduction

Write "visually impaired," "low vision," and "blind" on the board. Tell students a little about your job. Then begin to challenge students' preconceptions by explaining (adjusting the wording to fit your own caseload):

> Many of the students I work with have low vision; a few others are blind. What do you think the difference is between having low vision and being blind?

Emphasize that eyeglasses do not help people with low vision to see normally. You may also want to mention that many people who are blind still have some visual abilities such as the perception of light or large forms.

To begin to correct students' misconceptions about blindness, start by asking:

> How would life be different for you if you were blind?

As students volunteer answers, briefly describe adaptations and accommodations that enable people who are blind to function independently at home, school, and work. Then have the students close their eyes, and ask them questions such as these:

> Would you like a lot of homework tonight?
>
> Do you like pizza?
>
> Do you enjoy playing in the playground?

Point out that the answers to these questions would be the same, whether their eyes were open or closed. Emphasize that children who are blind feel the same way inside as children who see.

Mobility Information

Although mobility is not directly related to braille, this is an ideal opportunity to teach regular education students the sighted guide technique and to demonstrate other mobility techniques such as trailing and the use of a cane. You can also review the importance of not interfering with a dog guide at work. Then review the information presented by asking:

> What are some ways that a person who is blind can travel safely?

Responses should include the sighted guide technique, trailing, a cane, or a dog guide.

Braille Reading

Find out and discuss what the children know about braille. Then pass out index cards with their names written on them in grade 1 braille, along with a copy of the braille alphabet (samples of the alphabet are provided in Appendix C; printed braille alphabet cards are also available from the American Foundation for the Blind; see Resources). Have the students compare the braille letters they see on their cards to the letters printed on their handouts. Encourage them to close their eyes and feel the special shape of their names. Use a large diagram of the braille cell with removable dots to demonstrate the dot positions of different letters and the capital sign. (The dots can be attached to the diagram with Velcro.) Then ask the students:

> Looking at your handout of the braille alphabet, who can tell me the dot numbers for *m*? For *y*?

The teacher can repeat the question for several other letters and demonstrate each one on the large diagram.

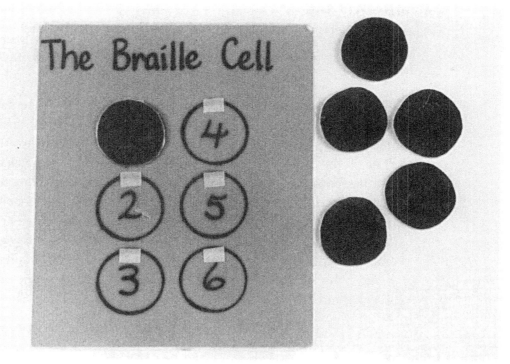

A diagram of a large braille cell with removable dots makes it easy for sighted students to understand how braille characters are formed.

After the children have become familiar with the braille characters, explain how the system was invented:

> Louis Braille was only a teenager when he invented the braille alphabet. He used a very logical system to form the dot pattern

for each letter. Notice that the letters are arranged in three rows on your handout. How did Louis Braille use the letters in the first row to make the letters in the second row? How did he use the letters in the second row to make the letters in the third row? Which letter in the third row does not follow this pattern?

Some children may notice that a dot 3 is added to each letter in the first row to make the second row, and a dot 6 is added to each letter in the third row. You may need to tell them that *w* is the exception to the pattern because there is no *w* in the French alphabet.

If you are speaking to older students, you can explain the number sign and contractions. Show several different types of books to illustrate the progression of skills mastered by a typical braille reader: a volume of *Touch and Tell* (1969) for very young children, a print-braille book, and a braille magazine or trade book with interpoint braille. Have your student read a few pages from a braille book aloud to the class.

Braille Writing

Insert a piece of paper and demonstrate the parts of the braillewriter.

Why do you think there are only six main writing keys on the braillewriter?

Help the children understand that each key makes one of the dots in the braille cell.

Have your student braille the alphabet while a primary class sings the alphabet song; or stage a race: You write the alphabet on the board while the braille student writes on the braillewriter. The student should win, and the class will be impressed with the speed and ease of braille writing. If you are speaking to a group alone, ask someone in the class to time you while you write the alphabet on the brailler as quickly as possible. You or your student may also wish to demonstrate the slate and stylus and talk about other means of writing braille, such as electronic notetakers, computers with braille embossers, and the Mountbatten Brailler.

After the students have learned about different methods of writing braille, you can ask them

If you were blind, which would you rather use, a slate or a braillewriter? Why?

After several children answer, summarize the advantages and disadvantages of each, such as weight, cost, and ease of use, and note that most students learn to use both.

Adaptive Aids

Ask your student to talk about several favorite adapted learning tools. Examples might include flat-sided crayons with braille color names, a raised-line drawing board, a braille clock or watch, and a braille ruler. If the student uses an electronic notetaker, he or she may wish to demonstrate how to write with it.

ACTIVITIES

Depending on the time available, the teacher can supplement the presentation with a variety of hands-on activities and materials. Many of these can be used as follow-up activities by the classroom teacher.

Slate and Stylus

Students who express a strong interest in braille often enjoy learning to write on the slate and stylus. Plastic slates that students can purchase are available at relatively low cost from the American Printing House for the Blind (see the Resources section). Give students the Braille Alphabet Backwards sheet from Appendix C to help them write letters correctly on the slate.

Rotating Groups

Divide the class into groups that will rotate among three centers. Group 1 tries puzzles, pegboards, money identification, raised-line drawing boards, telling time with an old braille watch, and other fine motor or tactile discrimination activities while blindfolded. Group 2 practices the sighted guide technique with a blindfolded partner. Group 3 takes turns using the brailler to write their names, assisted by the student who is blind or visually impaired. While waiting to use the brailler, the others try the slate and stylus, decode riddles written in grade 1 braille, and complete worksheets like those in Appendix C.

"Bean Braille"

Have students create their names in braille using split peas, popcorn kernels, or white beans. To facilitate correct placement of the dots, give each child a small template of the braille cell made from half an index card with holes punched out for each dot. The student places the template on a blank sheet of construction paper and makes a mark where each dot should go for the desired letter. Then he or she can glue the beans in place on the marks.

Hands-on Materials

Leave one or more braille worksheets (see Appendix C) and a basket of "hands-on" items for students to examine at a classroom center, such as a volume of *Touch and Tell,* print-braille book, copy of a braille magazine or trade book, slate and stylus, folding cane, braille ruler, braille calendar, raised-line map of the United States, and assorted pamphlets and books.

SUMMARY

Classroom activities that promote awareness of braille reading and writing, particularly when presented by a mainstream student, help the other children in the class, as well as the classroom teacher, gain an appreciation of the usefulness and versatility of braille. They realize that it is indeed possible for someone who is blind to accomplish the same work expected of sighted students, only in a different medium. At the same time, the mainstreamed child benefits from his or her status as an "expert" in a skill that most people know nothing about. The result can be a sharing of information, questions, and ideas that promotes better understanding and cooperation in the classroom.

Epilogue

Six-year-old Andrew seats himself at the front of the room, his newly published book of braille poems in front of him. His classmates listen attentively as they watch his fingers move fluently from line to line. Andrew is enjoying himself. He meows like a cat, makes splashing noises, and squeals "Whee!" at appropriate moments in the text. After closing the book, Andrew takes a large drum and recites the poems from memory, this time enhancing the words with a variety of complex rhythms. He is totally immersed in the rhythm, pattern, and meaning of the language he has created, and his excitement is contagious.

After six months of kindergarten, Andrew tackles braille tasks with enthusiasm and confidence. He reads and writes daily about subjects of interest to him: his cat, the playground, a dish of ice cream. Given frequent opportunities to use braille in meaningful contexts, he seems to absorb new contractions and words effortlessly. Even as I applaud Andrew's successes, I am aware that my next students may learn very differently. It is possible that they will require a larger dose of traditional structure, drill, and repetition to achieve braille literacy. I know, however, that as I plan for their individual needs, I will continue to seek out ways to make their learning purposeful—from their point of view as well as my own.

The language arts continuum offers a broad and flexible repertoire of instructional possibilities. As I seek to match my teaching to the learning style and interests of a particular child, I continue to learn and grow along with my student. In the end, it is motivation that provides children with the perseverance to master the very complex skills of reading and writing in braille. I want my students to be motivated less by a desire to please me than by a love of books and an eagerness to communicate their ideas in writing. These are the attitudes that will be with them for a lifetime.

References*

Anderson, R. C., Hiebert, E. H., Scott, J. A., & Wilkinson, I. A. G. (1984). *Becoming a nation of readers: The report of the Commission on Reading.* Washington, DC: National Institute of Education.

Bolton, F., & Snowball, D. (1993a). *Ideas for spelling.* Portsmouth, NH: Heinemann.

Bolton, F., & Snowball, D. (1993b). *Teaching spelling: A practical resource.* Portsmouth, NH: Heinemann.

Burton, L., Ormerod, A., & Kelzenberg, L. (1997, September). *Grade one first—grade two second: Linking technology to braille literacy.* Paper presented at the Third Biennial Getting in Touch with Literacy Conference, Minneapolis, MN.

Butler, A., & Turbill, J. (1987). *Towards a reading-writing classroom.* Portsmouth, NH: Heinemann.

Castellano, C., & Kosman, D. (1997). *The bridge to braille: Reading and school success for the young blind child.* Baltimore: National Organization of Parents of Blind Children.

Caton, H. (1991). *Print and braille literacy: Selecting appropriate learning media.* Louisville, KY: American Printing House for the Blind.

Caton, H. (1994). *TOOLS for selecting appropriate learning media.* Louisville, KY: American Printing House for the Blind.

Caton, H., Pester, E., & Bradley, E. J. (1982a). *Go and do.* Louisville, KY: American Printing House for the Blind.

Caton, H., Pester, E., & Bradley, E. J. (1982b). *Letters and you.* Louisville, KY: American Printing House for the Blind.

Caton, H., Pester, E., & Bradley, E. J. (1982c). *Patterns: The primary braille reading program.* Louisville, KY: American Printing House for the Blind.

Clemmons, J., Laase, L., Cooper, D., Areglado, N., & Dill, M. (1993). *Portfolios in the classroom: A teacher's sourcebook.* New York: Scholastic Professional Books.

Curran, E. (1988). *Just enough to know better: A braille primer.* Boston: National Braille Press.

D'Andrea, F. M. (1997). Teaching braille to students with special needs. In D. P. Wormsley & F. M. D'Andrea (Eds.), *Instructional strategies for braille literacy* (pp. 145–188). New York: AFB Press.

Dolch, E. W. (1942). *The Dolch basic sight word test.* Champaign, IL: Garrard Press.

Erin, J. N., & Koenig, A. J. (1997). The student with a visual disability and a learning disability. *Journal of Learning Disabilities, 30*(3), 309–320.

Fowler, D., Jackson, R., & McCallum, S. (1995). *Primary purposes language arts resource guide: Reading.* Fairfax, VA: Department of Instructional Services, Fairfax County Public Schools.

Fowler, D., Jackson, R., & McCallum, S. (1996). *Primary purposes language arts resource guide: Spelling.* Fairfax, VA: Department of Instructional Services, Fairfax County Public Schools.

---

*For the reader's convenience, children's books mentioned in the text appear in a separate reference list following this one.

Fowler, D., & McCallum, S. (1995a). *Primary purposes language arts resource guide: Assessing.* Fairfax, VA: Department of Instructional Services, Fairfax County Public Schools.

Fowler, D., & McCallum, S. (1995b). *Primary purposes language arts resource guide: Writing.* Fairfax, VA: Department of Instructional Services, Fairfax County Public Schools.

Godwin, A., Grafsgaard, K., Hanson, N., Hooey, P., Martin, J., McNear, D., Rieber, C., Tillmanns, E. (1995). *Minnesota braille skills inventory: A resource manual.* Little Canada, MN: Minnesota Educational Services.

Graves, D. H. (1983). *Writing: Teachers and children at work.* Portsmouth, NH: Heinemann.

Graves, D. H. (1997, April). *Putting writing to work across the curriculum.* Workshop sponsored by Heinemann Press, Fairfax, Virginia.

Hansen, J. (1987). *When writers read.* Portsmouth, NH: Heinemann.

Harley, R. K., Truan, M. B., & Sanford, L. D. (1997). *Communication skills for visually impaired learners.* Springfield, IL: Charles C Thomas.

Heydt, K., Clark, M. J., Cushman, C., Edwards, S., & Allon, M. (1992). *Perkins activity and resource guide.* Watertown, MA: Perkins School for the Blind.

Hudson, C., & O'Toole, M. (1983). *Spelling: A teacher's guide.* Victoria, Australia: Landmark Educational Supplies Pty.

Hudson, L. (1997). *Classroom collaboration.* Watertown, MA: Perkins School for the Blind.

Huebner, K. M., Prickett, J. G., Welch, T. R., Joffee, E. (Eds.). (1995). *Hand in hand: Essentials of communication and orientation and mobility for your students who are deaf-blind.* New York: AFB Press.

Hurray, G. (1993). *A braille spelling dictionary for beginning writers.* Boston: National Braille Press.

Johns, J. (1997). *Basic reading inventory: Pre-primer through grade twelve and early literacy assessments* (7th ed.). Dubuque, IA: Kendall/Hunt Publishing.

Koenig, A. J., & Farrenkopf, C. (1994). *Providing quality instruction in braille literacy skills: A companion guide to "Invitations: Changing as Teachers and Learners K–12."* Portsmouth, NH: Heinemann.

Koenig, A. J., & Farrenkopf, C. (1994–95). *Assessment of braille literacy skills.* Houston: Region IV Education Service Center.

Koenig, A. J., & Holbrook, M. (1995). *Learning media assessment of students with visual impairments* (2nd ed.). Austin: Texas School for the Blind and Visually Impaired.

Lamb, G. (1996). Beginning braille: A whole language-based strategy. *Journal of Visual Impairment & Blindness, 90*(3), 184–189.

Layton, C. A. (1997). Assessing the literary skills of students who are blind or visually impaired. In D. P. Wormsley & F. M. D'Andrea (Eds.), *Instructional Strategies for Braille Literacy* (pp. 231–268). New York: AFB Press.

Maggart, X. R., & Zintz, M. V. (1990). *Corrective reading.* Dubuque, IA: Wm. C. Brown.

Mangold, P. (1993). *Teaching the braille slate and stylus: A manual for mastery.* Castro Valley, CA: Exceptional Teaching Aids.

Mangold, S., (1977). *The Mangold developmental program of tactile perception and braille letter recognition.* Castro Valley, CA: Exceptional Teaching Aids.

Miller, D. (1985). Reading comes naturally: A mother and her blind child's experiences. *Journal of Visual Impairment & Blindness, 79,* 1–4.

Miller, C., & Levack, N. (1997). *A paraprofessional's handbook for working with students who are visually impaired.* Austin: Texas School for the Blind and Visually Impaired.

Olson, M. (1981). *Guidelines and games for teaching efficient braille reading.* New York: American Foundation for the Blind.

Rex, E. J., Koenig, A. J., Wormsley, D. P., & Baker, R. L. (1994). *Foundations of braille literacy.* New York: AFB Press.

Routman, R., (1988). *Transitions: From literature to literacy.* Portsmouth, NH: Heinemann.

Routman, R., (1991). *Invitations: Changing as teachers and learners K–12.* Portsmouth, NH: Heinemann.

Sanchez, R. (1998, March 19). A mixed approach to reading. *Washington Post,* p. A2.

Sewell, D. (1997). *Assessment tools for teacher use.* Austin: Texas School for the Blind and Visually Impaired.

Sharpe, M. N., McNear, D., & McGrew, K. S. (1996). *Braille assessment inventory.* Columbia, MO: Hawthorne Educational Services.

Swallow, R. M., Mangold, S., & Mangold, P. (1978). *Informal assessment of developmental skills for visually handicapped students.* New York: American Foundation for the Blind.

Swenson, A., & Norrish, C. (1994, July). *Using a whole language approach to teach braille reading and writing at the elementary level.* Paper presented at the biennial international conference of the Association for Education and Rehabilitation of the Blind and Visually Impaired, Dallas.

Teale, W. (1985). The beginnings of literacy. *Dimensions, 13,* 5–8.

Touch and Tell. (1969). Louisville, KY: American Printing House for the Blind.

Troughton, M. (1992). *One is fun: Guidelines for better braille literacy.* Brantford, Ontario: Author.

Wormsley, D. P. (1997). Learning to read, reading to learn: Teaching braille reading and writing. In D. P. Wormsley & F. M. D'Andrea (Eds.), *Instructional strategies for braille literacy* (pp. 57–109). New York: AFB Press.

Wormsley, D. P., & D'Andrea, F. M. (Eds.). (1997). *Instructional strategies for braille literacy.* New York: AFB Press.

CHILDREN'S BOOKS CITED

Campbell, Rod. (1984). *Dear Zoo.* New York: Puffin Books.

Carle, Eric. (1969). *The Very Hungry Caterpillar.* New York: Philomel.

Carle, Eric. (1972). *The Secret Birthday Message.* New York: Crowell.

Carle, Eric. (1984). *The Very Busy Spider.* New York: Philomel.

Cowley, Joy. (1986). *Ice Cream.* Bothall, WA: The Wright Group.

Cowley, Joy. (1990). *Mrs. Wishy-Washy.* Bothell, WA: The Wright Group.

Emberley, Ed. (1992). *Go Away, Big Green Monster!* Boston: Little, Brown.

Fowke, E. (1966). *Sally go round the sun.* Toronto, Ontario, Canada: McClelland & Stewart.

Freeman, Don. (1955). *Mop Top.* New York: Puffin Books.

Hutchins, Pat. (1968). *Rosie's Walk.* New York: Scholastic.

Keats, Ezra Jack. (1976). *The Snowy Day.* New York: Puffin Books.

Martin, Bill, Jr. (1983). *Brown Bear, Brown Bear, What Do You See?* New York: Holt, Rinehart & Winston.

Neasi, Barbara. (1984). *Just Like Me.* Chicago: Childrens Press.

Nelson, JoAnne. (1989). *Lions and Gorillas.* New York: Simon & Schuster.

Numeroff, Laura Joffe. (1985). *If You Give a Mouse a Cookie.* New York: Scholastic.

Petrie, Catherine. (1982). *Joshua James Likes Trucks.* Chicago: Childrens Press.

Rosen, Michael. (1989). *We're Going on a Bear Hunt.* New York: Margaret K. McElderry Books.

Resources

This Resources section is designed to furnish information to teachers who provide instruction in braille reading and writing to young blind and visually impaired children. It includes the sources for the products and publications mentioned throughout this book. Readers can find additional information and detailed listings of products, services, organizations, readings, and braille materials in *Instructional Strategies for Braille Literacy* (Wormsley & D'Andrea, 1997) and the *AFB Directory of Services for Blind and Visually Impaired Persons in the United States and Canada*, both of which are published by the American Foundation for the Blind (see the listing in this section).

This Resources listing is divided into four major sections: Resources for Teachers, Resources for Parents, Products and Materials, and Readings for Students about Blindness.

RESOURCES FOR TEACHERS

In addition to using the listings in this section, teachers and paraprofessionals may also want to review the information provided for parents, both for their own use and so that they are prepared with appropriate referrals.

National Organizations

American Foundation for the Blind

11 Penn Plaza, Suite 300
New York, NY 10001
(212) 502-7600 or (800) 232-5463
TDD: (212) 502-7662
FAX: (212) 502-7777
E-mail: afbinfo@afb.net
http://www.afb.org

Provides services to and acts as an information clearinghouse for people who are blind or visually impaired and their families, professionals, organizations, schools, and corporations. Conducts research and mounts program initiatives to improve services to visually impaired persons, including the National Initiative on Literacy; advocates for services and legislation; maintains the M. C. Migel Library and Information Center and the Helen Keller Archives; provides information and referral services; operates a National Technology Center and a Careers and Technology Information Bank; produces videos and Talking Books; and publishes books, pamphlets, the *Directory of Services for Blind and Visually Impaired Persons in the United States and Canada,* and the *Journal of Visual Impairment & Blindness.* Maintains the following offices throughout the country in addition to the headquarters' office:

AFB Midwest
401 N. Michigan Avenue, Suite 308
Chicago, IL 60611
(312) 245-9961
FAX: (312) 245-9965
E-mail: chicago@afb.net

AFB Southeast
National Initiative on Literacy
100 Peachtree Street, Suite 620
Atlanta, GA 30303
(404) 525-2303
FAX: (404) 659-6957
E-mail: atlanta@afb.net
blmit@afb.org

AFB Southwest
260 Treadway Plaza
Exchange Park
Dallas, TX 75235
(214) 352-7222
FAX: (214) 352-3214
E-mail: afbdallas@afb.net

AFB West
111 Pine Street, Suite 725
San Francisco, CA 94111
(415) 392-4845
FAX: (415) 392-0383
E-mail: sanfran@afb.net

Governmental Relations Group
820 First Street, N.E., Suite 400
Washington, D.C. 20002
(202) 408-0200
FAX: (202) 289-7880
E-mail: afbgov@afb.net

American Printing House for the Blind
1839 Frankfort Avenue
Louisville, KY 40206-0085
(502) 895-2405 or (800) 223-1839
FAX: (502) 899-2274
E-mail: info@alpha.org
http://www.aph.org
Produces materials in braille and large print and on audiocassette; manufactures computer-access equipment, software, and special education devices for persons who are visually impaired; and maintains an educational research and development program and reference-catalog service providing information about volunteer-produced textbooks in accessible media.

Braille Authority of North America
c/o Dolores Ferrara-Godzieba, Chairperson
Associated Services for the Blind
919 Walnut Street
Philadelphia, PA 19107
(215) 627-0600 or (215) 922-0692
Serves as a U.S.-Canadian standard-setting organization whose member agencies strive to promulgate codes regarding usage of braille and to promote and facilitate its use, teaching, and production. Publishes an *Annual Directory.*

Braille Revival League
c/o Ms. Kim Charlson, President
57 Grandview Avenue
Watertown, MA 02172
(617) 926-9198
E-mail: klcharlson@delphi.com
Fosters the use, production, and instruction of braille. Encourages people who are blind to read and write in braille and advocates mandatory braille instruction in educational facilities for individuals who are blind. Publishes the newsletter *BRL Memorandum.*

California Transcribers and Educators of the Visually Handicapped
741 North Vermont Avenue
Los Angeles, CA 90029
(213) 666-2211
Serves as a national organization of braille transcribers and educators. Provides support to teachers, holds a yearly conference, and publishes a quarterly journal.

Council for Exceptional Children
Division of the Visually Impaired
1920 Association Drive
Reston, VA 22091-1589

(703) 620-3660 or (800) 328-0272

TDD: (703) 620-3660

FAX: (703) 264-9494

Acts as a professional organization for individuals serving children with disabilities and children who are gifted. Is the largest such international organization, with 17 specialized divisions. Primary activities include advocating for appropriate government policies; setting professional standards; providing continuing professional development; and helping professionals obtain conditions and resources necessary for effective professional practice. Publishes numerous related materials, journals, and newsletters.

International Reading Association

800 Barksdale Road

P.O. Box 8139

Newark, DE 19714-8139

(302) 731-1600

FAX: (302) 731-1057

Serves as the professional membership organization for reading teachers. Publishes several journals and is a source of information and publications on the teaching of reading.

National Braille Association

3 Townline Circle

Rochester, NY 14623

(716) 427-8260

FAX: (716) 427-0263

Assists in the development of skills and techniques required for the production of reading materials for individuals who are print handicapped through seminars, workshops, consultation, and publications on the production of braille, tape recording, tactile graphics, and computer-assisted transcription. Provides braille textbooks and materials at below cost to students and professionals. Publishes the *NBA Bulletin*.

National Library Service for the Blind and Physically Handicapped

Library of Congress

1291 Taylor Street, N.W.

Washington, DC 20542

(202) 707-5100 or (800) 424-8567

FAX: (202) 707-0712

Conducts a national program to distribute free reading materials of a general nature to individuals who are blind or who have physical disabilities. Provides reference information on all aspects of blindness and other physical disabilities that affect reading. Conducts national correspondence courses to train sighted persons as braille transcribers and blind persons as braille proofreaders.

Recommended Readings for Teachers

Anderson, R. D., Hiebert, E. H., Scott, J. A., & Wilkinson, I. A. G. (1985). *Becoming a nation of readers. The report of the Commission on Reading.* Washington, DC: National Academy of Education, National Institute of Education.

Braille Authority of North America. (1994). *English braille, American edition.* Louisville, KY: American Printing House for the Blind.

Burns, M. F. (1991). *The Burns braille transcription dictionary.* New York: American Foundation for the Blind.

Edman, P. K. (1992). *Tactile graphics.* New York: American Foundation for the Blind.

Harley, R. K., Truan, M. B., & Sanford, L. D. (1997). *Communication skills for visually impaired learners.* Springfield, IL: Charles C Thomas.

Hudson, L. (1997). *Classroom collaboration.* Watertown, MA: Perkins School for the Blind.

Koenig, A. J., & Farrenkopf, C. (1994). *Providing quality instruction in braille literacy skills: Companion guide to "Invitations: Changing as Teachers and Learners K–12."* Houston, TX: Region IV Education Service Center.

Koenig, A. J., & Holbrook, M. C. (1993). *Learning media assessment of students with visual impairments: A resource guide for teachers.* Austin: Texas School for the Blind and Visually Impaired.

Koenig, A. J., and Holbrook, M. C. (1995). *Braille enthusiasts dictionary.* Nashville, TN: SCALARS Publishing.

Mangold, P. (1993). *Teaching the braille slate and stylus: A manual for mastery* (rev. ed.). Castro Valley, CA: Exceptional Teaching Aids.

Mangold, S. S. (Ed.). (1982). *A teachers' guide to the special educational needs of blind and visually handicapped children.* New York: American Foundation for the Blind.

Olson, M. R. (1981). *Guidelines and games for teaching efficient braille reading.* New York: American Foundation for the Blind.

Rex, E. J., Koenig, A. J., Wormsley, D. P., & Baker, R. L. (1994). *Foundations of braille literacy.* New York: AFB Press.

Routman, R. (1994). *Invitations: Changing as teachers and learners K–12.* Portsmouth, NH: Heinemann.

Stratton, J. M., & Wright, S. (1991). *On the way to literacy.* Louisville, KY: American Printing House for the Blind.

Wormsley, D., & D'Andrea, F. M. (Eds.). (1997). *Instructional strategies for braille literacy.* New York: AFB Press.

Recommended Videotapes for Teachers

Mangold, S. S., & Pesavento, M. E. (1994). *Personal touch: Braille for lifelong enrichment.* Winnetka, IL: Hadley School for the Blind.

Mangold, S. S., & Pesavento, M. E. (n.d.). *Teaching the braille slate and stylus.* Castro Valley, CA: Exceptional Teaching Aids.

Understanding braille literacy. (1993). New York: AFB Press.

Sources of Professional Publications, Curricula, and Assessments

The organizations and entities listed in this section publish many professional publications. The specific ones mentioned in each entry are those cited in this book.

American Foundation for the Blind

11 Penn Plaza, Suite 300
New York, NY 10001
(212) 502-7600 or (800) 232-5463 or (800) 232-3044 for book orders only
TDD: (212) 502-7662
FAX: (212) 502-7774
E-mail: afbinfo@afb.net
http://www.afb.org
Publishes *Informal Assessment of Developmental Skills for Visually Handicapped Students* and *Instructional Strategies for Braille Literacy,* both of which contain assessment forms and checklists.

American Printing House for the Blind

1839 Frankfort Avenue
Louisville, KY 40206-0085
(502) 895-2405 or (800) 223-1839
FAX: (502) 899-2274
E-mail: info@aph.org
http://www.aph.org http://www.aph.org
Publishes the following curricula for teaching braille reading and writing to young children: *Touch and Tell; Preparatory Reading Program for Visually Handicapped Children (PREP); Patterns Prebraille Program; Patterns: The Primary Braille Reading Program; Patterns Library Series;* and *Patterns: The Primary Braille Spelling and English Program.* Also publishes *Print and Braille Literacy: Selecting Appropriate Learning Media* and *TOOLS for Selecting Appropriate Learning Media.*

Exceptional Teaching Aids

20102 Woodbine Avenue
Castro Valley, CA 94546
(510) 582-4859 or (800) 549-6999
FAX: (510) 582-5911
Publishes *The Mangold Developmental Program of Tactile Perception and Braille Letter Recognition* and *Teaching the Braille Slate and Stylus: A Manual for Mastery.*

Hawthorne Educational Services

800 Gray Oak Drive

Columbia, MO 65201

(573) 874-1710

Publishes the *Braille Assessment Inventory.*

Heinemann

361 Hanover Street

Portsmouth, NH 03801-3912

(800) 793-2154

FAX: (800) 847-0938

http://www.heinemann.com

Publishes professional books and other resources for educators.

Minnesota Educational Services

Capitol View Center

70 West Country Road B2

Little Canada, MN 55117-1402

(612) 483-4442 or (800) 848-4912, ext. 2401

FAX: (612) 483-0234

Publishes the *Minnesota Braille Skills Inventory.*

Region IV Education Service Center

7145 West Tidwell

Houston, TX 77092-2096

(713) 550-7412

FAX: (713) 744-8148

E-mail: dspence@tenet.edu

Publishes the *Assessment of Braille Literacy Skills (ABLS).*

Texas School for the Blind and Visually Impaired

1100 West 45th Street

Austin, TX 78756-3494

(512) 454-8631

FAX: (512) 454-3395

Publishes *Learning Media Assessment of Students with Visual Impairments* and the *Kit of Informal Tools for Academic Students with Visual Impairments,* which includes:

    Part 1: Assessment Tools for Teacher Use

    Part 2: Large Print Reading Assessments for Student Use

    Part 3: Braille Reading Assessments for Student Use

    Part 4: Basic Reading Inventory: Pre-Primer through Grade Twelve and Early Literacy Assessments

RESOURCES FOR PARENTS

National Organizations

American Council of the Blind
1155 15th Street N.W., Suite 720
Washington, DC 20005
(202) 467-5081 or (800) 424-8666
FAX: (202) 467-5085
E-mail: ncrabb@access.digex.net
http://www.acb.org
Promotes effective participation of blind people in all aspects of society. Provides information and referral, legal assistance, scholarships, advocacy, consultation, and program development assistance. Affiliated groups include the Council of Families with Visual Impairment. Publishes *The Braille Forum.*

American Foundation for the Blind
11 Penn Plaza, Suite 300
New York, NY 10001
(212) 502-7600 or (800) 232-5463
TDD: (212) 502-7662
FAX: (212) 502-7777
E-mail: afbinfo@afb.net
http://www.afb.org
See under "Resources for Teachers"

Exceptional Parent
Psy-Ed Corporation
209 Harvard Street, Suite 303
Brookline, MA 02146-5005
(613) 951-1581
FAX: (613) 951-1584
Publishes a magazine devoted to issues of interest to families of exceptional children, including resources and support information.

Hadley School for the Blind
700 Elm Street
Winnetka, IL 60093-0299
(847) 446-8111 or (800) 323-4238
FAX: (847) 446-9916
Provides tuition-free home studies in academic subjects as well as braille reading and writing, vocational and technical areas, personal enrichment, parent-child issues, and compensatory/rehabilitation education. Also offers courses for parents and family members of blind individuals.

National Association for Parents of the Visually Impaired

P.O. Box 317

Watertown, MA 02272-0317

(800) 562-6265

FAX: (617) 972-7444

Provides support to parents and families and youths who have visual impairments. Operates a national clearinghouse for information, education, and referral. Publishes a newsletter, *Awareness.*

National Federation of the Blind

1800 Johnson Street

Baltimore, MD 21230

(410) 659-9314

FAX: (410) 685-5653

http://www.nfb.org

Strives to improve social and economic conditions of blind persons, evaluates and assists in establishing programs, and provides public education and scholarships. Affiliated groups include the National Organization of Parents of Blind Children. Publishes *The Braille Monitor* and *Future Reflections.*

Recommended Books and Videotapes for Parents

Ashcroft, S. C., Henderson, F. M., Sanford, L. R., & Koenig, A. J. (1991). *New programmed instruction in braille.* Nashville, TN: SCALARS.

A programmed instruction course designed to teach the braille code.

Castellano, C. & Kosman, D. (1997). *The bridge to braille: Reading and school success for the young blind child.* Baltimore: National Organization of Parents of Blind Children.

A clearly written, comprehensive look at how a young child learns braille and uses it in the regular classroom. The authors offer numerous suggestions for adapting and organizing materials, developing efficient reading strategies, and working in Nemeth Code.

Curran, E. (1988). *Just enough to know better: A braille primer.* Boston: National Braille Press.

A step-by-step introduction to the basics of reading braille, designed especially for parents. The text includes braille passages for transcription practice that were written by a parent about her blind child. The book comes with helpful braille flash cards and a braille code reference sheet.

Holbrook, M. C. (1996). *Children with visual impairments: A parents' guide.* Bethesda, MD: Woodbine House.

A thorough discussion of how children with visual impairments grow and develop at home and at school. The book includes a chapter related to literacy.

Mangold, S. S., & Pesavento, M.E. (1994). *Personal touch: Braille for lifelong enrichment.* Winnetka, IL: Hadley School for the Blind.
An upbeat and informative videotape showing how braille is used throughout the lifespan.
Understanding Braille Literacy. (1993). New York AFB Press.
A motivational video featuring parents, teachers, and school administrators discussing how braille skills contribute to the literacy, independence, and educational success of students and their own roles in fostering braille literacy. Students and teachers demonstrate how braille is learned and used.

PRODUCTS AND MATERIALS

Publishers of Braille Books for Children

American Action Fund for Blind Children and Adults

18440 Oxnard Street
Tarzana, CA 91356
(818) 343-2022
Lends Twin-Vision and braille-only books free of charge.

American Printing House for the Blind

1839 Frankfort Avenue
Louisville, KY 40206-0085
(502) 895-2405 or (800) 223-1839
FAX: (502) 899-2274
E-mail: info@aph.org
http://www.aph.org
Sells the *On the Way to Literacy* series of print-braille books with colorful tactile pictures for preschoolers and early primary students; also produces many textbooks, curricula, and adapted materials for school use.

Braille International

The William A. Thomas Braille Bookstore
3290 S.E. Slater Street
Stuart, FL 34997
(561) 286-8366 or (800) 336-3142
FAX: (561) 286-8909
E-mail: braille@gate.net
Sells fiction and nonfiction books for children and adults.

National Braille Press

88 St. Stephen Street
Boston, MA 02115

(617) 266-6160 or (800) 548-7323
FAX: (617) 437-0456
E-mail: orders@nbp.org
Sells a variety of print-braille and braille-only books and sponsors a children's Braille Book-of-the-Month Club.

National Library Service for the Blind and Physically Handicapped
Library of Congress
1291 Taylor Street, N.W.
Washington, DC 20542
(202) 707-5100 or (800) 424-8567
FAX: (202) 707-0712
Lends print-braille and braille-only books to braille readers free of charge through state and regional libraries.

Seedlings: Braille Books for Children
P.O. Box 51924
Livonia, MI 48151-5924
(313) 427-8552 or (800) 777-8552
E-mail: seedlink@aol.com
http://www.22cent.com/seedlings
Publishes and sells a wide variety of well-known print-braille and braille-only books.

Volunteer Braille Services
3730 Toledo Avenue, North
Robbinsdale, MN 55433
(612) 521-0372
FAX: (612) 588-4912
Produces print-braille books for younger readers.

Publishers of Emergent Reader Books in Print
Rigby
P.O. Box 797
Crystal Lake, IL 60039-0797
(800) 822-8661
FAX: (815) 477-3998
http://www.rigby.com
Publisher of the Literacy 2000 Series in ten stages (K–4), as well as other collections of fiction and nonfiction in print.

The Wright Group
19201 120th Avenue, N.E.
Bothell, VA 98011
(206) 486-8011 or (800) 523-2371
FAX: (206) 486-7704 or (800) 543-7323

Publisher of the Storybox and Sunshine collections for grades K–3, as well as other collections of fiction and nonfiction in print.

Sources for Products and Materials

Listed here are sources of materials and equipment for teachers, many of which have been described in this book. Also included are a selection of other organizations and companies that carry a variety of products related to braille reading and writing, including teaching aids, tactile materials, and materials for producing braille. Catalogs are available on request from many of these sources. An index to the products mentioned in the text appears after the address listings.

Sources

American Printing House for the Blind

1839 Frankfort Avenue
Louisville, KY 40206-0085
(502) 895-2405 or (800) 223-1839
FAX: (502) 899-2274
E-mail: info@aph.org
http://www.aph.org

American Thermoform Corporation

2311 Travers Avenue
City of Commerce, CA 90040
(213) 723-9021
FAX: (213) 728-8877

Blazie Engineering

101 East Jarretsville Road
Forest Hill, MD 21050
(410) 893-9333
FAX: (410) 836-5040
http://www.blazie.com

Carolyn's Enhanced Living Products

P.O. Box 14577
Bradenton, FL 34207-4577
(800) 648-2266
FAX: (941) 739-5503
E-mail: magnify@bhip.infi.net

Exceptional Teaching Aids

20102 Woodbine Avenue
Castro Valley, CA 94546
(510) 582-4859 or (800) 549-6999
FAX: (510) 582-5911

Flaghouse
601 Flaghouse Drive
Hasbrouck Heights, NJ 07604-3116
(800) 221-5185
E-mail: info@flaghouse.com
http://www.flaghouse.com

Lighthouse Enterprises
36-20 Northern Boulevard
Long Island City, NY 11101
(718) 786-5620 or (800) 829-0500
FAX: (718) 786-0437

Los Olvidados
P.O. Box 475
Plaistow, NH 03865
(603) 382-1748 or (800) TACTILE (822-5845)
FAX: (603) 382-1748
E-mail: braille@tack-tiles.com
http://www.tack-tiles.com

LS&S Group
P.O. Box 673
Northbrook, IL 60065
(847) 498-9777 or (800) 468-4789
FAX: (847) 498-1482
E-mail: lssgrp@aol.com
http://www.lssgroup.com

Maxi-Aids
42 Executive Boulevard
P.O. Box 3209
Farmingdale, NY 11735
(516) 752-0521 or (800) 522-6294
FAX: (516) 752-0689
E-mail: sales@maxiaids.com

Pla-za
173 Madison Avenue
New York, NY 10016
(212) 689-2870
FAX: (212) 889-8634

Index to Products and Sources

Braillabels

    American Thermoform Corporation

Braille Lite, Braille 'n Speak, and Type 'n Speak braille notetakers

    Blazie Engineering

ClearLabels

    Exceptional Teaching Aids

Crayola Anti-Roll Crayons

    Exceptional Teaching Aids

Dycem

    Flaghouse

Form-A Line Tape

    Pla-za; art and office supply stores

Individual Calendar Kit

    American Printing House for the Blind (APH)

Letraline Flex-a-Tape

    Pla-za; art and office supply stores

Magnetic Braille Calendar

    Carolyn's Enhanced Living Products

Swing Cell

    APH

Touch and Color and *Touch and Color II* raised-line coloring books

    Exceptional Teaching Aids

Tack-Tiles Braille System

    Los Olvidados

Wikki Stix

    Exceptional Teaching Aids; craft stores

READINGS FOR STUDENTS ABOUT BLINDNESS

The pamphlets and books listed here are recommended for use during classroom presentations to sighted students about braille, blindness, or literacy, and they may be left in the classroom for follow-up reading. School librarians also may be interested in purchasing books featuring characters who are blind so that these resources can be enjoyed by a wider audience. They will also be of high interest to students who are blind or visually impaired.

Pamphlets

You Seem Like a Regular Kid to Me! by Anne L. Corn, Chris M. Cowan, and Elaine Moses (New York: American Foundation for the Blind, 1988).

    Jane, a girl who is blind, answers common questions about blindness. Numerous photographs show her at work and play in the school setting.

A Different Way of Seeing, by Robin L. Tannenbaum (New York: American Foundation for the Blind, 1989).

A question-and-answer format introduces young readers to basic information about how visually impaired students perform academic, mobility, and daily living skills.

More Alike than Different: Blind and Visually Impaired Children Around the World. (New York: American Foundation for the Blind, 1990).

Children from around the world who are blind or visually impaired are portrayed in this collection of photographs.

What Do You Do When You See a Blind Person? (New York: American Foundation for the Blind, 1970).

Cartoon sketches illustrate common rules of courtesy around blind people. (Appropriate for upper-elementary students.)

Books Featuring Characters Who Are Blind or Visually Impaired*

Adler, D. A. (1997). *A picture book of Louis Braille.* New York: Holiday House.
The story of Louis Braille is told in words and pictures. (Grades 3–6)

Adler, D. A. (1990). *A picture book of Helen Keller.* New York: Holiday House.
A picture book gives a brief biography of Helen Keller.

Aiello, B., & Shulman, J. (1988). *Business is looking up.* Frederick, MD: Twenty-First Century Books.
Renaldo Rodriguez, an 11-year-old child who is blind, sets up a greeting card service for stepfamilies. (Grades 3–6; audiocassette/braille)

Alexander, S. H. (1990). *Mom can't see me.* Books for Young Readers. New York: Simon & Schuster.
A 9-year-old girl tells about life with her mother, who is blind. (Grades K–3; audiocassette/braille)

Alexander, S. H. (1992). *Mom's best friend.* New York: Macmillan.
Sally Alexander and her family adjust to their new dog guide. (Grades 2–4; audiocassette)

Amdur, N. (1981). *One of us.* New York: Dial Press.
When Nora moves to a new town, she makes friends with Jerry, who is blind. (Grades 3–6; audiocassette)

Arnold, C. (1991). *A guide dog puppy grows up.* San Diego: Harcourt Brace.
The career of Honey, a dog guide, is followed from puppyhood through the training process to placement with a person who is blind. (Grades 4–6; photographs appropriate for all ages)

Barrett, M. B. (1994). *Sing to the stars.* Boston: Little, Brown.
Ephraim makes friends with Mr. Washington and his dog guide, Shilo. (Grades K–3; audiocassette)

---

*This bibliography was compiled by Janie Humphries, Preschool Consultant to Educational Services for Visually Impaired, Arkansas School for the Blind, Little Rock.

Bergman, T. (1989). *Seeing in special ways.* Milwaukee: Garth Stevens Children's Books.

The author interviews a group of children at the Tomteboda School in Sweden.

Brown, M. (1979). *Arthur's eyes.* New York: Avon.

Arthur's friends tease him about his new glasses, but he soon learns to wear them with pride. (Preschool–grade 3; audiocassette)

Cohen, M. (1983). *See you tomorrow, Charles.* New York: Greenwillow Books.

First graders learn to accept Charles, the new boy in their class, who is blind. (Preschool–grade 2; audiocassette)

Condra, E. (1994). *See the ocean.* Nashville: Ideals Children's Books.

One foggy day, Nellie is the first in her family to know when they reach the ocean on vacation. (Grades K–3; audiocassette)

Coutant, H. (1983). *The gift.* New York: Alfred A. Knopf.

A young girl searches for the perfect gift to give her elderly friend, who has returned home from the hospital after losing her vision. (Grades 3–6; audiocassette)

DeArmond, D. (1988). *The seal oil lamp.* San Francisco: Sierra Club Books.

A 7-year-old boy who is blind is left to die by the people of his village in this retelling of an Eskimo tale.

Dorris, M. (1996). *Sees behind trees.* New York: Hyperion.

A 16th-century Native American boy who is visually impaired earns the respect of his tribe and then undertakes a dangerous journey. (Grades 3–6)

Gellman, E. (1992). *Jeremy's Dreidel.* Rockville, MD: KAR-BEN Copies.

Jeremy signs up for a Hanukkah dreidel workshop and makes one with braille dots for his dad, who is blind.

Giff, P. R. (1987). *Watch out Ronald Morgan.* New York: Viking.

Ronald Morgan has an array of humorous mishaps until he gets his glasses. (Grades K–3; audiocassette)

Goldin, B. D. (1991). *Cakes and miracles (A Purim tale).* New York: Penguin.

After an angel in a dream tells Hershel to make what he sees in his head, he uses his hands and memories to make cookies for the Purim holiday in his village. (Preschool–grade 2; audiocassette/braille)

Heide, F. P. (1970). *Sound of sunshine, sound of rain.* New York: Parents Magazine Press.

A young boy listens carefully to the world around him as he makes his way through his day. (Grades 3–6)

Hermann, H., & Hermann, B. (1988). *Jenny's magic wand.* New York: Franklin Watts.

After attending a school for children who are blind, Jenny worries about going into a public school classroom. (Grade K–4; audiocassette/braille)

Karim, R. (1994). *Mandy Sue day.* New York: Houghton Mifflin.
>   *A young girl who is blind spends her special day with her horse, and together they drink in the sounds, tastes, smells, and feel of an autumn day.* (Grade K–3; audiocassette)

Keats, E. J. (1971). *Apt. 3.* New York: Macmillan.
>   *Sam and Ben meet the resident of Apt. 3, who is blind.* (Grades K–3; audiocassette/braille)

Keller, H. (1982). *Cromwell's glasses.* New York: Greenwillow Books.
>   *It is easier for Cromwell to see when he gets his glasses, but now his siblings tease him about how he looks.* (Preschool–grade 2; audiocassette)

Kroll, V. L. (1993). *Naomi knows it's springtime.* Honesdale, PA: Boyds Mill Press.
>   *A young girl who is blind experiences the first signs of spring.* (Grades K–3; audiocassette)

Leggett, L., & Andrews, L. (1979). *The rose-colored glasses: Melanie adjusts to poor vision.* New York: Human Sciences Press.
>   *A young girl adjusts to wearing glasses and helps her classmates understand what it means to have low vision.*

Levinson, M. (1989). *The fourth-grade four.* New York: Henry Holt.
>   *Afraid that his friends will tease him about wearing glasses, fourth-grader Alex refuses to wear them anywhere but at home.*

Litchfield, A. B. (1977). *A cane in her hand.* Mortin Grove, IL: Albert Whitman.
>   *Valerie learns new skills and techniques from a vision specialist as her vision changes.* (Grades 1–4; audiocassette/braille)

MacLachlan, P. (1980). *Through grandpa's eyes.* New York: HarperCollins.
>   *A young boy learns a different way of seeing from his grandfather, who is blind.* (Grades K–3; audiocassette/braille)

McMahon, P. (1995). *Listen for the bus: David's story.* Honesdale, PA: Boyds Mill Press.
>   *A real-life look at David, who is blind and hearing impaired, as he begins kindergarten.* (Grades 2–4; braille)

Moon, N. (1994). *Lucy's picture.* New York: Dial Books for Young Readers.
>   *Lucy creates a special picture for her grandfather, who is blind.* (Preschool–grade 2)

Naylor, P. R. (1994). *Jennifer Jean, the cross-eyed queen.* Minneapolis: Carolrhoda Books.
>   *Jennifer Jean likes her big, green, crossed eyes and doesn't want to wear a patch.*

Pearson, S. (1987). *Happy birthday, Grampie.* New York: Dial.
>   *Martha takes care to make just the right gift for her Swedish grandfather, who has lost his vision.* (Grades K–3; audiocassette)

Peterson, P. (1974). *Sally can't see.* New York: John Day.
>   *A 12-year-old girl who is blind learns to read, swim, and ride a horse.*

Raskin, E. (1980). *Spectacles.* New York: Atheneum.

Iris sees things that aren't really what they seem to be, until an optometrist gives her glasses.

Reuter, M. (1979). *My mother is blind.* Chicago: Children's Press.

A young boy describes how everyone comes to terms with his mother's blindness. (Grade 2; audiocassette)

Rosenberg, M. (1993). *My friend Leslie.* New York: Lothrop Lee & Shepard Books.

Leslie, a kindergarten child, is deaf-blind. (Grades K–3; audiocassette)

Smith, E. S. (1987). *A guide dog goes to school.* New York: William Morrow.

A puppy goes through training to become a dog guide. (Grades 2–4)

Thomas, W. E. (1980). *The new boy is blind.* New York: Julian Messner Books.

Ricky and his sighted classmates adjust to his blindness when he becomes the new student in their fourth-grade classroom.

Wild, M. (1992). *All the better to see you with.* Morton Grove, IL: Albert Whitman.

Because Kate is the quiet one in her family, her parents are slow to notice she is nearsighted.

Wiley, S. (1995). Sounds and voice by Stevie Wonder. *Little Stevie Wonder in places under the sun.* New York: Golden Books.

Little Stevie Wonder goes to Japan with his friends to play a concert.

Yolen, J. (1997). *The seeing stick.* New York: Thomas Crowell.

The emperor's daughter is blind, and a mysterious old man with a "seeing stick" teaches her to see with her fingers, her mind, and her heart. (Grades K–3; audiocassette)

Young, E. (1982). *Seven blind mice.* New York: Philomel Books.

Seven blind mice explore and discover different parts of an elephant. (Grades K–3; braille)

APPENDIX A

TEMPLATES FOR SIMPLE BOOKS

Texture Book

This template can be enlarged by 130 percent to make a full-size book. The dotted outline indicates the size of the book's brailled pages in relation to the cover.

Human Figure for
Experience Book

B BLANK RECORD FORMS AND CHECKLISTS

Spelling Record

Name:_____

Week:			
Focus:			
1.			
2.			
3.			
4.			
5.			
6.			
7.			
8.			
9.			
10.			
11.			
12.			
13.			
14.			
15.			
16.			
17.			
18.			
19.			
20.			

Indicators of Readiness for a Functional Literacy Program

Student _____

Date _____ Evaluator _____

Yes	No	No Opportunity	Behavior
____	____	____	Attends to and responds meaningfully when others read.
____	____	____	Anticipates activities and events.
____	____	____	Differentiates sounds and spoken words, gestures, or signs.
____	____	____	Attaches meaning to sound or spoken words, gestures, or signs.
____	____	____	Differentiates objects visually and/or tactually.
____	____	____	Demonstrates an association of pictures or objects with stories or books.
____	____	____	Identifies objects visually and/or tactually.
____	____	____	Associates signs in the home or community with important events (such as the golden arches mean "time to eat").
____	____	____	Chooses independently to examine books, letters, and/or symbols.
____	____	____	Notes likenesses and differences in words when presented in print or braille.
____	____	____	Follows simple directions of two or three steps.
____	____	____	Generalizes directional concepts (such as top, bottom).
____	____	____	Generalizes the ability to sequence a series of objects, activities, or events.
____	____	____	Generalizes the use of primitive symbolic communications systems such as real objects or miniatures.
____	____	____	Generalizes the use of abstract symbolic communication.
____	____	____	Initiates interactive communication through systems such as sign, gestures, or augmentative communication devices.
____	____	____	Recognizes that words in print or braille have meaning.
____	____	____	Recognizes name in print or braille.

Anna M. Swenson, *Beginning with Braille: Firsthand Experiences with a Balanced Approach to Literacy.* New York, AFB Press, 1999. This page may be copied for educational use.

Grade 2 Braille—Oral Reading

Over a period of readings, monitor the student's level of braille reading using the following list of contractions and short-form words. Place a check mark next to those that the student is able to identify consistently.

about	beneath	dis	him	necessary	receiving	tion
above	beside	do	himself	neither	rejoice	to
according	between	ea	his	ness	rejoicing	today
across	beyond	ed	immediate	not	right	together
after	ble	either	in	o'clock	said	tomorrow
afternoon	blind	en	ing	of	sh	tonight
afterward	braille	ence	into	one	shall	under
again	but	enough	it	oneself	should	upon
against	by	er	its	ong	sion	us
ally	can	ever	itself	ou	so	very
almost	cannot	every	ity	ought	some	was
already	cc	father	just	ound	spirit	were
also	ch	ff	know	ount	st	wh
although	character	first	knowledge	ourselves	still	where
altogether	child	for	less	out	such	which
always	children	friend	letter	ow	th	whose
ance	com	from	like	paid	that	will
and	con	ful	little	part	the	with
ar	conceive	gg	lord	people	their	word
as	conceiving	gh	many	perceive	themselves	work
ation	could	go	ment	perceiving	there	world
bb	day	good	more	perhaps	these	would
be	dd	great	mother	question	this	you
because	deceive	had	much	quick	those	young
before	deceiving	have	must	quite	through	your
behind	declare	here	myself	rather	thyself	yourself
below	declaring	herself	name	receive	time	yourselves

Comments:

Anna M. Swenson, *Beginning with Braille: Firsthand Experiences with a Balanced Approach to Literacy.* New York, AFB Press, 1999. This page may be copied for educational use.

Name: _____

Week of: _____

Planned Objectives/Activities:

Anecdotal Records/Comments

Name: _____

Week of: _____

Planned Objectives/Activities:

Anecdotal Records/Comments:

Task List

Name: _____

Week of: _____

Task	Monday	Tuesday	Wednesday	Thursday	Friday

I = Completed *independently*; **A** = Completed *almost* independently—with minimal assistance; **H** = Completed with *help*

Anna M. Swenson, *Beginning with Braille: Firsthand Experiences with a Balanced Approach to Literacy.* New York, AFB Press, 1999. This page may be copied for educational use.

Beginning Braille Alphabet Skills Checklist

Name:_____

Letter	Identifies Letter	Reads Whole-Word Contraction	Writes Letter or Contraction	Recognizes Sound 9/20 10/25
a				
b		but		
c		can		
d		do		
e		every		
f		from		
g		go		
h		have		
i		I		
j		just		
k		knowledge		
l		like		
m		more		
n		not		
o				
p		people		
q		quite		
r		rather		
s		so		
t		that		
u		us		
v		very		
w		will		
x		it		
y		you		
z		as		
0			Other words:	
1				
2				
3				
4				
5				
6				
7				
8				
9				
10				

Anna M. Swenson, *Beginning with Braille: Firsthand Experiences with a Balanced Approach to Literacy.* New York, AFB Press, 1999. This page may be copied for educational use.

Tactile Sight Words and Familiar Names

Name:_____

Write the date that the child learns to read each of the words below in grade 2 braille.

go_____	you_____	can _____
I_____	we_____	like _____
have_____	the_____	a _____
do_____	but_____	just_____
that_____	people_____	not _____
me_____	to (uncontracted)_____	and _____
with_____	get_____	will _____
for_____	it _____	in _____

Other tactile sight words and names

_____ _____ _____

_____ _____ _____

_____ _____ _____

_____ _____ _____

_____ _____ _____

Anna M. Swenson, *Beginning with Braille: Firsthand Experiences with a Balanced Approach to Literacy.* New York, AFB Press, 1999. This page may be copied for educational use.

Braille Oral Reading Individual Checklist

Name:_____

Book Read:_____

Date:_____

	Check	Comments
Reads familiar material fluently with appropriate expression		
Matches one spoken word to each braille word		
Uses efficient tracking movements		
Self-corrects to preserve meaning		
Takes risks in pronunciation		
Recognizes braille contractions		
Observes punctuation		
Notices when reading does not make sense		
When confronting unfamiliar words:		
• rereads the sentence		
• uses context clues		
• skips unknown words, reads on, returns to word		
• uses phonics clues		
• substitutes words that make sense (*little* for *small*)		

Anna M. Swenson, *Beginning with Braille: Firsthand Experiences with a Balanced Approach to Literacy.* New York, AFB Press, 1999. This page may be copied for educational use.

Early Braille Writing Development Checklist

Name: _____

Directions: Date entries every 3 or 4 weeks. Comment on the child's progress.

	Date	Comments
Imitates writing behavior by randomly pressing keys and speaking message		
Writes a line of full cells		
Isolates fingers, pressing one key at a time		
Inserts paper into the brailler		
Writes random letters		
Uses letter-sound relationships to write words (temporary spelling)		
Uses grade 2 braille contractions		
Leaves spaces between words		
Uses some conventional spelling		
Reads writing to others		
Organizes writing in time order		
Organizes writing around a topic or event		
Uses capital sign at the beginning of a sentence		
Uses end punctuation		
Marks words not spelled correctly		
Uses more conventional spelling than approximations		
Other:		

Anna M. Swenson, *Beginning with Braille: Firsthand Experiences with a Balanced Approach to Literacy.* New York, AFB Press, 1999. This page may be copied for educational use.

Braille Writing Assessment

Name: _____

Date: _____

Title: _____

Student plans writing by:	Check	Comments
• discussing with others		
• orally rehearsing sentences		
• reading		
• brailling a sample list or outline		
• other		
Student revises writing by:		
• rereading to see if it makes sense		
• checking for a beginning and an end		
• adding information		
• deleting or substituting information		
• reorganizing ideas		
• carefully choosing the best word		
• other		
Student edits writing by using:		
• capital letters (sentence beginnings)		
• capital letters (proper nouns)		
• end punctuation		
• commas in a series		
• conventional spelling/grade 2 braille		
• apostrophes (contractions/possessions)		
• other		

DOLCH WORD LIST

Name: _____ Date/%: _____ Date/%: _____ Date/%: _____

a	down	in	over	think
about	draw	into	own	this
after	drink	is		those
again		it	pick	three
all	eat	its	play	to
always	eight		please	today
am	every	jump	pretty	together
an		just	pull	too
and	fall		put	try
any	far	keep		two
are	fast	kind	ran	
around	find	know	read	under
as	first		red	up
ask	five	laugh	ride	upon
at	fly	let	right	us
ate	for	light	round	use
away	found	like	run	
	four	little		very
be	from	live	said	
because	full	long	saw	walk
been	funny	look	say	want
before			see	warm
best	gave	made	seven	was
better	get	make	shall	wash
big	give	many	she	we
black	go	may	show	well
blue	goes	me	sing	went
both	going	much	sit	were
bring	good	must	six	what
brown	got	my	sleep	when
but	green	myself	small	where
buy	grow		so	which
by		never	some	white
	had	new	soon	who
call	has	no	start	why
came	have	not	stop	will
can	he	now		wish
carry	help		take	with
clean	her	of	tell	work
cold	here	off	ten	would
come	him	old	thank	write
could	his	on	that	
cut	hold	once	the	yellow
	hot	one	their	yes
did	how	only	them	you
do	hurt	open	then	your
does		or	there	
done	I	our	these	
don't	if	out	they	

Source: Adapted from E. W. Dolch, *The Dolch Basic Sight Word Test* (Champaign, IL: Garrard Press, 1942).

C BRAILLE WORKSHEETS FOR SIGHTED CHILDREN

THE BRAILLE ALPHABET

a b c d e f g h i j

k l m n o p q r s t

u v w x y z

The Braille Cell

1 4
2 5
3 6

THE BRAILLE ALPHABET

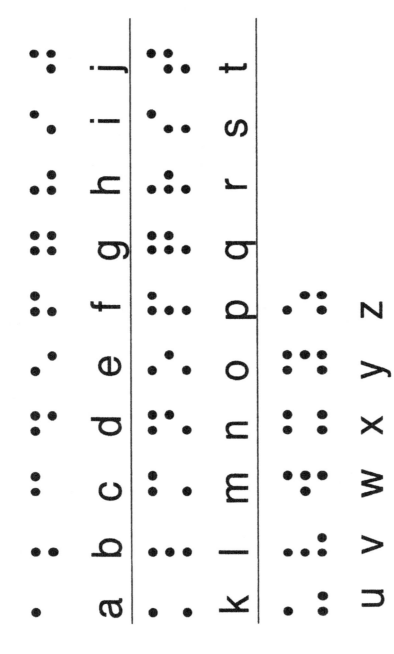

BRAILLE NUMBERS

THE BRAILLE ALPHABET
(FOR SLATE WRITING)

a b c d e f g h i j

k l m n o p q r s t

u v w x y z

The Braille Cell

1 4
2 5
3 6

BRAILLE NUMBER WORDS

Can you read the braille letters and write the number words?

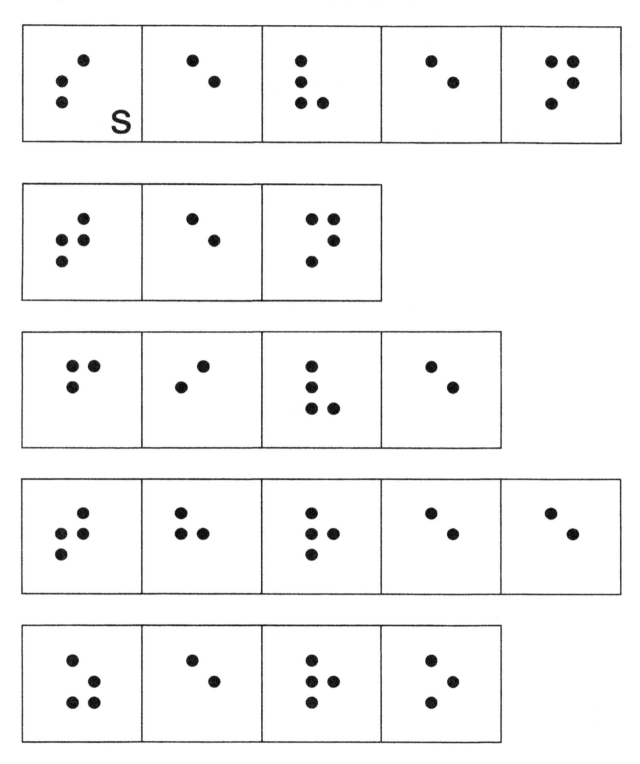

RIDDLES

Can you solve these riddles using the braille alphabet?

1. What smells the most in a perfume shop?

2. What asks no questions, but requires many answers?

3. What can speak in every language, but never went to school?

4. What goes up white and comes down yellow and white?

5. What rises and waves all day?

6. What is easy to get in to, but hard to get out of?

BRAILLE WRITING

Write your name in braille.

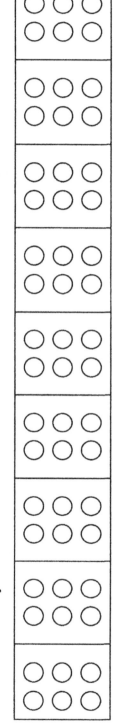

Write another word you know in braille.

Source: Adapted with permission from a worksheet by Martine Pistell, Fairfax County Public Schools, Fairfax, VA.

Index

About the Author

Anna M. Swenson, M.Ed., is a Teacher of the Visually Impaired in the Fairfax County Public Schools in Fairfax, Virginia. She has published articles on her approach to teaching students who are visually impaired in numerous professional journals such as the *Journal of Visual Impairment & Blindness, RE:view,* and *Teaching Exceptional Children* and has presented workshops at professional conferences nationwide. Ms. Swenson has been honored with the Outstanding Educator Award from the Virginia Chapter of the Association for Education and Rehabilitation of the Blind and Visually Impaired.

The mission of the American Foundation for the Blind (AFB) is to enable persons who are blind or visually impaired to achieve equality of access and opportunity that will ensure freedom of choice in their lives.